I Never Knew That

About

COASTAL
ENGLAND

Christopher Winn

I Never Knew That

About

COASTAL
ENGLAND

ILLUSTRATIONS
BY
Mai Osawa

EBURY
PRESS

1 3 5 7 9 10 8 6 4 2

Published in 2019 by Ebury Press an imprint of Ebury Publishing,
20 Vauxhall Bridge Road,
London SW1V 2SA

Ebury Press is part of the Penguin Random House group of companies
whose addresses can be found at global.penguinrandomhouse.com

Penguin
Random House
UK

Text © Christopher Winn 2019
Illustrations © Mai Osawa 2019

This edition published by Ebury Press in 2019

www.penguin.co.uk

A CIP catalogue record for this book is available from the British Library

Series design by Peter Ward

ISBN 9781785039539

Typeset in 9.5/11 pt Adobe Garamond Pro
by Integra Software Services Pvt. Ltd, Pondicherry

Printed and bound in Great Britain by Clays Ltd, Elcograf S.p.A.

MIX
Paper from
responsible sources
FSC® C018179

Penguin Random House is committed to a sustainable future
for our business, our readers and our planet. This book is
made from Forest Stewardship Council' certified paper.

For Martin and Rachel
Thank you
for your support and friendship
Over the years.

And in memory of two irreplaceable friends whose humour, generous
spirit, kindness and inspirational example I miss every day.
Hugh Montgomery-Massingberd and Sir Terry Wogan.

Acknowledgements

My thanks to the home team at Ebury for all their hard work in putting together this book. Special thanks to Samantha Crisp for knocking the book into shape with such skill and professionalism and for always being there to help.

Thanks also to Steve Dobell for his sympathetic and masterly editing.

Particular thanks to Carey Smith, my editor, whose patience, wisdom, forbearance and support are unwavering and without whom this book – and this series – would never have happened.

And for Mai, my wife and illustrator, my admiration and love are unbounded.

Contents

Preface

'This precious stone set in the silver sea'
William Shakespeare

Coastal England is England at its most wild and dramatic, both in nature and in history. From England's gateway, the white cliffs of Dover, to the grey granite cliffs of Land's End in Cornwall, from the bubbling brown mudflats of the Wash to the gurgling green creeks of Essex, from the crackling creamy pebbles of Dorset's Chesil Beach to the seafoam salt marshes of Cumbria, from the wide, shifting marmalade sands of Morecambe Bay to the ochre flats of Somerset, from the bird-speckled cliffs of Yorkshire to the red cliffs of Devon, from the blue, boat-filled inlets of Chichester and the south to the golden, castle-strewn beaches of Northumberland, coastal England is spectacular and colourful, ever changing, thrilling.

England's coastal communities are as distinctive and picturesque as the scenery, laden with history and legend, places from where generations of English men and women have gone out to fish or trade, to explore or build new communities across the world. Tiny fishing villages like Clovelly in Devon or Staithes in Yorkshire, made quaint and picture perfect by a daily life battling 'gainst the sea, smuggling haunts like Dymchurch in Kent, working coastal towns like Workington in Cumbria or Tynemouth in Durham, from where coal and iron were sent across the world, forgotten harbours like Sunderland in Cumbria or Charleston in Cornwall, mighty fortresses built to repel invaders at Dover and Deal and Bamburgh, busy modern ports like Felixstowe and Immingham, naval bases like Portsmouth or Plymouth, all have the sea running rich in their veins. And the coast is where the English go to get better, with resorts such as Scarborough and Dr Brighton attesting to the health-giving qualities of the coastal air and brash and breezy holiday towns like Clacton in Essex or Blackpool in Lancashire built exclusively for fun.

Nowhere in England is more than 70 miles from the coast and there is no excuse not to visit. When next you do, take this book with you. *I Never Knew That About Coastal England* can point you to the best bits and help you find the stories that will make you exclaim, again and again, 'I never knew that!'

SCOTLAND

Northumber-land

Durham

Cumbria

Yorkshire

Lancs

Cheshire

Derbys

Notts

Lincs

Shropshire

Staffs

Leics

1

Norfolk

Warwicks

Northants

Cambs

WALES

Hereford

Worcs

2

Suffolk

Beds

Glos

Oxon

Bucks

Herts

Essex

London

Berks

Wilts

Surrey

Kent

Somerset

Hants

Sussex

Devon

Dorset

Cornwall

1... Rutland
2... Huntingdonshire

Introduction

The England Coast Path

I Never Knew That About Coastal England travels anti-clockwise around the length of the English coastline, from the Solway Firth in the northwest to Berwick-on-Tweed in the northeast, uncovering along the way the highlights and the stories to be found on or near the England Coast Path.

At 2,795 miles long the England Coast Path is the longest managed and waymarked coastal path in the world. Completed in the early 2020s, the path fills in the gaps between England's 11 pre-existing coast paths, creating one continuous trail around the coast of England.

Each chapter covers the coastline of a different county, while Devon, being the only English county to have two separate coasts, has two chapters, north and south. Cornwall, with two very different coastlines north and south, also has two chapters.

The Isle of Wight, once part of Hampshire, is now a county in its own right and has its own chapter.

Coastal Paths

The 11 coastal paths combined in the England Coast Path are:

The Cumbria Coastal Way that runs for 185 miles from Burgh by Sands to Silverdale in Lancashire

The Lancashire Coastal Way – 66 miles from Silverdale to Freckleton near Lytham St Annes

The West Somerset Coast Path – 25 miles from Brean Down south of Weston-super-Mare to Minehead

The South West Coast Path – 630 miles from Minehead in Somerset, through Devon and Cornwall to Poole Harbour in Dorset

The Bournemouth Coast Path – 20 miles from Bournemouth to Milford-on-Sea

The Solent Way – 60 miles from Milford-on-Sea to Emsworth

The Isle of Wight Coastal Path – 70 miles around the coast of the Isle of Wight

The Saxon Shore Way – 163 miles from Hastings in Sussex to Gravesend in Kent

The Suffolk Coast Path – 50 miles from Felixstowe to Lowestoft

The Norfolk Coast Path – 63 miles from Sea Palling south of Cromer to Hunstanton on the Wash

The coastal section of the Cleveland Way in Yorkshire – 48 miles from Filey to Saltburn-by-the-Sea

CHAPTER ONE
CUMBRIAN COAST

Solway Firth to Arnside
110 miles

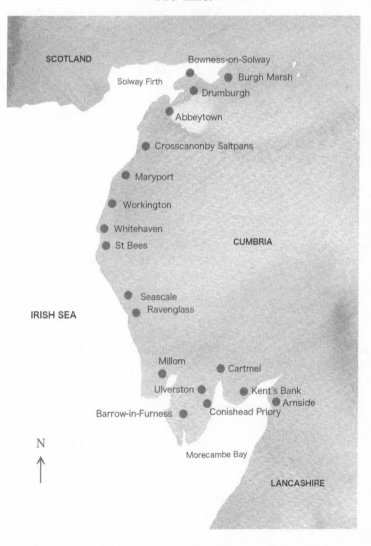

SCOTLAND

Bowness-on-Solway

Solway Firth

Burgh Marsh

Drumburgh

Abbeytown

Crosscanonby Saltpans

Maryport

Workington

Whitehaven

St Bees

CUMBRIA

Seascale

Ravenglass

IRISH SEA

Millom

Cartmel

Ulverston

Kent's Bank

Arnside

Barrow-in-Furness

Conishead Priory

N

Morecambe Bay

LANCASHIRE

The west coast of England begins in Cumberland, on the south bank of the River Esk where it runs into the wild Solway Firth, Britain's third largest estuary. Across on the north bank of the Solway lies Scotland.

Highlights of the Cumberland coast include a forlorn monument to a warrior king, a unique fortified church, the largest peat bog in Britain, the western end of Hadrian's Wall, the burial place of Robert the Bruce's father, Britain's best preserved medieval saltworks, Alfred Waterhouse's first commission, a queen's refuge, the town that inspired New York, the world's first undersea mine, the largest nuclear site in Europe, the highest Roman wall in Britain, the first public narrow-gauge railway in England, the largest indoor shipbuilding hall in Europe and the world's only Laurel and Hardy museum.

Burgh Marsh

The first man-made feature we come to as we travel south from Scotland down the west coast of England is a tall column of bluff red sandstone standing alone on the barren Burgh Marsh south of the River Eden, more than a mile from the nearest road or house. It marks the desolate spot where, at daybreak on 7 July 1307, the mighty King of England, EDWARD I, 'Hammer of the Scots', breathed his last, his dying gaze cast at Scotland, the land he had come to subdue, lying tantalisingly close across the waters of the Eden and Solway.

Edward, 68 years old and failing, had been provoked into marching north by the rising threat of the Scottish nobles under Robert the Bruce. Too ill to ride any distance, he was carried in a litter to Carlisle, where he mounted his white war horse for the last time and rode forth to crush the rebellious Scots once and for all. Forced to make camp on the marshes, he died in the arms of his manservant within sight of Scotland. A monument was first placed at the scene in 1685 by Henry Howard, Duke of Norfolk, and this was restored by the Earl of Lonsdale in 1803. A plaque inscribed in Latin survives from the original monument which translates as something like, *'In memory of Edward who was preparing for war against the Scots when he died here in camp on 7 July 1307.'*

This is a strangely melancholy place, perhaps haunted by the spirit of the dead king. The view across the Solway towards the beckoning hills of Galloway cannot have changed in the 700 years since – is that the shrieking of the gulls on the wind or the anguished cry of a warrior king denied his final victory?

With his last words Edward bade his men to carry his bones into battle and not to bury them until the Scots were overcome. But his last wishes were denied. Instead Edward's body was carried back to Burgh by Sands, a 30-minute walk to the south, and there in the magnificent Norman church it lay in state before being taken back to London for burial in Westminster Abbey.

Drumburgh

The tiny hamlet of Drumburgh sits at the top of a gentle rise on the site of the Roman fort of Concavata, the smallest station on Hadrian's Wall, which was built to guard the southern

end of a ford across the Solway. Stone from the fort was used in the construction of the glorious old three-storey farmhouse that stands at the centre of the village. This was once Drumburgh Castle, built by Lord Dacre in 1518 out of a 12th-century peel tower crenellated in the early 14th century as a defence against the Scots after the death of Edward I. The house still has a grand stone stairway leading up to the ancient studded front door on the first floor. A Roman altar is incorporated into the door frame while Lord Dacre's initials and coat of arms are mounted on the wall above. Two stone eagles keep watch from a parapet on the roof.

Immediately south of the village is Drumburgh Moss, one of four peat bogs along this section of coast that together form THE LARGEST AND BEST AREA OF PEAT BOG IN BRITAIN.

Bowness-on-Solway

Bowness is a village of about a hundred buildings, old cottages made with Roman stone, Victorian houses and a school, a pub, a Methodist chapel of 1872 and a fine Norman church. The village marks the western end of Hadrian's Wall and stands on the site of the Roman fort of Maia, the second largest fort on the wall. Those who have walked the length of the wall from Wallsend on the east coast, some 84 miles, can collect a stamp from

the village hall to commemorate their achievement.

St Michael's church, mainly 12th century but restored in the 19th century, boasts two Norman doorways, a double bellcote and a beautifully carved Norman font. In 1626 raiders from Scotland crossed the Solway and stole the church bells. Hotly pursued by angry villagers the raiders dropped the bells in the sea, where they rest to this day in a spot known as Bell Pool. In retaliation for this dastardly insult the men of Bowness mounted their own raid on Annan across the water and returned carrying church bells from the nearby villages of Dornock and Middlebie. These bells are still in the church in Bowness and every new vicar of Annan, on his or her induction, traditionally makes a request for their return – and is politely refused.

Although Bowness was the end of Hadrian's Wall it was not the end of the Roman fortifications, and a line of coastal forts was built all the way down the Cumbrian coast to the south to prevent the Picts from sailing around the wall and attacking from the sea.

Solway Junction Railway

This was constructed to carry iron ore from Cumberland to the Scottish ironworks without having to pass through Carlisle, and consisted of a mile-long iron girder viaduct across the mouth of the Solway Firth with rail links at either end to connect with the main line. The line opened in 1869 but proved expensive to maintain, constantly being damaged by ice and fast-flowing tides, and was finally closed in 1921, although it remained in situ for some years after that and provided a popular excursion for walkers, particularly for those on the Scottish side who would walk across on a Sunday, when alcohol was banned in Scotland, to get a drink in England. It was finally demolished in 1932, allegedly because too many Scots visitors were falling into the sea when returning home the worse for wear.

Parts of the causeway's embankment are still visible down by the shore, and some rusting iron girders are sometimes revealed at low tide.

Abbeytown

As you enter the village from the north a lofty hangar-like structure suddenly rears up from the cluster of farm buildings and it takes a moment to realise that this is not a great barn but the remains of the abbey from which Abbey Town takes its name. HOLME CULTRAM ABBEY was founded here in 1150 by Cistercian monks from Melrose, at a time when Cumberland was held by the Scottish crown. Seven years later Henry II reclaimed Cumberland for England and despite the turbulent times Holme Cultram became the largest monastery in Cumberland, its 256 foot (78 m) length surpassing that of Carlisle Cathedral, and with a tower 110 feet (34 m) high. Its splendour reflected the wealth earned from sheep and cattle and

a thriving trade in salt from the marshes of the River Weaver estuary. Edward I, King of England, came here on his way to Scotland in 1300 and again in 1307, a few days before he died on Burgh marsh to the north. Robert the Bruce, King of Scotland, came in 1319 and sacked the monastery despite the fact that his father, Sir Robert de Brus, 6th Lord of Annandale, had been buried here only 15 years earlier. His tombstone, carved with a cross, can still be seen inside. At the Dissolution of the Monasteries in 1538 the abbey's buildings were plundered for stone, but the villagers persuaded Henry VIII to let them keep the abbey church itself for use as a parish church and for protection against the Scots. In 1600 the tower fell down, and not long after that there was a fire and the nave was reduced to the six bays we see today. Nonetheless what remains, while stark, is impressive, and Holme Cultram is unique in that it is the only Cistercian abbey in England whose nave is still used as a church. There are some lovely arcades inside, a fine Norman west doorway and a splendid Tudor porch outside built in 1507 by the Abbot, Robert Chamber. His crest of a bear in chains can be seen on his tomb in the porch.

Milefortlet 21 &
the Crosscanonby Saltpans

Milefortlet 21, a couple of miles south of Allonby, is one of a chain of Roman mileforts running down the Solway coast from Bowness to Maryport and the only one to be fully excavated. These mileforts were constructed at the same time as Hadrian's Wall to defend the shore from any Scots who might try to outflank the wall by sailing around it and landing on the coast. There was no wall but watchtowers were built between the mileforts at intervals of a third of a mile, creating a continuous line of observation for 30 miles along the Cumberland coast.

Across the road on the seaward side are the Saltpans of Crosscanonby, built around 1634 and the best preserved direct boiling saltworks in Britain. Until the 19th century salt was the only means of preserving meat and fish and the basis for a highly lucrative industry. Here at Crosscanonby sea water was collected into tanks on the foreshore and allowed to settle. It was then pumped into a large round storage pool sealed with clay from where it trickled into panhouses and was boiled in iron pans until the salt crystallised. The remains of the round storage pool and the stone-lined circular collecting tanks are remarkably intact and in the 1990s the historical importance of the site was finally realised. A wall was subsequently built to protect the pans from being washed away by the tide.

Milefortlet 21 and the Crosscanonby Saltpans are a designated World Heritage Site.

Maryport

Maryport is the southernmost town on the Solway Firth. It takes its name from

Mary, the wife of local landowner Humphrey Senhouse, who founded the port in 1749 and built the docks to handle coal from the Cumbrian coalfields and iron from the local ironworks – iron rails made in Cumberland were sent from Maryport to make railways all over the world. Maryport's neat Georgian terraces and streets, a favourite subject of the painter L.S. Lowry, and in particular the lovely sloping town square, reflect the wealth the docks brought to the town in the 18th and 19th centuries. However, the General Strike of 1926 and the opening of Workington's deep-water dock in 1927 hit the town's trade badly, and today the docks, which were closed to cargo ships in the 1960s following the closure of Cumbria's remaining coalfields, are used only by fishermen and pleasure boats. THOMAS ISMAY, founder of the White Star Line, was born in Maryport in 1837. His son Joseph was instrumental in the building of the *Titanic* and survived the sinking of the ship after it hit an iceberg in the Atlantic Ocean in 1912.

Workington

Workington, Cumbria's second largest town, sits at the mouth of the River Derwent where it empties into the Irish Sea. Workington's origins are Roman. There was a small fort on the north bank of the Derwent and a watchtower on the south side, both forming part of the coastal defences stretching from Bowness-on-Solway to Ravenglass.

Once the Romans had departed, Workington settled into being a fishing village, and then in the 18th century a small dock was built to handle locally mined coal. In the 19th century an iron industry developed to exploit the haematite iron ore fields that lie to the south of the town, which were acknowledged to be THE FINEST HAEMATITE IRON ORE FIELDS IN THE WORLD. Haematite is important in steel making and in 1857 Sir Henry Bessemer came to Workington to build the first mills in the world to use his revolutionary Bessemer process for the mass production of steel. In 1872 Bessemer's company, the Workington Haematite Iron Company, opened THE FIRST LARGE-SCALE STEEL MAKING PLANT IN THE WORLD at Moss Bay south of the Derwent and a few years later the plant began to produce the first ever commercial quantities of rolled mild steel rails for the railway industry. For much of the 19th century Workington was THE LARGEST AND MOST IMPORTANT PRODUCER OF STEEL IN THE WORLD and it was said that Workington steel 'held the world together'. Steel making declined in the 20th century and the last steelworks in Workington was closed in 2006 with most of the plant buildings being converted into offices.

MARY QUEEN OF SCOTS spent her first night in England in Workington on 16 May 1568 after crossing the Solway Firth from Dundrennan Abbey in Scotland in a fishing boat. Forced to abdicate in favour of her son James and defeated by the Scottish nobles at the Battle of Langside, she fled to England to seek the help of her cousin Elizabeth I and was received by the Curwens at their home Workington Hall. The following morning she wrote a letter to Elizabeth appealing to her to 'send for me as soon as possible, for I am in a pitiable condition … having nothing in the world but the clothes in which I escaped …' Mary then rode to Cockermouth and from there to Carlisle where she stayed in her apartments in the castle.

Workington Hall still stands amongst the trees on a hill to the east of the town, but as a roofless ruin. The house that Mary would have known was built in 1404 around a 14th-century peel tower and was added to in the 1780s by the architect John Carr. The Curwen family lived there for over five hundred years until 1929. Badly damaged by fire during the Second World War, while it was being used by the War Office to billet troops, the hall has remained a ruin ever since.

Whitehaven

Whitehaven started life in the 12th century as a port for St Bees Priory and remained a small fishing village, with just nine cottages and a single fishing boat called the *Bee*, until the end of the 16th century when it was obtained by the Lowther family. Over the next hundred years they built docks and developed Whitehaven as a port for shipbuilding and the export of Cumberland coal, and by the end of the 17th century Whitehaven had become the second largest port on England's west coast after Bristol, exporting coal to Ireland and importing tobacco from the New World. In designing their new town the Lowthers were inspired by Christopher Wren's vision for rebuilding the City of London after the Great Fire, and although Wren's plans for London were never fully realised the Lowthers were able to start Whitehaven more or less from scratch. The town's elegant grid pattern of streets was so admired that it was used as a blueprint for the expansion of New York in the early 19th century. Many fine Georgian buildings survive, in particular St James's Church, built in 1753 to the design of Lord Lonsdale's agent Carlisle Spedding, and said to have THE FINEST GEORGIAN INTERIOR IN CUMBERLAND.

American Connections

Importing tobacco and being the inspiration for New York's grid pattern are not Whitehaven's only connections to America. MILDRED GALE, paternal grandmother of the first US President, George Washington, is buried in the churchyard of St Nicholas in the centre of town. After the death of her first husband Lawrence Washington in 1698, Mildred married a sea merchant called George Gale who had interests on both sides of the Atlantic and they settled in his home town of Whitehaven. She died in 1701, just a year after their marriage.

In 1778, during the American War of Independence, the American privateer John Paul Jones, who had been born in Scotland and apprenticed in Whitehaven, sailed into the harbour in an attempt to destroy a fleet of coal ships at anchor there, but the town had been forewarned by one of Jones's own men and the American was able to inflict little damage before fleeing across the Solway to Scotland.

Mining

There are several reminders of Whitehaven's mining history dotted around the town. Standing high on a cliff above the old harbour is the CANDLESTICK CHIMNEY, built as an air shaft for the Duke coal-pit. The chimney was given its distinctive candlestick shape at the suggestion of the mine's owner Lord Lonsdale who, when asked over dinner by his architect if he had any particular design in mind for the chimney, pointed to a candlestick on the dining table and said, 'Build it like that!'

Set on a rock platform above the beach about a mile south of the harbour, are remnants of the SALTOM PIT, THE WORLD'S FIRST UNDERSEA MINE, which operated between 1729 and 1848 and reached a depth of 456 feet (139 m). The mine was sunk by Lord Lonsdale's agent Carlisle Spedding (1695–1755), an innovative pioneer who was the first mine operator to utilise the newfangled Newcomen steam engine to pump out water from his mines. He also invented THE FIRST 'SAFETY' LAMP, a device called a Steel Mill, consisting of brass and steel wheels turned by a handle to strike a flint and produce sparks for illumination. Still highly dangerous, it was at least less lethal than a naked flame. Alas, it didn't prevent poor Carlisle Spedding from dying in a mine explosion in 1755.

The American diplomat and inventor Benjamin Franklin went down the Saltom Pit in 1771 with Carlisle Spedding's son James and William Brownrigg, a Whitehaven doctor and scientist whose studies of mine gases led to his being made a fellow of the Royal Society. Brownrigg also discovered platinum by experimenting with a sample of material brought back to Whitehaven from Jamaica by his brother-in-law Charles Wood.

The remnants of the mine that survive include the winding engine house, a chimney, the footings of some ancillary buildings and the outline of a gin circle, which horses plodded around all day long lifting tubs of coal up from the bottom of the shaft. The mine shaft itself is protected by a concrete cover.

Inspiring Stuff

In 1668 a sickly one-year-old boy who would grow up to enthral the world with his writings arrived in Whitehaven from Ireland. He had been kidnapped by his nurse, a Whitehaven girl who had returned to her home town from Dublin to attend the deathbed of a relative from whom she expected a legacy. The nurse was loath to leave her beloved charge with his struggling widowed mother in their impoverished Dublin home and so she took him with her and, once safely ensconced in Whitehaven, she wrote to the boy's mother telling her of what she had done. The mother, not wanting her son to be exposed to another perilous sea crossing, told the nurse to keep him until it was safe to return to Dublin; and so JONATHAN SWIFT, future author and Dean of St Patrick's Cathedral, lived in Whitehaven until he was four, by which time he was able to read every chapter in the Bible. The house where he lived was a grim-looking 17th-century place called BOWLING GREEN HOUSE set high on the cliffs overlooking the harbour, and it was his memory of watching the tiny people moving about in the town below that provided Swift with the inspiration for the kingdom of Lilliput in *Gulliver's Travels*.

St Bees Head

Whitehaven stands at the northern end of 4 miles of precipitous red sandstone cliffs, the only major cliffs on the coast between Scotland and Wales. The coast path climbs along the cliff tops, past Birkham's Quarry, which is still supplying the St Bees red sandstone used for so many Cumbrian buildings, to St Bees Head, the westernmost point of northern England. St Bees lighthouse sits on the crest and from here, on a clear day, there are fine views of the Isle of Man. St Bees Head is home to an RSPB bird reserve and is the only breeding place in England of the Black Guillemot. It is also the start of the Coast to Coast Walk devised by Alfred Wainwright in 1972, which runs for 192 miles from the Irish Sea at St Bees to the North Sea at Robin's Hood Bay in North Yorkshire.

St Bees

The coast path now slopes down to the village of St Bees, which sits beside a wide sandy beach at the end of a long valley formed by the Pow Beck. The name St Bees comes from a legendary Irish princess called 'Bega' who fled Ireland in the 9th century to avoid a forced marriage to a Viking prince. She was washed up on the coast of Cumberland and appealed to the local landowner, Lord Egremont, for some land on which to build a nunnery. Now milord was not one to give anything away for free but he didn't want to appear mean, so he told the princess that she could have as much land as was covered by snow the next day – and since that was Midsummer's Day, Lord Egremont went to bed feeling pretty pleased with himself. Well, imagine how disgruntled he must have been when he woke up to find a huge tract of land between his castle and the sea deep in snow. Damned unsporting.

The nunnery Princess Bega established was sacked by the Vikings a hundred years later – serves her right, Lord Egremont might have said had he still been alive – and then rebuilt by the first Norman Lord Egremont as a Benedictine priory in 1120. Much of the priory was destroyed in 1539 during the Dissolution of the Monasteries, but the priory church was saved for use as the parish church, and although it was much restored by the Victorian architect William Butterfield in the 19th century some good features

of the Norman church survive. There are a number of fine Norman pillars in the nave, and the west doorway is considered the best Norman doorway in Cumbria. Outside, forming the lintel of an alcove set in the wall opposite the west door, is the carved Beowulf Stone, which portrays St Michael slaying the Dragon, and is thought to have come from the original pre-Conquest nunnery.

St Bees Man

In 1981 an archeological dig in a ruined area of the priory uncovered a lead coffin containing the body of a man of about 40. It was wrapped in a linen shroud impregnated with a resinous substance that had preserved his body to such an extent that his nails, skin and major organs were found to be in almost perfect condition, the best preserved body from medieval times ever found in England. St Bees Man, as he came to be known, is now thought to be a knight called Anthony de Lucy who died in 1368.

Across the road to the east of the priory is St Bees School, founded in 1583 by Edmund Grindal, the son of a local farmer, who became Archbishop of Canterbury under Elizabeth I. He was born in a big grey house called Cross Hill, which still sits at the top of the lovely sloping main street across the Barrow to Whitehaven railway which divides the village from the priory and school.

Old boys of St Bees School include CAPTAIN WILLIAM LEEFE ROBINSON (1895–1918), who won the Victoria Cross for being the first to shoot down an airship over Britain, in 1916, and ROWAN ATKINSON, TV comic and the creator of Mr Bean.

Ravenglass

Ravenglass is Cumberland's oldest seaport and the only coastal town that lies within the Lake District National Park. It is also one of the locations that claim to be the birthplace of St Patrick. It consists of a breezy main street lined with rosy cottages that straggles along the now sanded-up estuary where three rivers meet, the Irt, the Mite and the Esk. The Romans established an important naval base here in AD 79, which they called Glannoventa, and built a fort to protect it, the final link in a chain of fortifications that ran down the Cumberland coast from Hadrian's Wall at Bowness. The remains of the fort's bath house lie at the end of an avenue of trees running south from Ravenglass and form one of Britain's largest and best preserved Roman ruins. Parts of the wall around the fort are 12 feet (3.7 m) high, THE HIGHEST SECTION OF DEFENSIVE ROMAN WALL LEFT STANDING IN BRITAIN.

Sharing the railway station with the Cumbrian Coast Line is the Ravenglass and Eskdale Railway, THE FIRST PUBLIC NARROW-GAUGE RAILWAY IN ENGLAND, which was opened in 1875 to transport iron ore from workings above Boot in Eskdale, a distance of 7 miles. The line is known as 'Rat Trod', an old Cumbrian dialect name meaning 'rat track', and is today a popular tourist attraction.

Barrow-in-Furness

Barrow grew up around Furness Abbey whose resplendent rose-pink ruins fill the leafy Vale of Deadly Nightshade on the northeastern edge of the town. The abbey was founded in 1123 by the future King Stephen and grew into a great Cistercian house second only in power and wealth to Fountains Abbey in Yorkshire. In 1322 Robert the Bruce was royally entertained there by the abbot in a partially successful attempt to prevent the Scottish king from sacking the place, but in 1537, during the Reformation, Furness became the first major abbey to voluntarily dissolve, fearful of being charged with treason for having taken part in the Pilgrimage of Grace, a northern uprising against the Dissolution of the Monasteries.

In 1839 iron prospector Henry Schneider discovered huge iron ore deposits on the Furness Peninsula and in 1846, along with other investors, built the Furness Railway to bring the iron ore to the harbour. By 1870, the blast furnace that Schneider and his colleagues built in Barrow had made the town into of the largest steelworks in the world, while the population of Barrow increased from 700 in 1851 to 47,000 in 1881.

The ready availability of high-quality steel and Barrow's safe harbour encouraged the town to become a shipbuilding centre. In 1897 the Barrow Shipbuilding Company was taken over by the Sheffield steel firm Vickers and Barrow and became a leading producer of naval warships including the *Mikasa*, the Japanese flagship during the 1905 Russo-Japanese War, and the aircraft carrier *Invincible*, which found fame during the Falklands War.

In 1935 a Barrow ship became the first in the world to be launched by radio when the Duke of Gloucester, who was standing in the City Hall in Brisbane, Australia, 11,000 miles away, declared 'I name you *Orion*' and pulled a switch which sent an electronic signal to Barrow to release the ship into the water.

Iron and steel production ceased in Barrow in the 1980s, but the Vickers shipyard remained active and Barrow became synonymous with submarine manufacture, having produced THE ROYAL NAVY'S FIRST SUBMARINE *Holland 1* in 1901 and BRITAIN'S FIRST NUCLEAR SUBMARINE HMS *Dreadnought* in 1960.

Today the shipyard is part of BAE Systems and is manufacturing Britain's latest class of nuclear submarines, the Astute class. Barrow is currently BRITAIN'S LARGEST OPERATIONAL SHIPBUILDING TOWN by workforce numbers, and the DEVONSHIRE DOCK HALL, where the submarines are put together, is not only THE TALLEST BUILDING IN CUMBRIA at 167 feet (51 m) in height, but the largest indoor shipbuilding hall in Europe outside Germany. It covers an area of over 6 acres (2.4 ha) and is visible from Blackpool, 20 miles away.

The heart of Barrow that grew up around the shipyards is a town of wide, tree-lined boulevards and High Gothic buildings of the Victorian era. Particularly fine is the imposing red sandstone Town Hall, with its 164 foot (50 m) high clock tower, which was opened in 1887 to mark Queen Victoria's Golden Jubilee.

Piel Island

During the summer months a small ferry boat runs between Roa Island, south of Barrow, and Piel Island, half a mile due south and occupied only by a ruined castle and the Ship Inn. In the 12th century the monks of Furness Abbey built a warehouse on the island to handle cargo travelling between the abbey and its landholdings in Ireland and the Isle of Man. In the 14th century the warehouse was fortified with a motte and bailey castle for protection against pirates and the Scots, and as a base for smuggling, in which the abbey was much involved. The castle was the largest such fortification in the north-west and after it fell into decay in the 16th century the vast red sandstone ruins became known as the Pile of Fouldrey – which may explain how Piel Island got its name. The castle is today looked after by English Heritage.

In 1487 the 14-year-old Yorkist Pretender LAMBERT SIMNEL landed on Piel Island, accompanied by two thousand men-at-arms from Ireland, at the start of his unsuccessful campaign to win the throne away from Henry VII. Simnel claimed to be the Earl of Warwick and the rightful King of England, but he was defeated at the Battle of Stoke two weeks later and then allowed to join Henry's household as a kitchen boy.

In mock homage to Lambert Simnel the landlord of the 300-year-old Ship Inn is known as the King of Piel. Each new landlord is crowned King in a ceremony that involves him sitting in an ancient chair holding a sword and wearing a helmet while having alcohol poured over his head. The inn is popular with fishermen and yachtsmen, as well as day-trippers visiting the castle.

Rampside

Rampside, south of Barrow, has a long main street running alongside the muddy shingle beach which at low tide extends 2 miles out into the bay. In the late 18th century Rampside was bigger than Barrow, then still a small hamlet, and was popular as a bathing resort. William Wordsworth visited Rampside

in the early 1800s and wrote of the view towards Piel Castle:

I was thy neighbour once, thou rugged Pile!
Four summer weeks I dwelt in sight of thee:
I saw thee every day, and all the while,
Thy form was sleeping on a glassy sea.

On the beach opposite Clarke's Hotel is Rampside Lighthouse, known as 'The Needle'. Built in 1875 it is 66 feet (20 m) tall and made of red-and-yellow bricks, the only remaining example of 13 such navigation beacons that were dotted around Barrow Harbour in the 19th century to guide ships into port.

A little further on, to the left, is the 17th-century RAMPSIDE HALL, a local landmark with 12 chimneys all in a row that go by the name of 'the 12 apostles'.

Conishead Priory

On the coast just south of Ulverston is Conishead Priory, home since 1976 to the Manjushri Kadampa Meditation Centre, dedicated to the teaching of Buddhism and the art of Buddhist meditation. The site has been occupied since 1160, when a hospital was founded here for the 'poor, decrepit, indigent and lepers', which later became an Augustine priory and something of a rival to Furness Abbey. One of the monks would always be on hand to guide people across the treacherous Leven Sands of Morecambe Bay.

At the Dissolution of the Monasteries in 1537 the priory was demolished and the materials used for building a large private house for William Stanley, Lord Mounteagle, whose son would uncover the Gunpowder Plot in 1605. In 1821 the new owner, Colonel Braddyll, commissioned the architect Philip Wyatt to remodel the house in an extravagant Gothick style similar to that of Horace Walpole's Strawberry Hill House in London. The cost ruined the Colonel and he had to sell up, unaware that enough iron ore ran beneath the property to have made him richer than he could have dreamed. The priory then passed though a number of hands, becoming a hydropathic hotel known as the 'Paradise of Furness', a convalescent home for Durham miners, a military hospital and finally the Buddhist retreat it is today. In 1997 THE WORLD'S FIRST KADAMPA WORLD PEACE TEMPLE opened in the grounds of Conishead Priory, the Mother Temple of a series of international temples dedicated to world peace being built in major cities around the world. Inside is THE LARGEST

BRONZE STATUE OF BUDDHA YET
CAST IN THE WEST.

Ulverston

A mile further north the coast path comes to Canal Point, the seaside end of the Ulverston Canal and a pleasant spot with an inn, a lock-keeper's cottage, some dilapidated lock gates and fine views across the sands. The canal was built by the engineer John Rennie in 1796 to link Ulverston with the sea and runs dead straight into the town for just over a mile. At 65 feet (20 m) wide and 15 feet (4.6 m) deep it is THE SHORTEST, WIDEST AND DEEPEST CANAL IN BRITAIN. A vast pharmaceutical plant lurks behind trees along one side of the canal.

Ulverston itself is an ancient market town of narrow, winding cobbled streets and comely old buildings set between green hills and the sea. It is the birthplace of Stanley Jefferson, better known to the world as STAN LAUREL, the smaller half of the comedy duo Laurel and Hardy, who was born in his grandparents' tiny terraced house in Argyll Street in 1890 – the house is still there. There is a statue of Laurel and Hardy leaning on a lamp-post outside the Coronation Hall, and housed in the Roxy Cinema complex behind the hall is the world's only Laurel and Hardy museum, containing THE BIGGEST COLLECTION OF LAUREL AND HARDY MEMORABILIA EVER ASSEMBLED.

Overlooking the town from Hoad Hill to the northeast is the HOAD MONUMENT, put up in 1850 as a tribute to Sir John Barrow, born in a small cottage in Dragley Beck, Ulverston, in 1764 – the tiny house is still there beside the A5087 coast road

as it enters the town from the south. The monument is 100 feet (30 m) tall and built to resemble John Smeaton's Eddystone Lighthouse. Visitors can climb 122 steps to a viewing room near the top from where it is possible on a clear day to see the whole of Morecambe Bay, the Yorkshire Dales, the Lakeland Fells, Blackpool Tower and Snowdonia.

Sir John Barrow

SIR JOHN BARROW (1764–1848) was Second Secretary to the
Admiralty for over 40 years, from 1804 to 1845. The Battle of
Trafalgar took place under his watch, and as Nelson stepped aboard
HMS *Victory* at Portsmouth before sailing off to battle, Sir John was
the last man to shake his hand. After the Battle of Waterloo in 1815,
Barrow proposed the island of St Helena as Napoleon Bonaparte's
place of exile, and as a founder of the Royal Geographical Society,
he promoted a number of Arctic expeditions, including those of
John Ross, William Parry and Captain John Franklin. Point Barrow
and the city of Barrow in Alaska are named after him, as are the
Barrow Strait in the Canadian Arctic, Barrow Island, off Western
Australia, and Mount Barrow on Tasmania.

Kent's Bank

Kent's Bank lies, appropriately enough,
on the west bank of the Kent estuary.
Until the arrival of the railway in 1857
there was almost nothing there except
Abbot Hall, now a hotel but originally
a rest house built by the monks of
Furness Abbey in 1160 for those travelling across Morecambe Bay. The present
building was put up in 1840. The sweet
little Victorian station incorporates a
weather-boarded art gallery with a huge
chimney that looks as if it dates from
Tudor times.

Kent's Bank is at the western end of
one of the ancient routes across the
Kent estuary portion of Morecambe
Bay taken by those travelling between
Lancaster and Carlisle, and a little north
of Kent's Bank, right on the edge of
the estuary, is the 700-year-old Guide's
Farm, complimentary home of the
Queen's Guide to the Sands, who is
appointed by the Crown to guide
people along the treacherous paths
through the shifting sands. Until the
Dissolution of the Monasteries the
monks from Conishead Priory and
Furness Abbey provided guides, but this
role was taken over by the Duchy of
Lancaster on behalf of the Crown, with
the first official guide, THOMAS
HOGESON, being appointed in 1548.
Today the Queen's Guide leads regular
summer crossings of the sands between
Arnside and Kent's Bank, usually to raise
money for charities.

Well, I never knew this
about
THE CUMBRIAN COAST

ROCKCLIFFE MARSH, beside the Solway Firth, is THE BIGGEST SALT MARSH IN ENGLAND.

Standing marooned on the greensward between the road and the beach in ALLONBY, a quaint fishing village and resort developed in the 18th century by Quakers, is the first solo commission of the architect ALFRED WATERHOUSE, who would go on to bring us such monumental creations as London's Natural History Museum and Manchester Town Hall. It was built for the Quakers in 1862 as a Reading Room, a place where the people of Allonby could go to read and educate themselves.

SELLAFIELD nuclear fuel reprocessing site is THE LARGEST NUCLEAR SITE IN EUROPE, home to 80 per cent of the UK's nuclear waste and the birthplace of the nuclear age. Sellafield also incorporates Windscale, the site of the original nuclear reactor that produced the plutonium for Britain's first nuclear bomb in the 1950s, and Calder Hall, where THE WORLD'S FIRST COMMERCIAL NUCLEAR POWER STATION opened in 1956. Both Windscale and Calder Hall are now being decommissioned and there is a visitor centre telling the story of the plant.

MILLOM is the southernmost town in the old county of Cumberland. It began life as a small settlement that grew up around a Norman church and castle, the latter now ruined and with a 16th-century farmhouse built amongst the ruins. They stand about a mile north of the new town of Millom, which came into existence in 1855 when iron ore was discovered nearby. Towards the end of the 19th century Millom boasted 11 shafts and THE BIGGEST AND BUSIEST IRONWORKS IN THE WORLD.

WALNEY ISLAND is 12 miles long and a quarter mile wide at most – in some places it is no more than 100 yards wide – but it still acts as a natural breakwater for Barrow-in-Furness. Walney was the inspiration for the Isle of Sodor, where the steam engines lived in the Revd W. Awdry's *Thomas the Tank Engine* stories, while Vickerstown is the model for Vicarstown.

ULVERSTON claims to have invented polevaulting as a competitive sport by adapting the practice of local farmers who would leap over their farm gates using their shepherd's crooks. One such farmer, Ulverston's Tom Ray, became the World Pole Vaulting Champion in 1887.

HUMPHREY HEAD, at the southeastern tip of the Cartmel Peninsula, is a long, thin limestone ridge with cliffs up to 172 feet (52 m) high that projects a mile into Morecambe Bay at the mouth of the Kent estuary. The hawthorn trees atop the ridge are bent almost flat by the fierce winds. At the base of the cliffs on the western side, where the road peters out, is St Agnes Well, whose waters are said to cure gout and worms. It was on Humphrey Head, in 1390 or thereabouts, that local landowner SIR JOHN HARRINGTON is said to have cornered and killed the last wolf in England.

A mile inland from Grange is the little stone village of CARTMEL, dominated by its noble priory church, which is all that survives, along with a gatehouse, of the Augustinian priory founded here by William Marshal, 1st Earl of Pembroke, in 1190. Although much rebuilt over the years the church is renowned for its glorious east window, the tomb of Lord Harrington, ancestor of the wolf slayer, and some beautifully carved misericords. The church tower is unique in England, having been added to in the 15th century by a new upper section placed at a 45-degree angle – ENGLAND'S ONLY DIAGONAL CHURCH TOWER.

CHAPTER TWO
LANCASHIRE COAST

Silverdale to Preston
75 miles

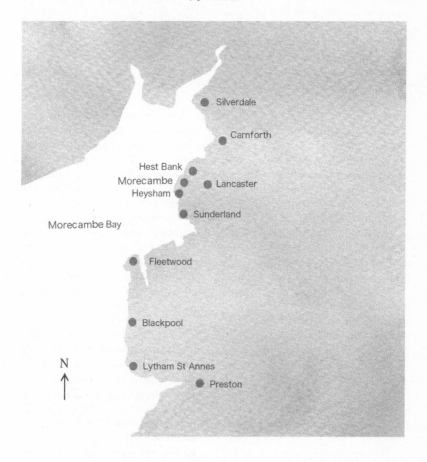

Silverdale

Carnforth

Hest Bank
Morecambe
Heysham

Lancaster

Sunderland

Morecambe Bay

Fleetwood

Blackpool

N

Lytham St Annes

Preston

Highlights of the Lancashire coast include a Brief Encounter, Britain's largest expanse of mudflats and sands, the finest neolithic site in northern Europe, the Taj Mahal of the North, the only mainland community in England cut off by the tide, the first planned town of the Victorian era, the home of the Fisherman's Friend, Britain's only surviving Victorian tramway, the only town in England to boast three piers, Britain's tallest roller-coaster, the site of the last major battle fought on English soil and Europe's biggest bus station.

Silverdale

Silverdale welcomes us into Lancashire at the meeting place of two coastal paths, the Cumbria Coastal Way north to Scotland and the Lancashire Coastal Way south to Freckleton, near Blackpool. The Victorian Lancashire poet Edwin Waugh spoke of 'Pleasant Silverdale, all in the blossomtide', and the village sits at the heart of an Area of Outstanding Natural Beauty. The beguiling scenery attracted *Cranford* author ELIZABETH GASKELL to come and visit in 1843 and she returned regularly for the next 20 years, often staying at LINDETH TOWER south of the village, where she wrote her novel *Ruth*, published in 1853. The three-storey tower was built by Preston banker and shipowner HESKETH FLEETWOOD, whose family founded the town of Fleetwood further down the coast. From here he could watch as his ships made their way in and out of Barrow, across Morecambe Bay.

In 1826 Charlotte and Emily Brontë were sent to stay at Cove House in Silverdale, the summer home of the Revd Carus Wilson, the headmaster of their school at Cowan Bridge, to escape the fever that had killed two of their sisters.

Carnforth

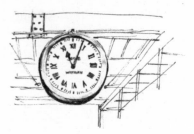

In the 19th century Carnforth grew rapidly from a small village into an industrial town thanks to steel and the railways. Iron ore from Cumbria and locally mined limestone provided the materials for steel making, while the meeting here of the Furness Railway, the Carnforth to Leeds line and the main west coast London to Glasgow line made the town an important railway junction. In 1937 the London Midland and Scottish Railway Company rebuilt the station to include a 900 foot (274 m) long platform, sheltered by THE LONGEST UNSUPPORTED SINGLE-PIECE CONCRETE ROOF IN BRITAIN, which is now used by northbound trains on the Furness Line. Mainline trains no longer stop at Carnforth, but the railway station is famous world-wide as the location for David Lean's classic 1945 film *Brief Encounter* starring Trevor Howard and Celia Johnson. The station has been converted into a heritage centre where you can watch *Brief Encounter*, pose beneath the iconic station clock which featured prominently in the film and take tea in the Refreshment Room, which has been carefully refurbished to replicate the studio set used in the film. Just northwest of the station, a unique Victorian stone signal box built in 1882 for the Furness Railway survives, although it is no longer in use.

Hest Bank

Hest Bank stands at the southern end of the ancient route across the sands of Morecambe Bay to Kent's Bank, 11 miles to the northwest. Until 1857 a horse-drawn service operated between Hest Bank and Ulverston, described by the poet William Wordsworth as 'the only acceptable route into the Lake District'. Due to the shifting sands the walk between Hest Bank and Kent's Bank is no longer possible and the Queen's Guide to the Sands now takes those wishing to walk the sands on a shorter 6 mile walk between Arnside and Kent's Bank.

Morecambe Bay

Morecambe Bay is the largest expanse of mudflats and sands in the British Isles and supports one of the largest populations of sea birds in the world. It is a magical seascape of sweeping sands, mudflats and salt marshes that covers an area of 120 square miles and stretches from Barrow-in-Furness in the northwest to the Lancashire coast towns of Morecambe and Heysham in the southeast. Five rivers drain into the bay, the rivers Leven, Kent, Keer, Lune and Wyre, and their estuaries create a number of peninsulas, the largest being the Furness and Cartmel peninsulas formed by the Leven and Kent estuaries. Crossing the sands of Morecambe Bay used to be an important route from

Lancaster to the north avoiding the Lakeland mountains, but the shifting sands and treacherous tides made the route hazardous, and guides were essential (*see* Hest Bank, left).

Morecambe

Morecambe grew out of three fishing villages to become a popular Victorian resort with the arrival in the 1850s of the railway bringing holiday-makers from Yorkshire and Scotland. It has a bracing promenade that curves for 4 miles along the edge of the bay and was originally laid out in red brick and black diamonds as the first two-coloured promenade in England. The panoramic views across the bay are spectacular with sunsets that have inspired artists including J.M.W. Turner.

As holiday patterns changed and more people went abroad, the 1980s and 90s saw a period of decline in Morecambe with the demolition of the town's two piers and the closing of many of its other attractions including Marineland, Europe's first oceanarium, which had opened in 1964. The town is now being revived as a holiday desti-nation and in 2002 was chosen by the RNLI to be the site for their FIRST ACTIVE HOVERCRAFT LIFEBOAT.

Midland Hotel

Landmarks include the red-brick neo-Gothic Winter Gardens, opened in 1897, the beautifully restored art deco Midland Hotel opposite the station, a former railway hotel with sculptures by Eric Gill, and Graham Ibbeson's prancing statue of Morecambe's most famous son, ERIC MORECAMBE, of the comedy duo Morecambe and Wise. He was born here in 1926 as John Eric Bartholomew, and changed his name to Morecambe in honour of his beloved home town.

Heysham

A little to the north of the port of Heysham, at the northern end of Half Moon Bay, is the rocky promontory of HEYSHAM HEAD, or the Barrows, forming the only sea cliffs on the Lancashire coast. Heysham Head lies due east of the southeastern tip of Walney Island and the line between the two marks the southern boundary of Morecambe Bay.

Sheltered behind Heysham Head is the quaint stone village of Old Heysham, its narrow, twisting streets a complete and welcome contrast to the industrial sprawl of Heysham's newer incarnation to the south. Main Street, lined with rose-decked stone cottages, tea shops and pubs, leads to ST PETER'S CHURCH, built low and solid against the sea winds from the north. The view from the churchyard, north across wide

Morecambe Bay to the Furness Hills, is exhilarating, especially when the hills are tipped with winter snow.

There has been a church here since the 7th century, first of wood and then of Saxon stone, the latter recorded on the site in 1080. Just inside the south door is St Peter's great treasure, ENGLAND'S FINEST VIKING HOG-BACK TOMBSTONE, decorated along the sides with carved figures of men and animals illustrating a stag hunt or, perhaps, the ancient Viking legend of Sigmund and Sigurd. A bear hugs the tomb at each end.

On the headland above St Peter's stand the gaunt ruins of the only single-cell Saxon chapel left in England. The chapel is dedicated to St Patrick, for the headland is said to be where St Patrick himself landed when he came to Britain from Ireland in the 5th century.

A few steps away from the chapel, on the cliff top, are two remarkable sets of graves cut into the living rock, one group of six and one of two. They are shaped for a human head and body, with a socket at the head to hold a cross, and would have been covered by stone slabs. Bones recovered from the rock coffins have been dated to the 10th century, but numerous artefacts from the neolithic period have been excavated from beneath them, making

Heysham THE FINEST NEOLITHIC
SITE IN NORTHERN EUROPE.

Sunderland

A little to the northeast of the point on
the west bank of the Lune estuary is
Sunderland, one of those gloriously
remote and atmospheric former ports
that seem to proliferate along this coastline of estuaries and shifting sands. The
road across the marsh from Overton is
covered by the high tide twice a day,
making SUNDERLAND THE ONLY
MAINLAND COMMUNITY IN ENGLAND
CUT OFF BY THE TIDE. Small boats
wallow in the mud in front of two
terraces of a dozen sturdy dark sandstone
houses and warehouses and one elegant
stone gatepost. They stand on the crumbling dockside to remind us of what was
an important entry port for Lancaster,
developed in the early 18th century by
a Quaker, Robert Lawson. The port only
lasted for 20 years or so before losing
its custom to Lancaster, but its importance to the Lancashire cotton trade,
and hence the Industrial Revolution, is
historic, for it was at Sunderland in 1701
that the first ever bales of raw cotton
from the New World were landed – and
left on the quayside for a year because
no one knew what it was or what to do
with it. A cotton tree, or black poplar,
native to America, stood beside one of
the cottages for more than two hundred

years, since the days of Sunderland's
prosperity, and was thought to have
sprung from a seed spilled from an
imported bale of cotton. It was blown
down in a storm on New Year's Day in
1998. A section of the trunk can still be
seen in front of the cottage.

Sunderland was part of the slave
triangle between Africa, America and
Europe, and across the headland from
the village, reached by a path from the
Old Brewery, is SAMBO'S GRAVE, the
burial place of a young African slave
brought here from the West Indies in
1736 by the captain of a ship sailing to
Lancaster. The young man was left at
the old brewery while his master went
on to Lancaster to conclude his business
but fell ill and died, and was buried in
an unmarked grave on the seashore.
Sixty years later the grave was discovered by a retired schoolteacher who
raised some money for a memorial and
wrote a moving epitaph that can still
be seen inscribed on a plaque embedded
in the gravestone.

Lancaster

During the 18th century Lancaster
handled trade with the West Indies and
was the fourth busiest port in England
after London, Bristol and Liverpool. St
George's Quay, beside the River Lune
and lined with tall 18th-century warehouses, is redolent of those days. The
handsome Palladian Custom House
was built in 1764 by RICHARD
GILLOW, son of the founder of the
Gillow furniture making company.

Looking down over the quayside
from its situation on Castle Hill is
Lancaster's mighty Norman castle, built
on the site of the Roman fort that gave
the town its name – Lunecastra, or the
fort on the Lune. The castle has a huge

12th-century keep, 80 feet (24 m) square and 66 feet (20 m) high with walls 10 feet (3 m) thick, and a magnificent 15th-century gatehouse that has been described as one of the finest fortified gatehouses in England.

Since it was built the castle has been in constant use as a prison and courthouse, and the 13th-century Well Tower, named after its two wells, has three stone dungeons where prisoners were kept while awaiting trial, including the ten Lancashire Witches from Pendle whose notorious trial and execution took place at the castle in 1612. The Lancashire Assizes has been held at Lancaster Castle since 1176, and it is thought that more people have been sentenced to death on this spot than anywhere else in England. At the end of the 18th century the old Great Hall where the court sat was replaced by a new Shire Hall, where the Crown Court still sits, making it THE OLDEST CONTINUOUSLY SITTING CROWN COURT IN ENGLAND. On show inside is the last official criminal branding iron that survives in England, used for burning the hands of malefactors with a 'M' – it was last used in 1811.

Nearby on Castle Hill is the medieval parish church, Lancaster Priory, founded as a Benedictine priory in 1094 on the site of a 6th-century Saxon church. Roman artefacts excavated on the site suggest that there has been Christian worship here since the 2nd century, one of the few sites in Roman Britain where Christianity was practised before it became legal throughout the Roman Empire. The priory is famous for its beautifully carved oak choir stalls and misericords, dating from 1345, the third oldest in England, and regarded as amongst the most impressive sets of medieval church furniture in England.

Just down the hill from the castle and overlooked by the imposing Georgian façade of the Judge's Lodgings, is Market Square, where a cross stands from which the kings and queens of England have been proclaimed since medieval days – Charles II was proclaimed king here in 1651, nine years before his Restoration to the throne in 1660.

Fleetwood

Fleetwood stands at the northern tip of the Fylde Peninsula, which stretches as far south as Lytham St Annes and is dominated by Blackpool on the middle. Greeting passengers arriving in Fleetwood on the ferry from Knott End-on-Sea to the east is the elegant Queen's Terrace, built in 1844 by Decimus Burton who, amongst other things, was responsible for the spectacular terraces lining Regent's Park and St James's Park in London. Burton was hired by local landowner PETER HESKETH-FLEETWOOD to develop Fleetwood as a seaport and resort town, and both Burton and his employer lived in Queen's Terrace from time to time while development was ongoing. Fleetwood was THE FIRST PLANNED TOWN OF THE VICTORIAN ERA and much of Burton's original 'halfwheel' layout remains.

Across from Queen's Terrace is the old railway station, built to welcome

Queen Victoria when she arrived in Fleetwood by boat from Scotland in 1847 and here transferred to the royal train. Fleetwood never became the transport hub that Hesketh-Fleetwood had intended but ferry services to Scotland, Ireland and the Isle of Man were introduced along with some cargo traffic, and the port found honest employment as one of Britain's leading deep sea fishing ports until the 1970s when the Cod Wars with Iceland and the imposition of Europe's Common Fishing Policy brought about the collapse of Britain's fishing industry. The ferry service to the Isle of Man was withdrawn in 1961, the service to Larne in Northern Ireland ceased in 2010, and the dockside is now used as a marina.

Fleetwood is the only town in England that can boast three lighthouses, and just around the corner from Queen's Terrace is the tallest of the three, the Upper Lighthouse, popularly known as the 'Pharos' after the Pharos of Alexandria, one of the seven wonders of the ancient world. The Fleetwood Pharos, an 1840 design by Decimus Burton, 93 feet (28 m) high, made of pink sandstone and still functioning, is the only working lighthouse in Britain that stands in the middle of the street. The second of the lighthouses is the

Lower or Beach Lighthouse which sits on the seafront to the north of the Pharos. Also still functioning and also designed by Decimus Burton in 1840, this lighthouse is 44 feet (13 m) high. The third lighthouse, the 40 foot (12 m) high WYRE LIGHT, stands 2 miles offshore on a sandbank and is no longer operational. It was designed by a blind Irish engineer called Alexander Mitchell, who was the inventor of the screw pile, an anchoring system for structures requiring deep foundations, and it was THE FIRST SCREW PILE LIGHTHOUSE IN THE WORLD EVER TO BE LIT. When the lights of the three lighthouses were lined up they marked the path of the deep-water channel into the Wyre estuary.

Across the road from the Lower Lighthouse is the imposing crescent façade of the NORTH EUSTON HOTEL, Fleetwood's crown jewel and another of Decimus Burton's designs. At the time of its opening in 1841 there was no rail link across the Lake District Hills for those travelling between London and Scotland, and Peter Hesketh-Fleetwood's idea was that Fleetwood should serve as a rail terminus where travellers could disembark from the train and board a boat to Scotland. The hotel was built as somewhere for these rail travellers to stay, and since the railway station where they would have boarded the train in London was Euston he named the hotel the North Euston. However, in the 1850s, the main west coast railway line between London and Scotland was completed to the east and Fleetwood's days as a boat and rail link were over, although the town's glorious sandy beach has ensured that it remains a popular resort.

A few hundred yards south is the Mount, a landscaped sandhill topped by a pagoda-style summer house from which there are wondrous views in all directions.

Decimus Burton used this, the tallest of the seafront sandhills, as the hub of his half-wheel design for Fleetwood, and from here it is possible to make out the residential streets that form the spokes of the wheel leading to the rim created by commercial area of Dock Street.

On the seafront further south is Fleetwood's Model Yacht Pond, believed to be THE LARGEST MODEL YACHT POND IN EUROPE. And Fleetwood has a couple more claims to fame, as the site of BRITAIN'S FIRST FULLY AUTOMATED TELEPHONE EXCHANGE, which opened in 1922, and as the home of the Lofthouse Company, makers of FISHERMEN'S FRIEND throat lozenges, developed to protect the fishermen of Fleetwood from the chill winds of the northern seas. A favourite of Prime Minister Margaret Thatcher, Fishermen's Friends are so strong that local children like to dare each other to try and eat more than three lozenges without crying.

Fleetwood is also the only town in Britain where trams share the full length of the main shopping street with cars. The tramway was built in the 1890s and links Fleetwood with Blackpool, 11 miles down the coast.

Blackpool

Blackpool – 7 miles of honey-coloured sands, amusements and illuminations, theatres, grand hotels and traditional guesthouses (many with free use of cruet), three piers, one tower, a Golden Mile, a Pleasure Beach frequently voted the UK's best theme park while being among the top 20 most visited amusement parks in the world, BRITAIN'S ONLY SURVIVING VICTORIAN TRAMWAY, constructed in 1885, and THE WORLD'S FIRST LITTLEWOODS STORE, opened in 1937.

It was during the 19th century that Blackpool developed from a small coastal hamlet into the 'archetypal English seaside resort'. During the 18th century the health-giving properties of sea air were starting to be recognised, and those who could afford it began to make their way to the coast during the summer months. New roads were built from Manchester and Halifax to the sandy beaches of Blackpool, and a number of small hotels went up to accommodate the visitors. Then in the 1840s the railway arrived, allowing workers from the industrial cities of Lancashire to get to Blackpool quickly and cheaply, and the town boomed. In 1801 the population of Blackpool was 473. In 1901 it was 47,000, a total hugely boosted by some three million visitors every summer.

Blackpool proper begins just past Bispham station where an archway across the road heralds the start of the famous Blackpool Illuminations, consisting of over a million bulbs and dubbed 'THE GREATEST FREE LIGHT SHOW ON EARTH'. First put up in 1879, the Illuminations now run for 6 miles along the seafront as far as Starr Gate at the south end of Blackpool, and are switched on annually from late August to early November as a way of extending Blackpool's holiday season.

After about 2 miles the road and the tramway come up against Blackpool's oldest hotel, the Metropole, which opened in 1785 as Bailey's Hotel. It is the only hotel in Blackpool that sits directly on the shore and the road and tramway must divert inland to get around it. Blackpool's first stretch of promenade, which opened in 1856, ran from here for about a mile to where the Houndshill shopping centre is now. Since then the promenade has been extended in both directions and now you can walk all the way along the seafront to Fleetwood 12 miles away.

North Pier

Next up, past the tall obelisk War Memorial, erected in 1923, is the North Pier, the oldest and longest of Blackpool's three piers. (Blackpool is, in fact, the only town in England to boast three piers.) The North Pier opened in 1863 and is 550 yards long. Until recently it tended to provide more genteel entertainments, such as orchestral concerts and 'clean' comic performances and charged admission right up until 2011. Harry Corbett bought his original Sooty puppet on the pier in 1948, as a gift for his son Matthew.

Golden Mile

We now embark on the Golden Mile, which is the name given to the stretch of promenade between the North and South Piers, an actual distance of some 1½ miles. The name came about because of the high number of slot machines to be found along the way.

The first building we come to on the seafront of the Golden Mile is

Blackpool's futuristic new Wedding Chapel, which opened in 2011 and offers weddings 'almost at sea'. Meanwhile, across the road, Victoria Street leads off to the Winter Gardens entertainment complex, which opened in 1878 and contains three reception halls, an exhibition hall, a banqueting hall, a ballroom and two theatres, including the Opera House Theatre, one of the largest theatres in the country and home TO THE LAST NEW WURLITZER TO BE INSTALLED IN BRITAIN. Victoria Street was also the site of Blackpool's first entertainment venue, the Assembly Rooms, built in 1837 and finally demolished in 1989.

Blackpool Tower

Blackpool Tower, the most famous landmark on the northwest coast, is visible from the Lake District hills to the north and Snowdonia to the south. Inspired by the Eiffel Tower in Paris, it opened in 1894 and stands 518 feet (158 m) high. For its first six years it was the tallest structure in the UK, until overtaken in 1900 by the New Brighton Tower on the Wirral, which reached 567 feet (173 m) in height before being dismantled in 1919. There is an observation deck at a height of 380 feet (120 m) which is known as the Blackpool Tower Eye and is the highest observation deck in the northwest of England.

The tower rises out of a three-storey block which contains an aquarium, a circus and a celebrated ballroom.

Central Pier

Known as the 'People's Pier' because it specialised in dancing, an activity frowned upon by the posher types who frequented the North Pier, the Central Pier was built in 1868 and is 500 yards (460 m) long. It is today dominated by a 108 foot (33 m) high Ferris Wheel, erected in 1990.

A bit further on, past a pedestrian crossing and across the road, is the Foxhall pub, housed in a fairly unprepossessing red-and-yellow striped brick building with a round tower at the entrance. This is the spot where Blackpool began, for it stands on the site of Fox Hall, a house put up in the late 17th century by Royalist supporter Edward Tyldesley near to the peaty or 'black' pool, full of dark water from Marton Moss, that gave the town its name. Fox Hall, which was so called because the Tyldesleys kept a fox chained up beside the front door, survived in some form until the end of the 1980s when it was demolished to make way for the present delight.

South Pier

The South Pier opened as the Victoria Pier in 1893. At 492 feet (149 m) long it is shorter but wider than the other two piers and was designed to accommodate a number of pavilions providing orchestral and theatrical performances. Today the pier offers amusement arcades and fairground rides and is only open from March until September.

Next door is Britain's largest indoor water park, the Sandcastle Water Park, home to THE MASTERBLASTER, THE WORLD'S LARGEST INDOOR ROLLER-COASTER WATER SLIDE and THE SIDEWINDER, THE FIRST VERTICAL INDOOR DROP SLIDE IN THE WORLD.

Pleasure Beach

Across the road is Blackpool's Pleasure Beach, one of the world's first and greatest amusement parks, founded in 1896 and today attracting some six million visitors every year. In 1904 the park introduced its first ride, a rotary swing ride designed by the machine-gun inventor Sir Hiram Maxim to replicate flight. SIR HIRAM MAXIM'S CAPTIVE FLYING MACHINE still operates today and is THE OLDEST AMUSEMENT PARK RIDE IN EUROPE.

Blackpool Pleasure Beach has ten rollercoasters, more than any other amusement park in Britain. In 1979 the park opened EUROPE'S FIRST FULLY LOOPING ROLLERCOASTER, REVOLUTION. In 1994 came THE BIG ONE, then THE TALLEST, FASTEST AND STEEPEST ROLLERCOASTER IN THE WORLD. At 213 feet (65 m) high with a first drop of 205 feet (62 m), it is still THE TALLEST ROLLERCOASTER IN BRITAIN. In 2018 the park introduced BRITAIN'S FIRST MULTI-LAUNCH ROLLERCOASTER, Icon. The park's water ride, known as VALHALLA, which opened in 2000, is THE LONGEST INDOOR DARK RIDE IN THE WORLD.

Lytham St Annes

Founded in 1875 by businessman ELIJAH HARGREAVES, St Annes is a quiet Victorian seaside resort that makes up the northwestern part of the township of Lytham St Annes and was the original home of ERNIE, the computer which selects Premium Bonds winners. It has a wide sandy beach backed by sand dunes and the northern section of the beach was internationally famous for sand-yachting until 2002, when a visitor died after being hit by a sand yacht and the sport was banned from the beach.

Set in a sunken garden just before the pier is a statue of the comedian LES DAWSON who lived in St Annes for many years. St Annes Pier was built in 1885 and has a quaint Edwardian mock-Tudor entrance with gables and timbers. Close by, in the Promenade Gardens beyond the bandstand, is the St Annes Lifeboat Monument, commemorating BRITAIN'S WORST EVER LIFEBOAT DISASTER when 27 lifeboatmen from St Annes and Southport lost their lives while attempting to rescue the crew of a German barque called *Mexico*, which had been driven on to a sandbank during a gale in 1886. The entire 13-man crew of the St Annes lifeboat was lost.

Further along the Inner Promenade, the road that runs between the beach and the houses, at No. 199, is the former home of entertainer GEORGE FORMBY, once Britain's highest paid performer, famous for his banjo and ukelele and remembered especially for the song 'Leaning on a Lamp-post'. Formby bought the house from the Irish tenor JOSEPH LOCKE and lived there from 1953 until his death in 1961. He called the house Beryldene after his formidable wife Beryl. A later occupant was the astrologer RUSSELL GRANT.

Preston

'a pretty town with an abundance of gentry in it, commonly called Proud Preston'
Edmund Calamy (1671–1732)

Proud Preston it still is. As well as being Britain's 50th city, having gained city status in 2002, Preston is Britain's second oldest borough, with a market charter dating from 1179, the former capital of the Duchy of Lancaster, and the current administrative centre of the county of Lancashire. It possesses one of Britain's finest museums and art galleries, the Harris Museum, has BRITAIN'S TALLEST PARISH CHURCH SPIRE, which soars 308 feet (94 m) high above St Walburge's Roman Catholic church, built by Joseph Hansom (of Hansom cab fame) in 1847, and can also claim the title of first place in the UK to have a Kentucky Fried Chicken outlet – it opened in 1965 on the main shopping street, Fishergate.

The city sits at the crossroads of two Roman roads, while the name Preston comes from 'Priest's Tun' – 'tun' being the Old English word for settlement – referring to a priory built by St Wilfrid in the 7th century at the lowest crossing point of the River Ribble (now marked by Old Penwortham Bridge).

There have been two Battles of Preston. The first was fought along the marshy banks of the Ribble in 1648 when Oliver Cromwell's New Model Army defeated an army of Royalists and Scots under the Duke of Hamilton, a definitive victory that finally ended the English Civil War in Parliament's favour. The second Battle of Preston, which was fought in the town itself in 1715, brought to an end the first Jacobite Rising and was THE LAST MAJOR BATTLE FOUGHT ON ENGLISH SOIL.

Once Lancashire's most important cotton town, Preston is also one of the birthplaces of the Industrial Revolution, for here, in 1732, was born RICHARD ARKWRIGHT, the inventor of the cotton spinning frame and creator of the modern factory system. Still standing in Stoneygate, near the city centre, is the fine Georgian house of 1728, now called ARKWRIGHT HOUSE, where in 1769 he developed his spinning machine, or water frame, which enabled the mass production of textiles. The cotton workers of Preston protested, fearful of losing their jobs to Arkwright's machines, and forced Arkwright to go and create his first factory elsewhere, but eventually mass production did come to Preston when John Horrocks built Preston's first factory in Dale Street, not far from Stoneygate, in 1791. After this Preston boomed and cotton mills sprang up all over the town, putting it at the forefront of the Industrial Revolution. Not many of the mills remain and those that do have been turned into shops and apartments, but the large, elegant Georgian houses of Winckley Square at the heart of the city give us some idea of how the mill owners lived.

Another indication of the town's increasing prosperity came in 1816 when Preston became THE FIRST TOWN OUTSIDE LONDON TO BE LIT WITH GAS.

On the other side of the coin, poverty amongst the mill workers drove many to drink, and in answer to this Preston gave birth to the TEMPERANCE MOVEMENT when Preston-born reformer JOSEPH LIVESEY set up the Preston Temperance Society in 1833. At one of the Society's meetings a member called Richard Turner, who had a stammer, tried to take the Pledge of 't-t-t-total' abstinence, giving rise to the word 'teetotal', meaning someone who abstains from alcohol.

The plight of Preston's cotton workers also attracted a number of different religious organisations to descend on the town. In 1837 Preston became THE SITE OF THE FIRST MORMON MISSION OUTSIDE AMERICA, and on 30 July that year the first nine English Mormon converts were baptised in the River Ribble. Today Preston is home to THE WORLD'S OLDEST CONTINUOUS MORMON CONGREGATION.

As the mid-way point between London and Glasgow, Preston has for centuries been a transport hub, and today it can boast THE BIGGEST BUS STATION IN EUROPE. In 1958 the town was bypassed by BRITAIN'S FIRST STRETCH OF MOTORWAY, now part of the M6, which during its construction was policed by Britain's first traffic cones. The railway arrived in Preston in 1838 and was extended to Glasgow in the 1850s. At that time London to Glasgow took more than 12 hours by rail and most passengers preferred to break the journey half-way at Preston, and so a number of huge railway hotels were built to accommodate them. The finest of them all, the Park Hotel, built in 1883, still stands in beautiful grounds between the station and the river but, no longer a hotel, is now used as offices.

For much of the late 19th century and early 20th century Preston was the largest and busiest port in Lancashire, and when it opened in 1892 it had THE LARGEST SINGLE DOCK IN EUROPE.

Preston Dock declined during the 1970s thanks to strikes and the silting up of the River Ribble, and finally closed in 1981. The 40 acre (16 ha) dock area is now given over to commercial and leisure activities and housing.

Preston's football club, PRESTON NORTH END, goes back to 1880. In 1888 it was one of the 12 founder members of the Football League and was also the first winner of the Football League, remaining unbeaten in the 1888/89 season. Preston North End also won the FA Cup that season to become THE FIRST CLUB TO WIN THE DOUBLE. In 1875 the club's forerunners, the North End sports club, moved into Deepdale, where Preston North End still play their home games today, making Deepdale THE OLDEST CONTINUOUSLY USED FOOTBALL STADIUM IN THE WORLD.

Well, I never knew this
about
THE LANCASHIRE COAST

Described as one of the wonders of the waterways, the LUNE AQUEDUCT carries the Lancaster Canal across the River Lune at Lancaster at a height of 53 feet (16 m). Designed by John Rennie and built in 1797 by Alexander Stevens, using traditional bridge building techniques, it is formed of five 70 foot (21 m) wide semi-circular arches and is 664 feet (202 m) long.

Visible from the sea and dominating the Lancaster skyline the 150 foot (46 m) tall Portland stone ASHTON MEMORIAL, with its copper dome, sits on a hill in Williamson Park, east of the city centre. Known as the Taj Mahal of the North, it was built in 1909 by industrialist Lord Ashton in memory of his wife Jessy at a cost of some £8 million in today's money. There is a viewing gallery at first-floor level which provides wide views of Lancaster and the surrounding countryside, Morecambe Bay and the Lakeland Hills.

BLACKPOOL AIRPORT, at Squire's Gate, south of Blackpool, was one of the first aviation sites in the country and where BRITAIN'S FIRST PUBLIC FLYING MEETING TOOK PLACE IN 1909. Hull-born Amy Johnson, THE FIRST WOMAN TO FLY SOLO TO AUSTRALIA, used to visit her sister at her home near Blackpool's Stanley Park, and it was on a flight south from Blackpool in January 1941 that Amy was killed when her plane ran out of fuel and crashed into the Thames estuary near Herne Bay.

Separated from the sea at St Annes by the railway and several streets of houses, Royal Lytham & St Annes is the most famous of Lytham's four golf courses and one of the world's best links courses. The club was founded in 1886 and has hosted ten Open championships and two Ryder Cups. Lying at the southeastern end of the golf course, on the landward side of the railway, is the village of Ansdell, named after the artist Richard Ansdell (1815–1885) who had a 'summer house' in the area. Ansdell is THE ONLY PLACE IN ENGLAND NAMED AFTER AN ARTIST.

CHAPTER THREE
MERSEYSIDE COAST

Southport to Parkgate
50 miles

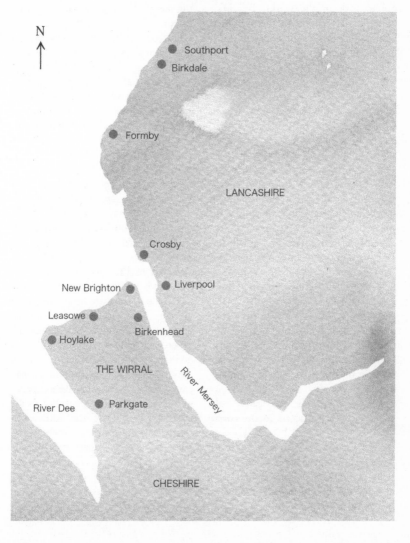

Highlights of the Merseyside coast include the oldest and longest iron pier in Britain, the ruins of the world's first lifeboat station, the fields where potatoes were grown for the first time in England, the world's largest brick warehouse, the largest clock faces in England, the largest single collection of Grade 1 listed buildings in Britain, Britain's biggest cathedral, the first public park in the world, Britain's oldest brick lighthouse and the first building in the world to be entirely heated by solar energy.

Southport

And so we come to Southport, which is held well back from its own beach by the huge Marine Lake, covering 91 acres (37 ha) and buzzing with boats and water sports of every kind. The lake, Marine Drive, shops and entertainments are all built on land reclaimed from the sea throughout the course of the 20th century.

Southport began life as a small inn and bathing house built amongst the sand dunes in 1792 by WILLIAM SUTTON. He was an innkeeper from an old village a mile or so to the northeast called CHURCHTOWN, now a part of Southport, and he was known as the Old Duke. His bathing house became known as Duke's Folly because no one thought the inn would succeed, but the opening of the nearby Leeds to Liverpool Canal in the early 19th century gave easy access to the coast, and 'Southport', as it became known, the little port south of Churchtown, boomed. The site of the original Duke's Folly is marked by the Duke's Folly Hotel, built in 1861 a few years after the original was demolished in 1854.

Duke's Folly Hotel sits at southern end of Southport's main shopping street, LORD STREET, a wide, leafy boulevard which runs north from the hotel for over a mile. The street is lined with gardens and fountains and memorials and a glorious confection of Victorian buildings of every shape and style, Gothic, Queen Anne, art deco, Classical, Jacobean, Tudor. Many of the shopfronts have attractive glazed canopies.

PRINCE LOUIS-NAPOLEON BONAPARTE, nephew of the first Emperor Napoleon, lived on Lord Street for a while in 1846 and was clearly impressed, for one of the things he did when he returned to France to become Emperor Napoleon III was to demolish the medieval centre of Paris and redesign the city as we see it today. The celebrated tree-lined boulevards of Paris are, in truth, mere copies of Southport's very own tree-lined boulevard, Lord Street.

About half-way along Lord Street, beside the tall obelisk-style war memorial, Nevill Street leads off west to the Marine Lake and the entrance to SOUTHPORT PIER, which was opened in 1860 and is THE OLDEST AND LONGEST IRON PIER IN BRITAIN. At 3,635 feet (1,108 m) long it is also the second longest surviving pier in Britain, after Southend. When it was built the entire length passed over the beach with the entrance being on the shore line. Today less than half the pier passes over the beach while the rest passes over reclaimed land and a section of the Marine Lake, while the entrance is quarter of a mile from the beach. At one point the pier goes over the Lakeside Miniature Railway, opened in 1911 and now THE OLDEST CONTINUOUSLY RUNNING 15-INCH GAUGE RAILWAY IN THE WORLD.

Birkdale

Birkdale's firm sands provided the runway for BRITAIN'S FIRST REGULAR SCHEDULED PASSENGER AIR SERVICE which began between Manchester and Blackpool via Southport in 1919. In 1936 aviation pioneer Dick Merrill took off from Southport on the return leg of the Ping Pong Flight, THE WORLD'S FIRST TRANSATLANTIC ROUND TRIP.

Home to 15 of England's finest golf courses, the Lancashire coast between Blackpool and the Wirral is known as England's Golf Coast, and Royal Birkdale is one of three courses on the Golf Coast to have hosted the Open Championship. The Open has been played here ten times, the first time in 1954. The club was formed in 1889 and moved to its present location in 1894. The distinctive art deco clubhouse was built in 1935.

Formby

Lying between Southport and Formby is the largest area of unspoiled sand dune terrain in Britain, some 1,700 acres (688 ha) of sand dunes and nature reserves in all. South of Ainsdale the coast path runs between the Ainsdale Sands National Nature Reserve, where access to the beach is restricted to specified paths through the dunes, and RAF Woodvale, which opened in 1941 as a base for fighter planes and was home to the very last operational Spitfires – the last Spitfire with military markings ever to fly on an operational mission took off from RAF Woodvale in 1957.

Set amongst the pine woods on the coast at Formby is the National Trust's Red Squirrel Reserve, one of the few places in England where red squirrels can be seen. Red squirrels love pine cone seeds which are difficult for the heavier grey squirrels to reach as they grow at the end of branches, and hence red squirrels tend to flourish in pine forests where they have less competition for food from greys. On the beach at Formby Point are the ruins of THE WORLD'S FIRST LIFE-BOAT STATION, which was established here in 1776 by Liverpool Dockmaster William Hutchinson, who also compiled THE FIRST KNOWN CONTINUOUS TIDAL RECORDS. The

original station was rebuilt in 1793 and closed in 1918.

Somewhere along the coast near Formby are the fields where potatoes were grown in England for the first time. In 1575 a ship laden with vegetables from the New World was wrecked off what is now Southport, and the newfangled potatoes were washed ashore to be found and propagated by enterprising local folk.

Liverpool Docks

Approaching Liverpool from Crosby you come first to SEAFORTH DOCK, opened in 1972 as Liverpool's largest dock facility. In 2016 the dock was expanded to include Liverpool 2, a container port capable of managing the largest of the world's container ships. Containers are handled by five giant red-painted Megamax cranes built in China. At 300 feet (90 m) high, the cranes are taller than the Liver Building and can be seen from miles away.

Access to Seaforth Dock from the Mersey is via GLADSTONE DOCK to the south, which is entered through a vast lock with what were ONCE THE LARGEST LOCK GATES IN THE WORLD. Gladstone Dock, which stretches for 3 miles along the Bootle waterfront, became fully operational in 1927, although Gladstone's Dry Dock, which

was built to handle the largest transatlantic liners, opened well before, in 1913. The dock was named, not after the four-times Prime Minister William Gladstone, who was born in Liverpool's Rodney Street in 1809, but his cousin Robert Gladstone, a Liverpool merchant.

South of Gladstone Dock is a series of Victorian docks, all opened in the 19th century as part of the northward expansion of Liverpool's dock system in response to the boom in trade. STANLEY DOCK, opened in 1848, is the only one of these docks built inland rather than standing out from the shore. In 1897 the south section of the dock was filled in to create the foundations for the STANLEY DOCK TOBACCO WAREHOUSE, which covered 36 acres (15 ha) and was, at the time, the world's largest building. It still stands as THE WORLD'S LARGEST BRICK WAREHOUSE and is the centrepiece of a regeneration scheme which includes shops and apartments and an extension of the Liverpool and Leeds Canal.

Liverpool

Liverpool's rise from a fishing village into one of the biggest and wealthiest ports in the world began in the early 18th century, when the River Dee started to silt up, cutting off the Roman port of Chester from the sea. In 1715 THE WORLD'S FIRST COMMERCIAL WET DOCK, the OLD DOCK, was built on the River Mersey around the natural 'liver' (dark or muddy water) tidal pool that gave the city its name. The Old Dock soon became too small and in 1826 was filled in, but the original Old Dock walls have been preserved beneath the Liverpool One shopping centre, and tours of the site can be booked through the Merseyside Maritime Museum.

Throughout the 18th century the docks were expanded to service the transatlantic slave trade and business created by the Industrial Revolution. During the 19th century vast numbers of Irish and English emigrants left from Liverpool for North America, and Liverpool became the port of registry for ocean-going liners such as *Titanic, Lusitania* and *Queen Mary*, as well as home to shipping companies such as Cunard and the White Star Line. By the end of the 19th century over 40 per cent of the world's trade was carried on Liverpool-registered ships.

Pier Head

In 1899, one of the original 18th-century docks, GEORGE'S DOCK, which had opened in 1771 and was named after the reigning monarch George III, was filled in to create what is now Liverpool's iconic waterfront Pier Head, location of the 'Three Graces': the Cunard Building, completed in 1917, the Port of Liverpool Building, 1907, and the Royal Liver Building, completed in 1911 and sporting THE LARGEST CLOCK FACES IN ENGLAND.

The clock on the Royal Liver Building was started at the exact moment King George V was crowned in Westminster Abbey, 1.40 p.m. on 22 June 1911. Each of the twin clock towers is topped by a Liver Bird, one female, watching out over the sea, and one male, watching out over the city. The Liver Bird, a type of cormorant, has been a symbol of Liverpool since the 14th century and carries in its beak a sprig of laver, a type of edible seaweed found along this stretch of coast.

Mersey Tunnels

There are three tunnels under the Mersey between Liverpool and Birkenhead, and just behind the Port of Liverpool Building on the Pier Head is the dazzling art deco George's Dock Ventilation and Control Station, built in 1931 to a design by HERBERT ROWSE as one of the ventilation shafts for the QUEENSWAY TUNNEL. When the tunnel opened in 1934 it was, at just over 2 miles long, THE LONGEST ROAD TUNNEL IN THE WORLD (until

1948) and THE LONGEST UNDERWATER TUNNEL IN THE WORLD (until 1955). Herbert Rowse also designed the two delightful art deco tunnel entrances in Liverpool and Birkenhead. In 1971 the KINGSWAY ROAD TUNNEL was opened to relieve congestion in the Queensway Tunnel.

The first Mersey tunnel was the MERSEY RAILWAY TUNNEL, which opened in 1886 and was THE FIRST TUNNEL IN THE WORLD TO RUN BENEATH A TIDAL ESTUARY. It is still in use.

Royal Albert Dock

South of the Pier Head is the pioneering ALBERT DOCK, opened in 1846 as THE WORLD'S FIRST NON-COMBUSTIBLE WAREHOUSE SYSTEM, constructed entirely from cast iron, brick and stone, with no wood. The Albert Dock was the first dock in the world to feature a docking system whereby cargoes could be directly loaded into or unloaded from the warehouse, and a few years later the dock was modified to utilise the world's first hydraulic cranes. Today Royal Albert Dock, which received Royal status in 2018, contains THE LARGEST SINGLE COLLECTION OF GRADE I LISTED BUILDINGS IN BRITAIN, and has been developed into a major tourist attraction, home to the Merseyside Maritime Museum, the Beatles Story and Tate Liverpool.

The Pier Head and Albert Dock form the Liverpool Maritime Mercantile City World Heritage Site, along with the William Brown Street Conservation Area centred on ST GEORGE'S HALL, which overlooks the docks from a gentle rise to the east. St George's Hall, which is widely regarded as THE FINEST NEO-CLASSICAL BUILDING IN THE WORLD and, incidentally, was THE WORLD'S

FIRST AIR-CONDITIONED BUILDING, was designed by 25-year-old architect HARVEY LONSDALE ELMES and completed in 1854, seven years after Elmes had died. Originally a concert hall and courthouse, the hall is now used for conferences and events.

During the 18th and 19th centuries Liverpool became one of the most prosperous cities in the world and has a wealth of fine buildings to prove it – for instance, it has more Georgian houses than Bath and has also been described by English Heritage as England's 'finest Victorian city'. And the Martin's Bank building, which stands beside the Town Hall in Water Street, a short walk from the Pier Head, is regarded as one of the finest 20th-century neo-classical buildings in Britain. It was designed in 1932 by Herbert Rowse, architect of the tunnel entrances and ventilation buildings of the Queensway tunnel. Martin's Bank was the only one of Britain's national banks to have its headquarters outside London, and during the Second World War, in May 1940, Britain's entire gold reserve was brought from London and stored in Martin's Bank before being shipped to Canada for safety, as part of OPERATION FISH, THE BIGGEST MOVEMENT OF WEALTH IN HISTORY. A plaque on the wall of the building marks where the gold bullion was lowered into the vaults.

Liverpool's Cathedrals

Liverpool can also boast two outstanding cathedrals, facing each other along Hope Street on St James's Mount, a hill east of Albert Dock. The Roman Catholic cathedral, affectionately known as the 'Wigwam', was built in the 1960s and has THE LARGEST DISPLAY OF STAINED GLASS IN ENGLAND. The magnificent Anglican cathedral took 74 years to build, from 1904 to 1978. It was designed by Giles Gilbert Scott when he was 22 years old and can boast a whole host of superlatives. It is THE LARGEST CATHEDRAL IN BRITAIN, THE FIFTH LARGEST CATHEDRAL IN THE WORLD and, at 621 feet (189 m) in length, the second longest church in the world after St Peter's in Rome. The central tower, 331 feet (101 m) high, is THE HIGHEST CHURCH TOWER (WITHOUT SPIRE) IN THE WORLD, THE BIGGEST BELL TOWER IN THE WORLD AND CONTAINS THE HEAVIEST PEAL OF BELLS IN THE WORLD. Liverpool Cathedral is breathtaking and beautiful, arguably the greatest English building of the 20th century.

Liverpool's Music

Liverpool's greatest export of the 20th century was pop music, as exemplified by a band made up of four lads born in Liverpool, THE BEATLES, perhaps the most influential pop band of all time. They learned their trade at the Cavern Club in Mathew Street in the city centre. The original club closed in 1973 but has since been rebuilt on the same site using bricks from the old club. It reopened in 1984. On the wall outside is the Liverpool Wall of Fame, which pays tribute to all the Liverpool acts who have reached No. 1 in the British charts, including jazz singer LITA ROSA, THE FIRST LIVERPUDLIAN AND THE FIRST WOMAN TO REACH No. 1, with 'How Much is that Doggie in the Window?', in 1953.

It's not just pop music, though. Liverpool can also boast BRITAIN'S OLDEST SURVIVING CLASSICAL ORCHESTRA, THE ROYAL LIVERPOOL PHILHARMONIC ORCHESTRA, which was founded in 1840 and is the only orchestra in Britain that has its own concert hall.

The Wirral

The name Wirral comes from the Old English 'wir' meaning myrtle, and so means place where myrtle is found. The Wirral Peninsula is 15 miles long and 7 miles wide and juts out into the Irish Sea, with the River Dee to the west, forming the border with Wales, and the River Mersey to the east. North of Birkenhead the longest unbroken promenade in Britain runs for nearly 3 miles along the Mersey shoreline from Seacombe via Egremont to New Brighton and then west to Leasowe. From here the coast path runs along the sandy beaches of the Irish Sea shore to Hoylake and the Royal Liverpool Golf Club, where a boardwalk takes the path south along the Dee to join the Wirral Way, part of the Wirral Country Park which opened in 1973 as THE FIRST DESIGNATED COUNTRY PARK IN BRITAIN.

Birkenhead

Birkenhead began life as a 12th-century priory, then dozed quietly for 650 years, began to stir when the steamer service arrived from Liverpool in 1817 and eventually boomed throughout the 19th century when, thanks to shipbuilding and docks, it became the largest town in Cheshire.

Today the ferry from Liverpool's Pier Head arrives at Woodside in Birkenhead, a short walk from the remains of Birkenhead Priory, built by Benedictine monks in 1150 and the oldest building still standing on Merseyside. BRITAIN'S FIRST STREET TRAMWAY, which opened in 1860 and was horse-drawn, departed from Woodside for Birkenhead Park.

In about 1330 Edward III granted the monks from the priory the rights to run the first regular 'ferry 'cross the Mersey', which they continued to do until the Dissolution of the Monasteries in 1536, when the ferry service fell into private hands. Not much is left of the priory, but the Chapter House, which contains some Norman features, has been restored as an Anglican chapel. Also in the priory grounds is the tower of Birkenhead's first parish church, St Mary's, which was consecrated in 1821. The expansion of the docks and

approach roads to the Queensway
Tunnel eventually cut the church off
from much of its parish and it was
mostly demolished in 1974, leaving just
the tower. St Mary's Tower is dedicated
to the 99 men who died on HMS *Thetis*,
a submarine launched from Birkenhead
in 1938 which sunk during trials in
Liverpool Bay when a torpedo tube
door was left open.

From the top of St Mary's Tower
there are spectacular views of the
Mersey and its docks, and right in front
of the tower is one of Birkenhead's most
historic docks, CAMMELL LAIRD'S
No. 4 DRY DOCK, constructed in 1857
and birthplace of many famous ships
including the Confederate privateer
Alabama, launched in 1862. The first
dock in Birkenhead was the MORPETH
AND EGERTON DOCK which opened
in 1847. More docks followed and in
1857 the Birkenhead and Liverpool
docks were merged into one company.

Buried in family vaults in St Mary's
churchyard are the Scottish ship-
builder WILLIAM LAIRD and his son
John, who were among the first to
develop Birkenhead. William Laird
opened an ironworks in Wallasey
Pool, an inlet off the Mersey half a
mile north of the priory, in 1824. In
1828 his ironworks received an order
for an iron ship to be used on the
lakes of Ireland and as a result, in the
following year, Laird & Co. launched
THE FIRST IRON SHIP TO BE BUILT
IN BRITAIN.

In 1845 they built the celebrated
HMS *Birkenhead*, which sank off the
South African coast and inspired the
worldwide maritime protocol of
'women and children first', when the
soldiers on board 'stood fast' as it was
sinking, to avoid overwhelming the
lifeboats.

In 1858 the *Ma Robert*, THE WORLD'S
FIRST ALL-STEEL SHIP, was built for
David Livingstone's expedition up the
Zambezi.

In 1903 Laird's merged with Charles
Cammell & Company to become
Cammell Laird, after which they went
on to build THE WORLD'S FIRST ALL-
WELDED SHIP, the *Fullager*, launched
in 1938, BRITAIN'S FIRST AIRCRAFT
CARRIER, HMS *Ark Royal*, launched in
1938, and BRITAIN'S FIRST GUIDED
MISSILE DESTROYER, HMS *Devonshire*,
launched in 1960.

Three minutes' walk inland from the
priory is glorious HAMILTON SQUARE,
the centrepiece of the new town of
Birkenhead, developed by William
Laird in the early 19th century. If its
smart Georgian terraces are reminiscent
of Edinburgh, that is because the square
was designed by the same architect who
designed much of Edinburgh's New
Town, JAMES GILLESPIE GRAHAM. Laid
out in 1826, Hamilton Square has more
Grade 1 listed buildings in one square
than any other square in Britain, other
than London's Trafalgar Square. On the
west side there is a statue of JOHN LAIRD
(1805–1874), who in 1861 became the first
MP for Birkenhead. He lived at No. 63
Hamilton Square. On the east side of
the square stands Birkenhead's impressive Town Hall, completed in 1887 with
a 200 foot (61 m) tall clock tower
designed to be seen from across the
Mersey in Liverpool. The hall is

now used for a variety of functions and continues as the town's register office.

The first of the Mersey road tunnels, the Queensway Tunnel, which opened in 1934, runs under Hamilton Square. Herbert Rowse's picturesque art deco tunnel entrance is just off the southeast corner of the square, and standing in a small patch of parkland just back from the entrance is the Monument to the Mersey Tunnel, the only survivor of a pair of identical monuments that marked the tunnel entrances on either side of the river. Each had a light at the top which illuminated the tunnel entrance.

Birkenhead Park

Birkenhead Park opened in 1847 as THE VERY FIRST PUBLIC PARK IN THE WORLD. It was designed by Sir Joseph Paxton, architect of the Crystal Palace, and the idea was to recreate within the town a country landscape of woods, meadows and lakes where industrial workers could escape from the unhealthy conditions of the workplace. As well as a Grand Entrance Lodge, based on the Temple of Illysus in Athens, the park features a number of pavilions and structures in different architectural styles, including a Roman Boathouse and the Swiss Bridge, THE ONLY TRADITIONAL-STYLE WOODEN COVERED BRIDGE IN BRITAIN. The park influenced the design of urban parks around the world including, most famously, Central Park in New York. 'We have nothing like this in democratic America,' declared the American landscape architect Frederick Law Olmsted after visiting Birkenhead Park, and promptly went on to create Central Park along the same lines.

New Brighton

New Brighton is a part of Wallasey and sits at the northeastern tip of the Wirral Peninsula where the Mersey meets the Irish Sea. It boasts a sandy beach on the Irish Sea and spectacular views across the Mersey, and in 1830 Liverpool merchant JAMES ATHERTON began developing the area into a resort town along the lines of Brighton in Sussex – hence 'New' Brighton.

In 1829 a coastal defence battery called FORT PERCH was built on Black Rock, an isolated piece of rock at the very northeastern tip of the peninsula, with a lighthouse constructed further out in the bay. Fort Perch Rock is now used as a museum. A wooden pier was built in 1830, which was rebuilt in iron in 1865 and included a dock for a Mersey ferry. The Promenade Pier, as it was called, was regarded as 'one of the finest the country' but like so many piers suffered from the elements and was finally dismantled in 1978. In 1900 NEW BRIGHTON TOWER, a structure similar in design to Blackpool Tower, opened on the seafront. At 567 feet (173 m) high it was almost 50 feet higher than its Blackpool rival and was then the highest structure in Britain. However the tower was neglected during the First World War and had to be dismantled in 1919.

New Brighton for a while possessed THE LARGEST OUTDOOR SWIMMING POOL IN EUROPE. Opened in 1934, the main pool at New Brighton Baths was 330 feet (100 m) long and 225 feet (69 m) wide and held almost 1½ million gallons of seawater. The buildings, diving boards and terraces of the Baths were battered by hurricane force winds during a storm in 1990 and were bulldozed, along with the pool, not long afterwards.

Leasowe

Leasowe sits on the western edge of Wallasey. Much of it lies below sea level and is protected by a coastal embankment. LEASOWE CASTLE, just within the embankment, was built for the 5th Earl of Derby in 1593 as an observation tower from where he could watch the Wallasey races, which were run on the sands during the 16th and 17th centuries. The Wallasey races are seen as a forerunner of the Derby races inaugurated by the 12th Earl of Derby at Epsom in 1780. Leasowe lighthouse, which stands a few yards inland from the beach, was built in 1763 and is THE OLDEST BRICK LIGHTHOUSE IN BRITAIN. The foundations were built on bales of cotton salvaged from a stranded ship, which helped to bind the soft sand and vegetation into a firm base. The lighthouse was operational until 1908 and is now used as a visitor centre for the North Wirral Coastal Path. THE WORLD'S FIRST PASSENGER HOVERCRAFT SERVICE operated between Leasowe and Rhyl in North Wales from 1961 to 1962.

Hoylake

Hoylake sits at the northwestern tip of the Wirral Peninsula, where the River Dee meets the Irish Sea. It is named for the 'High' Lake, a deep channel of water protected by a sandbank that lay between Hilbre Island and the mainland and provided a safe anchorage. In 1690 William III set sail for Ireland from here with ten thousand troops before the Battle of the Boyne. Hoylake is home to the ROYAL LIVERPOOL GOLF CLUB, founded in 1869 and the second oldest golf links in England after the Royal Devon in Westward Ho! The club has hosted the Open Championship 12 times.

Well, I never knew this about
THE MERSEYSIDE COAST

The Reformation never got as far as LITTLE CROSBY, a tiny village of some 50 houses, a church and Jacobean manor house to the north of big Crosby. The village has been owned by the staunchly Roman Catholic Blundell family since the 1200s and until fairly recently only Roman Catholics were allowed to be residents, making Little Crosby THE OLDEST EXISTING ROMAN CATHOLIC VILLAGE IN BRITAIN. Crosby Hall, lived in by the Blundells since it was built in 1609, is mainly Georgian, having been remodelled in the 1780s.

Since 2007 CROSBY BEACH has been the permanent home of Anthony Gormley's Another Place sculpture exhibition, consisting of a hundred cast-iron figures facing out to sea. The figures, each 6 feet 2 inches (1.88 m) tall and based on the sculptor's naked body, spread across a couple of miles of beach.

Between 1866 and 2004 the BIDSTON OBSERVATORY on the Wirral was used to calculate both time and tides, based on tables compiled by Liverpool Dockmaster William Hutchinson from measurements taken at various points along the Liverpool shoreline. The observatory provided tidal information for ports all over the world and, crucially, for the D-Day landings in 1944. Its successor, the University of Liverpool Tidal Institute, is still one of the top three tide prediction organisations in the world.

The SOLAR CAMPUS at Leasowe on the north Wirral, formerly St George's Secondary School, stands on the eastern edge of Leasowe and is THE FIRST BUILDING IN THE WORLD – AND THE MOST NORTHERLY – TO BE ENTIRELY HEATED BY SOLAR ENERGY. It was built in 1961 and consists of a glass wall of 10,000 square feet on the south side and a windowless brick façade on the north side. Unfortunately the design was flawed and on sunny days the south side of the building became unbearably hot while the north side remained cold, but the concept of a building run on solar energy is now very much in vogue – Leasowe's solar campus was ahead of its time. Although no longer a school, the building is still used for educational purposes.

GEORGE FRIDERIC HANDEL disembarked at PARKGATE on the Wirral in August 1742 after staying in Dublin, where his *Messiah* had been performed for the very first time in April that year.

AMY LYON, who later found fame as Lord Nelson's mistress, Emma, Lady Hamilton, was known to have bathed in the sea at Parkgate as a girl. Daughter of the local blacksmith, she was born in nearby Ness.

CHAPTER FOUR
BRISTOL AND
SOMERSET COAST

Bristol to Culbone
(80 miles)

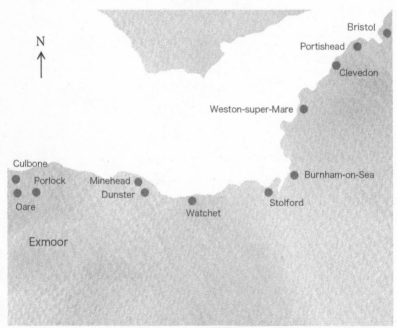

Bristol sits 5 miles inland from the Severn estuary, the eastern part of the Bristol Channel which laps the Somerset coast and has a tidal range of 48 feet (15 m), the second largest tidal range in the world after the Bay of Fundy in Canada. Highlights of Bristol and the Somerset coast include the first iron steamship to cross the Atlantic, the finest Norman room in Britain, Elizabeth I's favourite church, the oldest theatre in Britain, a rare 14th-century medieval hall house, England's oldest Victorian pier, England's shortest pier, the world's last mud horse fisherman, the home of the Ancient Mariner, the longest medieval church screen in England, wandering poets, Britain's steepest A-road, the smallest complete medieval church in England and the church that was the setting for the fateful wedding of Lorna Doone.

Bristol

Cradle of the New World

Bristol, which lies 5 winding miles inland from the Severn estuary, on the River Avon, was historically divided between Somerset and Gloucestershire until the late 14th century when it became a county of itself, still geographically a part of the larger counties but administratively separate. During the Middle Ages it was THE LARGEST AND BUSIEST TRADING PORT ON THE WEST COAST OF ENGLAND and a vital base for early exploration of the New World.

In 1497 Venetian explorer JOHN CABOT sailed from Bristol on the good ship *Matthew* and landed at what is now Bonavista Bay, Newfoundland, becoming THE FIRST EUROPEAN TO LAND ON THE NORTH AMERICAN MAINLAND since the Vikings in the 11th century. The voyage was commissioned on behalf of Henry VII and sponsored by the Merchants of Bristol, and every Bristolian knows that the New World was named in honour of the man who was Sheriff of Bristol at the time, RICHARD AMERIKE.

There is a bronze statue of John Cabot on the quayside and in 1897 Cabot Tower was erected in Brandon Hill Park, west of the city centre, to commemorate the 400th anniversary of his momentous voyage.

Merchant Venturers

In 1552 the Society of Merchant Venturers was founded in Bristol to exploit the new discoveries and underwrite the development of the early American colonies. They sent out ships to every part of the known world and the name of Bristol became a byword for efficiency and enterprise, hence the expression 'shipshape and Bristol fashion'.

On the pavement outside the Corn Exchange in the heart of the old city near the river are a number of bronze pedestals known as 'nails', used by merchants when making deals. When a deal had been agreed the money was placed on top of the nail – hence the expression 'to pay on the nail', meaning to pay straight away.

Nearby, on the quayside in cobbled King Street, is the LLANDOGER TROW, a glorious gabled and half-timbered inn built in 1664 and named after a type of Welsh sailing barge. It was here that Daniel Defoe met ALEXANDER SELKIRK, the sailor who inspired his tale of Robinson Crusoe. Selkirk had been marooned on an island in the South Pacific for four and a half years before being rescued by a Bristol privateer, CAPTAIN WOODES ROGERS, who would go on to be the first Royal Governor of the Bahamas. Rogers died at his home in Queen Square at the end of King Street in 1732, the site being marked with a plaque.

Opposite the Llandoger Trow is the Theatre Royal, home of the Bristol Old Vic. Opened in 1766, it is THE OLDEST CONTINUOUSLY WORKING THEATRE IN Britain.

Transatlantic Liners

The first transatlantic passenger liners were built in Bristol in the early 19th century, by Isambard Kingdom Brunel. In 1837 he launched the SS *Great Western*, the largest ship in the world at the time and THE FIRST STEAMSHIP BUILT SPECIFICALLY TO CROSS THE ATLANTIC. In 1843 he launched the SS *Great Britain*, THE LONGEST SHIP IN THE WORLD at the time, THE FIRST OCEAN-GOING LINER TO COMBINE AN IRON HULL WITH A SCREW PROPELLOR and THE FIRST IRON-HULLED STEAM-SHIP TO CROSS THE ATLANTIC. In 1886 the SS *Great Britain* was abandoned in the Falkland Islands as a rusting hulk, but in 1970 she was brought back to Bristol and restored. She now stands as a museum ship in the dry dock in Bristol Harbour where she was built.

Another contribution to maritime (and footwear) history that Bristol can take credit for is the Plimsoll Line, painted on the side of every ship to indicate when the vessel is loaded to its maximum safe capacity – if the line disappears below the waterline then the ship is overloaded. The Plimsoll Line was the idea of social reformer SAMUEL PLIMSOLL, born at 9 Colston Parade near the waterfront in Bristol in 1824. Plimsolls, shoes with rubber soles and canvas uppers, are so named because of the resemblance of the upper edge of the rubber on the canvas to the Plimsoll Line on a ship.

Bristol Churches

Bristol Cathedral was founded in 1140 as an Augustinian abbey. The Chapter House, built in 1160, is regarded as one of the finest and most beautiful Norman rooms in Britain while THE EARLY 14TH-CENTURY VAULTED CHOIR IS UNIQUE IN ENGLAND, having the aisles the same height as the main choir. The abbey became a cathedral in 1542 after the Dissolution of the Monasteries and the nave was completed in 1868 by G.E. Street (architect of the Law Courts in London) in the same unique style as the choir.

Down at the waterside is St Mary Redcliffe, described by Elizabeth I as 'the fairest, goodliest and most famous parish church in England'. A Gothic masterpiece, the church was built in the 14th century in Early English Gothic style and has a graceful spire, 285 feet (87 m) high, that serves as a prominent landmark for vessels entering Bristol Harbour.

Avonmouth

By the end of the 19th century ships had become too large to sail up the shallow River Avon into Bristol and in 1877 new docks were built at Avonmouth on the north bank of the mouth of the Avon. Avonmouth and the Royal Portbury deep-water dock on the south bank of the Avon, built in 1972, both with direct access to the Bristol Channel, took over from the old Bristol City Dock as the commercial docks for Bristol leaving the City Dock to be redeveloped for leisure, retail and residential use.

During the First World War Avonmouth was the UK centre for the production of mustard gas manufactured under the guise of the National Smelting Company (NSC). After the war the NSC became Consolidated Zinc and reverted to smelting zinc using the Imperial Smelting Process, a revolutionary process invented in the company's Britannia smelting works at Avonmouth. Today Avonmouth has THE ONLY ZINC SMELTING WORKS IN BRITAIN and is home to THE WORLD'S LARGEST BLAST FURNACE, unveiled in 1967.

Clevedon

Clevedon appears in the Domesday Book as a small farming community. It then expanded in the Victorian era to become Somerset's most dignified and unspoiled seaside resort. It has a wealth of fine Georgian and Victorian buildings, a fairytale clock tower in the town centre with a tall pyramid roof, built in 1897 to celebrate Queen Victoria's Diamond Jubilee, and the Curzon Cinema, opened in 1912 and ONE OF THE OLDEST SURVIVING PURPOSE-BUILT CINEMAS IN THE WORLD. Across Old Church Road from the cinema, at No. 55, is the cottage where the poet Samuel Tayler Coleridge spent his honeymoon with his new wife Sarah in 1795. He wrote his poem 'The Eolian Harp' while there in which he describes the cottage …

To sit beside our Cot, our Cot o'ergrown
With white-flowered Jasmin, and the
broad-leaved Myrtle …

Clevedon's development as a resort during the 19th century was largely driven by the Elton family of Clevedon Court, a glorious medieval manor house standing on Court Hill a little to the east of the town.

Clevedon Court

Clevedon Court was built in the early 14th century, around 1320, by lord of the manor Sir John de Clevedon, and despite the house being added to in the 16th and 18th centuries it remains one of the finest surviving examples of a medieval hall house in Britain. The estate was acquired by Sir Abraham Elton, a rich Bristol merchant, in 1709, and although the house was given to the National Trust in 1960 in lieu of death duties, it has remained the Elton family home ever since. The 6th baronet, Sir Charles Elton, was a writer in the early Victorian era and had many of the prominent writers of the day to stay at Clevedon Court, including William Makepeace Thackeray, who used Clevedon as the inspiration for the house Castlewood in his novel *The History of Henry Esmond* and also wrote some of *Vanity Fair* while at Clevedon.

Clevedon Pier

Striding out to the sea at the northern end of the town's rocky main beach is Clevedon's pride and joy, the delicate and graceful iron and steel Clevedon Pier, described by Sir John Betjemen as 'THE MOST BEAUTIFUL PIER IN ENGLAND'. It was designed by Hans Price in 1869 and is 1,024 feet (312 m) long with an elegant iron and glass pavilion at the pier head and a castellated stone toll booth at the landward end. The pier was built as a docking place for steamers from Devon and Wales and is made partly from iron rails intended for the southwest railway planned by Brunel but never completed. Clevedon Pier is, in fact, one of England's oldest surviving Victorian piers and THE ONLY FULLY INTACT GRADE I LISTED PIER IN BRITAIN. In 1970 two of the spans collapsed and the pier was threatened with demolition, but in the end it was dismantled and taken to Portishead for restoration and reconstructed in 1986, reopening in 1989. In the summer months the landing stage at the end of the pier is used by the *Waverley*, THE WORLD'S LAST SEAGOING PASSENGER PADDLE STEAMER.

A short walk from the beach at No. 5 Elton Road is the house where penicillin was first produced on a large scale. During the Second World War the Royal Navy set up a research laboratory here and manufactured the penicillin in a factory on land behind the house. After the war the factory was sold to the Distillers Company Ltd and the Clevedon site closed in 1961.

At the other end of the beach are a Victorian bandstand and a boating lake. The next stretch of coast path, which climbs up some steps to skirt two small hills, Church Hill and Wain's Hill, is known as Poet's Walk, as the views are said to have inspired the various poets who visited the town, including Samuel Taylor Coleridge, Alfred, Lord Tennyson and William Makepeace Thackeray. The first part of the path goes past the Sugar Lookout, a small stone hut built in 1835 for the Finzel family of sugar merchants from where they could watch out for their ships returning to Bristol from the West Indies laden with sugar. Wain's Hill is the site of an Iron Age fort while on Church Hill, crowning its own headland, stands the wonderfully weather-beaten 12th-century church of St Andrew, burial place in 1833 of Alfred, Lord Tennyson's tragic young friend Arthur Hallam, who died of a stroke aged 22. Hallam was the subject of one of Tennyson's greatest poems, *In Memoriam*, and in 1850, the year the poem was published, Tennyson visited Clevedon to pay respects to his lost friend

Woodspring Priory

Woodspring Priory was founded as an Augustinian priory by William de Courtenay in 1210. William inherited the estate from his grandfather Reginald Fitz-Urse, one of the four knights who murdered Archbishop Thomas Becket in Canterbury Cathedral in 1120, and he set up a priory dedicated to Becket at Woodspring as an act of penitence for his grandfather's misdeeds. The current priory church and tower, the infirmary, the great tithe barn and the prior's lodgings were built in the early 16th century, just before the Dissolution of the Monasteries, when the priory was given to a local nobleman. He leased it out to local farmers and the priory was used as a farmhouse until it was taken over by the National Trust in 1969. In 1989 the Landmark Trust converted the prior's lodgings into farmhouse holiday accommodation, while the National Trust continue to look after the infirmary and tithe barn.

Woodspring Priory

Kewstoke

The picturesque 14th-century tower of St Paul's, Kewstoke, north of Weston-super-Mare, peaks out from its own little rise beside the rather startling Cygnet mental hospital. The body of the church is mainly Norman and possesses a delightful Norman doorway with twisted pillars. In 1849, during restoration of the church, a broken wooden cup stained with blood was discovered hidden behind a sculpted figure built into the wall. The cup is thought to have contained the blood of Thomas Becket and was no doubt purchased from the monks of Canterbury by William de Courtenay and enshrined in Woodspring Priory (*see* above) as part of his atonement for his grandfather's part in Becket's murder. At the Dissolution of the Monasteries it was brought to St Paul's from the priory and hidden in the wall for safekeeping. The cup is now in the Museum of Somerset in Taunton.

Birnbeck Pier

The abandoned Birnbeck Pier to the north of Weston-super-Mare leads to Birnbeck Island and is the only pier in Britain linking the mainland to an island. The pier opened in 1867 and was designed by pier specialist Eugenius Birch, whose numerous other piers included Blackpool's North Pier, Brighton's West Pier and Margate Pier. A landing jetty was constructed on the island to allow steamers to land day-trippers from towns along both sides of the Bristol Channel and there was also a funfair, café and pavilion. With the decline of England's seaside resorts in the 1980s, Birnbeck Pier's allure faded and after being damaged in a storm in 1990 it was finally closed for safety reasons in 1994. Since then there have been many proposals of how to revive the pier but it remains sadly derelict and on the Heritage at Risk register.

The road now continues to the seafront in Weston-super-Mare.

Weston-super-Mare

Weston-super-Mare was made by Weston's super air, so they say, and the Victorians' love of sea air and sea bathing transformed Weston – named 'super Mare', meaning 'on Sea', to distinguish it from the numerous other Westons in Somerset – from a fishing village to the biggest west coast holiday resort between Land's End and Lancashire. As well as its health-giving air Weston has 3 miles of sandy beach to attract tourists, although the sea retreats for over a mile at low tide leaving acres of mud exposed, giving rise to the town's nickname of Weston-super-Mud. The mudflats are extremely deceiving as they are often covered by a thin layer of sand which breaks when trodden on, leaving unwary bathers stuck in the mud and at the mercy of the incoming tide. However, if the sea is out, there are a host of other seaside attractions to indulge in, most notably the Grand Pier, reborn after a bad fire in 2008. Opened in 1903, the pier is 1,201 feet (366 m) long and has a huge pavilion at the seaward end offering all kinds of amusements from concerts and circuses to fairground rides and restaurants.

North of the pier is Knightstone Island, once a bare piece of rock 50 yards out into the water that could only be reached at low tide, now a luxury apartment complex. In 1830 the island was purchased by a Dr Fox who built a therapeutic spa on it, and soon afterwards a causeway was built so that the island could be reached at high tide. Today it has been developed with condominiums and commercial outlets, although the original Victorian bath house has been partly preserved.

Boats trips can be taken from Knightstone to STEEP HOLM, the small island that can be seen lying out in the bay. It is now a nature reserve and is the only place in Britain where wild peonies grow. Beyond is the slightly larger island of FLAT HOLM, the most southerly point of Wales, from where Guglielmo Marconi sent THE FIRST OVERSEAS WIRELESS SIGNALS across to Lavernock on the South Wales coast.

Burnham-on-Sea

Burnham sits at the central point of the Somerset coastline by the mouth of the River Parrett. It began life long ago as a fishing village but because of the shifting sands and high tides, the seas off Burnham have always been hazardous. One stormy night in 1750 a fisherman's wife put a candle in the window of her cottage near the church to help her husband find his way home in the dark. She saved his life that night, and from then on the fishermen paid her to keep a candle burning in the window to guide them home.

After a few years the sexton of the church paid the fisherman's wife for the right to shine a light from the church tower, and at the turn of the 19th century the church curate, the Revd David Davies, bought the rights off the sexton and built a four-storey lighthouse in front of the church. He then extracted a toll from passing ships and used the money to sink a number of wells on the shore in the hope of turning Burnham into a spa. Alas, the waters were foul and 'smelled like a cesspool blended with bad horseradish' according to one unhappy visitor, and the spa failed to prosper, but the town nonetheless became firmly established as a resort, thanks largely to the miles of sandy beach and the bracing sea air.

The curate's lighthouse, known as the Round Tower, still stands on the Esplanade in front of the church but ceased operation as a lighthouse in 1832, after which the top two storeys were removed. It is now a guest-house.

In 1832 the Round Tower was replaced by the 110 foot (34 m) High Lighthouse built a hundred yards (90 m) inland on a hill further south,

and in 1834 this was complemented by the distinctive white-painted clapperboard Low Lighthouse which stands on the beach below on wooden stilts.

St Andrew's Church

St Andrew's Church is 14th century and stands just off the Esplanade, behind the Round Tower. It is noted for its leaning tower which inclines 3 feet (0.9 m) out of true, thanks to poor foundations. Dotted around the church inside are a series of superb sculptures, part of an altarpiece carved in 1687 by Grinling Gibbons for the chapel of James II's Whitehall Palace. Deemed too Popish by the Protestant William III, the altarpiece was taken down and later placed in the choir of Westminster Abbey. It 1820 it was removed again for the coronation of George IV and offered to then Bishop of Rochester, Walter King, who also happened to be vicar of St Andrew's.

A little further south along the Esplanade is Burnham's pier, built in 1914 and, with a length of just 900 feet (274 m), THE SHORTEST SEASIDE PIER IN BRITAIN.

Stolford

At low tide the tiny hamlet of Stolford, on Bridgwater Bay, is left high and dry as the sea recedes exposing a huge expanse of glistening mud deposited by the River Parrett. For hundreds of years fishermen would go out on to the mudflats to catch shrimps and prawns using a 'mud horse', a type of wooden sledge which they would push from behind to traverse the treacherous mud. Bridgwater Bay is the only place in the world where such mud horses are used, but since the building of the power

stations at nearby Hinkley Point the fishing has become almost unsustainable and now there is only one fisherman, Adrian Sellick, left to carry on the tradition.

Watchet

Watchet gets its name from 'wacet', a blue alabaster found in the local cliffs, and has been a active harbour town since the Dark Ages and possibly even earlier. Watchet's recorded story begins with the arrival at the end of the 7th century of St Decuman, who floated across from South Wales on a raft with his cow. He then lived as a hermit consuming only cow's milk while serving the local community as a physician and pastor. In a fit of temper one of the locals finally cut off Decuman's head but according to the legend the saint calmly picked it up, washed it off and put it back on, then helped to build a church beside the well where he was living, before finally succumbing to his injuries. The present 13th-century church of St Decuman now marks the spot high above the town. The view over Watchet harbour from the churchyard inspired Samuel Taylor Coleridge to set his famous poem *The Rime of the Ancient Mariner* in Watchet. Having walked here with William and Dorothy Wordsworth from his cottage in nearby Nether Stowey, mulling over the story, he declared, 'And here is where he shall set out on his fateful voyage.' A statue of the Ancient Mariner stands by the harbour in memory.

Narrow streets of colourful shops and houses lead down to that harbour which is still watched over by a 22 foot (6.7 m) high cast-iron lighthouse constructed in 1862 just after the harbour piers were built. The harbour remained in commercial use until the year 2000, after which it was converted into a marina.

Watchet has been famous for paper making since the 17th century, when a flour mill established by the local Wyndham family was taken over to produce paper, and by the end of the 19th century this mill had become THE LARGEST MANUFACTURER OF PAPER BAGS IN BRITAIN. The mill remained in operation throughout the 20th century producing container board and recycled envelopes and bags, but closed in 2015.

Dunster

A round watch tower and shipping landmark built in 1775 on top of Conygar Hill beckons us into the medieval streets of the Luttrell family's fiefdom of Dunster, just a mile inland from the sand and shingle of Dunster Beach. The view along the narrow High Street of quaint and crooked houses

dating from every century, towards the Tudor towers of the Norman castle on the hill, takes the breath away – an almost unique glimpse of medieval feudal England.

At the start of the High Street, on the left, is the medieval Luttrell Arms with its 15th-century gabled porch with crossbow slits, once the house of the Abbot of Cleeve. Opposite is the picturesque and much photographed YARN MARKET, built in 1609 by the Luttrells to reflect the importance of Dunster as a wool and cloth market.

Down the High Street with its latticed windows, bent chimneys, ancient wooden doors and timbers from wrecked ships, and around the corner as it climbs toward the church, on the right there is a long, charming, gabled house with overhanging storeys and pantiles patterned with diamonds at the front. This was THE NUNNERY, used mainly as a guest-house for the Benedictine priory which was established in Dunster in 1100.

The majestic 15th-century PRIORY CHURCH OF ST GEORGE stands proud on the hill behind. The villagers and the monks from the priory had to share the church, and to stop them from squabbling it was divided into two by THE LONGEST SCREEN IN ENGLAND, a sumptuous fan-vaulted wooden screen made by Flemish craftsmen in 1498. The monks got the transepts and the choir, while the villagers got the nave.

Behind the church on Priory Green is a round dovecote, probably 14th-century, with 540 nest holes, the lower ones blocked in the 18th century against rats. Across the road is the priory's tithe barn, again dating from the 14th century.

DUNSTER CASTLE occupies a steep hill called the Tor. The first castle was a timbered structure built by William de Mohun, who was given the land by William the Conqueror after the Norman Conquest. A stone keep was built not long afterwards and the castle was expanded over the centuries by the Luttrells, who owned the castle for six hundred years from 1376 until 1976 when it was gifted to the National Trust. The castle held out for six months as a Royalist stronghold during the Civil War, after which the medieval fortifications were largely destroyed by Cromwell's troops. The Luttrells then turned what was left of the castle into a family home and this was remodelled in picturesque Gothic style by the Victorian architect Anthony Salvin in the 1870s.

In the grounds south of the castle, beside the River Avill, there is a working 18th-century watermill on the site of a mill mentioned in the Domesday Book. Nearby is a medieval packhorse bridge.

It is thought that the 'purple headed mountains, the river running by' from Cecil Frances Alexander's much-loved hymn 'All Things Bright and Beautiful' were inspired by the heather-clad GRABBIST HILL, just west of Dunster, and the River Avill. Mrs Alexander visited Dunster frequently to stay with her friend Mary Martin, daughter of the owner of Martin's Bank.

Minehead

Somerset's oldest golf course and one of Britain's three remaining Butlins resorts welcome the coast path to Minehead, the Gateway to Exmoor. The name Minehead could have been derived from William de Mohun, the land's Norman owner – hence Mohun's headland – or from the Welsh 'mynydd' meaning mountain. At the far end of the sweeping bay with its wide golden sandy beach, the old village climbs the slopes of rounded North Hill from where the 15th-century tower of St Michael's Church still acts as a beacon guiding sailors and fishermen into the harbour, although no light has shone from there for many years.

Minehead has been a fishing port since 1380 and flourished in medieval times by trading local wool for coal from South Wales. By the start of the 18th century there were some 40 trading vessels working out of Minehead. Throughout the 19th century trade slumped as the harbour began silting up and bigger vessels had to transfer to larger ports. Today Minehead is used by pleasure boats and small fishing craft.

Modern apartment blocks line the eastern end of the seafront and give way to Victorian and Edwardian shops and houses built to accommodate the tourists who replaced the sailors and fishermen. The opening of Butlins in 1962 brought fresh waves of visitors.

Minehead's tree-lined shopping street, The Avenue, leads to Wellington Square where there is a fine statue of Queen Anne, one of two sculpted by Francis Bird in 1719 – the other stands in front of the steps of St Paul's Cathedral in London. Minehead's statue was given to the town by SIR JACOB BANKS, a Swedish naval officer who married a Luttrell and served as local M.P. St Andrew's Church on the edge of the square was designed by G.E. Street, architect of the Royal Court of Justice in London.

Running off the square is a row of almshouses built in 1630 by sea merchant ROBERT QUIRKE in gratitude for the safe delivery of his cargo from a storm. There is an inscription on one of the houses making clear his wish that the houses should always be reserved for the poor: 'Cursed be that man that shall convert it to any other use'.

From the almshouses a narrow road winds up North Hill to St Michael's Church, from where there are superb views across Minehead to the Quantocks and the wide sweep of Bridgwater Bay. The church boasts a magnificent 15th-century vaulted rood screen on top of which sits 'Jack Hammer', a little figure in hood and jerkin who used to hammer out the hours from the church clock.

Church Steps lead down from the church between colourful thatched and cob-walled cottages to Quay Street, where quaint 17th- and 18th-century cottages and their gardens nestle into the hillside and gaze out over the harbour wall.

On May Day, Minehead's brightly decorated Hobby Horse parades along Quay Street as it has done every year since no one knows when, recreating, it is said, the occasion when a charging Hobby Horse routed a pack of marauding Danes.

On the green at the bottom of Church Steps a sculpture of a pair of hands holding a map marks the original start of the South West Coast Path, although it has since been extended east as far as Weston-super-Mare. Before setting off, you can take 'Tea at the Quay' in one of Minehead's oldest

buildings – it used to be the Mermaid, home to Old Mother Leakey, Minehead's Whistling Ghost, who would 'whistle up a storm' whenever one of her son's ships came into port.

THE FISHERMAN'S CHAPEL, located in an old storehouse cellar on the quay, holds regular services for those at sea and for those about to start the steep climb on to Exmoor.

Exmoor

Exmoor is a world of purple heather and yellow gorse, rounded hills and dark woods, steep cliffs riven by deep ravines and strung with waterfalls, impossibly pretty thatched villages and glorious views in all directions. The moor covers an area of 267 square miles and its highest point is DUNKERY BEACON, which is 1,703 feet (519 m) above sea level.

ALLERFORD gathers around a much photographed 15th-century cobbled packhorse bridge, a working black-smith's forge and a thatched Victorian schoolroom, now a museum. Allerford House, by the bridge, was the child-hood home of Admiral John Moresby, famed for his explorations along the coastline of New Guinea. Port Moresby, capital of Papua New Guinea, is named after him.

The Lorna Doone Hotel in PORLOCK bears witness to the fact that this is Lorna Doone country (*see* page 60). The 13th-century Church of St Dubricius, dedicated to the saint who crowned King Arthur, sports a strangely truncated shingled spire, its top whipped off by a lightning storm in 1703. Inside is the splendid alabaster tomb of John Harington, who fought with Henry V at Agincourt, and his wife Elizabeth Courtenay, daughter of the Earl of Devon.

CHURCH at Culbone, just 35 feet (11 m) long and 12 feet (3.6 m) wide, with room for no more than 33 people, is THE SMALLEST COMPLETE MEDIEVAL CHURCH IN ENGLAND.

It was a 'person on business from Porlock' who, in 1797, interrupted Samuel Taylor Coleridge at his cottage in nearby Nether Stowey while the poet was half-way through writing down 'Kubla Khan', causing him to forget the details of his dream. While staying in the Quantocks, Coleridge and his friend William Wordsworth often wandered the moor at night, alarming the locals who thought they were French spies. The government sent an officer down to Somerset to investigate and he concluded, somewhat contemptuously, that they were 'mere poets'. Coleridge Way recreates some of those walks. Beginning at Nether Stowey, it used to end at Porlock but has recently been extended to Lynmouth.

The main road (A39) west out of Porlock climbs the notorious Porlock Hill, its 1 in 4 gradient THE STEEPEST ON ANY A-ROAD IN BRITAIN.

Culbone

Golden grey, steadfast and lovable, and seemingly bathed in sunlight whatever the weather, ST BEUNO'S

Culbone had been a place of pagan worship for a thousand years before the Welsh saint Beuno brought the Christian message to the southwest of England in the 6th century. While the walls of the present church are 12th-century Norman, the height of the nave indicates that the church has Saxon origins, and the Saxon font and a small Saxon two-light window in the north wall of the sanctuary, cut from a single block of sandstone, could only have come from an earlier Saxon church. At the top of the pillar dividing the two lights of the Saxon window there is a smiling feline face.

The porch is 13th century, while the spirelet was added in 1810. Inside, there is a wagon roof extending over both the nave and chancel, a 14th-century screen, benches and a Jacobean box pew for the use of the Squire of nearby Ashley Combe House.

Through the centuries the church has served many different communities: hermits, charcoal burners, French prisoners and even a 16th-century leper colony. In the autumn of 1797 the poet Samuel Tyler Coleridge walked to

Culbone from Porlock Weir seeking inspiration. Today it is mainly ramblers who visit, although there are also well-attended fortnightly services held in the church all year round.

Ancient Culbone may be, but it is also a significant cradle of the modern world. Up on the hillside above the church are the garden ruins of an exotic Italian-style mansion called Ashley Combe, bought by Lord King, later the Earl of Lovelace, in the early 18th century as a fairytale retreat for his wife Ada, daughter of the poet Lord Byron. The remnants of terraces and staircases, tunnels and follies and grottoes, set out amongst the woods, can still be explored. Ada took long walks in the gardens with her friend the great mathematician Charles Babbage, inventor of the Analytical Engine, a calculating machine programmed by punch cards, that is regarded as the first ever computer. During their walks Charles and Ada, a noted mathematician herself, discussed possible uses for his machine and programmes that might be created for it. Ada came up with numerous ideas and is hailed as being THE WORLD'S FIRST COMPUTER PROGRAMMER. In recognition, in 1979 the US Department of Defense named a secret software programme after her. ADA is still used as a programme today.

Well, I never knew this about
THE SOMERSET COAST

The NEW ROOM in BRISTOL was built in 1739 by John Wesley and is THE OLDEST METHODIST CHAPEL IN THE WORLD.

In 2017 DHL opened BRITAIN'S LARGEST SINGLE WAREHOUSE IN AVONMOUTH, occupying 55 achres (22 ha). Avonmouth's docks are still amongst the busiest on the west coast of Britain.

ALFRED LEETE (1882–1933), the artist who designed the First World War poster featuring Lord Kitchener and the words 'Your Country Needs You', grew up in Weston-super-Mare and is buried in the town's Milton Road cemetery, while *Monty Python* and *Fawlty Towers* star JOHN CLEESE was born in Weston in 1939.

BERROW BEACH, which runs for 7 miles from Brean Down, south of Weston-super-Mare to Burnham-on-Sea, is THE LONGEST STRETCH OF SAND IN EUROPE.

STEART, across the River Parrett from Burnham-on-Sea, marks the current start point of the newly extended South West Coast Path, BRITAIN'S LONGEST NATIONAL TRAIL, which runs for 650 miles round the coastlines of West Somerset, Devon, Cornwall and Dorset to Poole. It has been calculated that the total height climbed by anyone who walks the whole length of the South West Coast Path is almost 155,000 feet (47,000 m), the equivalent to climbing four Mount Everests.

CLEEVE ABBEY sits in lovely countryside just south of the village of Washford no more than 2 miles from the sea. Founded in 1198 for Cistercian monks, Cleeve Abbey is regarded as having the best preserved medieval monastic cloister buildings in Britain. Although the abbey church was demolished on the orders of Henry VIII, the rest of the complex was converted into a country house and the buildings are still roofed and habitable. There is a fine gatehouse, a low stone-vaulted chapter house, a 15th-century refectory with a magnificent wooden wagon roof decorated with carved angels, 13th-century painted tiles from the floor of an earlier refectory, a painted chamber with a large 15th-century wall painting and, perhaps best of all, an almost perfectly preserved 13th-century dormitory.

Just 2 miles inland and set in a purple fold of wild and beautiful moorland country, the 15th-century church of ST MARY AT OARE is where Lorna Doone married John Ridd in R.D. Blackmore's celebrated novel. Here is the window, glazed now but empty then, through which Carver Doone fired his pistol at the bride, whom he wanted for himself. People come from all over the world to relive the famous scene, and standing in the church it is hard not to think of Lorna Doone and all the drama as real – indeed, there was a real John Ride serving as churchwarden here as recently as 1925. The church has other attractions too, such as 18th-century box pews, a Norman font and a unique 15th-century piscina formed of a man's head held in two hands. There is also a memorial to Nicholas Snow, who lived in the nearby Manor House and often brought his friend the Prince of Wales, later Edward VII, to the church after they had been hunting on the moor.

CHAPTER FIVE
DEVON NORTH COAST

Lynmouth to Hartland
50 miles

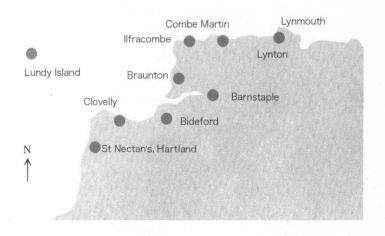

Highlights of Devon's north coast include the world's highest and steepest water-powered funicular railway, the highest sea cliff in England, the longest village street in England, Britain's oldest working lighthouse, the last abbey in England to be dissolved by Henry VIII, the largest area of sand dunes in England, Britain's oldest borough, the best lead broach spire in England, and the only town in Britain to have an exclamation mark after its name.

Lynmouth

A steep hill takes the coast road winding down into Lynmouth, a pretty former fishing village set where the West Lyn and East Lyn rivers converge before emptying into the sea. Here the South West Coast Path meets the Tarka Trail from Barnstaple, as taken by Tarka the Otter, the Two Moors Way linking Exmoor and Dartmoor, and the Coleridge Way from Nether Stowey.

Lynmouth prospered on herring until the start of the 17th century when the herring went elsewhere, and was then largely forgotten, although in 1746 the artist THOMAS GAINSBOROUGH honeymooned in the village with his bride Margaret and declared Lynmouth to be 'the most delightful place for the landscape painter this country can boast'.

When the Napoleonic Wars curtailed Continental travel and compelled people to explore Britain instead, Lynmouth was rediscovered as a Little Switzerland and was given a further boost by the poet SHELLEY who brought his new 16-year-old bride Harriet to Devon in 1812, seeking refuge from family disapproval. He extolled the virtues of Lynmouth to all his friends and was inspired to write his first major poem, *Queen Mab*, while staying in what is now Shelley's Hotel, a Victorianised Georgian cottage that stands above the spot where the roads into Lynmouth meet.

In August 1952 a savage storm deposited 9 inches (23 cm) of rain on Exmoor overnight and sent torrents of water laden with trees and boulders down both the Lyn valleys into Lynmouth, washing away over 100 buildings and 28 bridges, killing 34 people and making 420 people homeless. Afterwards the village was rebuilt and the river diverted, but the flood is not forgotten. There is a memorial garden where a group of houses once stood on the bank of the East Lyn and a memorial hall near the harbour. The strange-looking Rhenish Beacon Tower standing on the stone harbour pier is an exact replica of the tower built there in 1860 by General Rawdon as somewhere to store salt water for his bath tub, but subsequently carried away by the flood.

Today Lynmouth is made up mostly of Victorian hotels and guest-houses, but a delightful row of traditional thatched cottages survives down by the harbour.

When Lynmouth needed to expand as a result of its new-found popularity in the early 19th century there was nowhere left to build, and so it was decided to put up a new hotel in Lynton, 500 feet (150 m) up on the moor above the harbour, and at that time consisting of just a few cottages and a church.

Lynton

After the building of its first hotel in 1807, Lynton grew rapidly into a smart Victorian resort. Much of the development was financed by SIR GEORGE NEWNES, publisher of *Tit-Bits* magazine, the forerunner of popular journalism, which gave P.G. Wodehouse his first break, and the *Strand Magazine*,

for which Sir Arthur Conan Doyle created Sherlock Holmes. After watching some poor donkeys struggling to haul great loads up the hill from Lynmouth to Lynton, Sir George decided there must be some better way to connect the two villages and in 1890 he opened the LYNTON AND LYNMOUTH CLIFF RAILWAY, THE WORLD'S HIGHEST AND STEEPEST WATER-POWERED FUNICULAR RAILWAY, 862 feet (263 m) long with a rise of 500 feet (152 m). Each of the two cars has a 700 gallon water tank which is filled when the car is at the top and discharged when it is at the bottom. The heavier weight of the top car forces it to descend while the lighter lower car is hauled up to the top, with the speed controlled by a brakeman in each car.

Valley of the Rocks

The Valley of the Rocks is a dry valley edged with spectacular jagged pinnacles of rock, with names such as Ragged Jack, Devil's Cheesewring and Castle Rock, rising 800 feet (244 m) from the sea. The poet Robert Southey, visiting in 1799, described the valley as 'the very bones and skeletons of the earth; rock reeling upon rock, stone piled upon stone, a huge terrific mass'. R.D. Blackmore set some of *Lorna Doone* here and based the witch featured in the story on an old woman who lived in Mother Meldrum's Cave in the valley in the 19th century. Wild goats gaze down from the heights.

Combe Martin

Eight miles west of Lynton is the Great Hangman, at 1,043 feet (318 m) THE HIGHEST SEA CLIFF IN ENGLAND. From this unsurpassed viewpoint the path drops down into Combe Martin, where

THE LONGEST VILLAGE STREET IN ENGLAND winds its way up a long deep valley for 2 miles from a sandy beach. Half-way along, just before the 13th-century church of St Peter ad Vincula, is the extraordinary PACK O' CARDS INN, built in 1690 as a home by a local squire called George Ley with his winnings from a game of cards. It has four storeys, one for each suit in pack of cards, 13 doors and fireplaces on each floor for the number of cards in a suit, and 52 windows, one for each card in a pack.

Ilfracombe

Ilfracombe tumbles down a series of cliffs towards its attractive harbour, one of the few safe refuges along the North Devon coast and active as an important trading port during the 14th to 16th centuries. Like other Devon resorts it became popular during the Napoleonic Wars and more so with the coming of the railway, and boasts numerous extravagant Regency and Victorian hotels and holiday terraces overlooking the mainly Georgian quayside.

Thirteenth-century Holy Trinity Church looks down from its own hill to the west. The church tower finds itself half inside the north aisle, having been built around when the church was expanded. There is a Norman font, an Elizabethan pulpit and a magnificent, richly carved and colourful 15th-century wagon roof, regarded as the finest in the West Country. ANNA PARNELL, youngest sister of Irish nationalist Charles Stewart Parnell, is buried in the churchyard. She drowned while swimming off Ilfracombe in 1911.

Perched 100 feet (30 m) up on Lantern Hill, a rocky outcrop above the harbour entrance, is a 14th-century chapel dedicated to the patron saint of sailors, St Nicholas, which has long been used as a lighthouse to guide sailors safely into harbour. In the days of Henry VIII indulgences were granted to those who kept a lantern burning in the chapel window. No longer a chapel, St Nicholas's became an official lighthouse in 1819 and is still operational, very possibly BRITAIN'S OLDEST WORKING LIGHTHOUSE.

St Nicholas Chapel, one of Ilfracombe's oldest structures, looks straight down on one of its newest and most controversial, a 66½ foot (20 m) tall sculpture of a pregnant woman holding aloft a sword. Called *Verity*, the sculpture was loaned to the town for 20 years in 2012 by its creator Damien Hirst, who lives in nearby Combe Martin. The internal anatomy of the mother is shown, along with the foetus.

Never afraid of controversy, Ilfracombe is clearly enamoured of the female form, for just across town is the new, eye-catchingly conical LANDMARK THEATRE, opened in 1997 and known locally as Madonna's Bra – because that is indeed what it looks like.

Ilfracombe has no main beach but straggles along a series of rocky coves with patches of sand and it is quite easy for swimmers to be cut off by the tide. In 1820 Welsh miners were hired to carve four tunnels though the cliffs from the western edge of the town to give access by horse and carriage to two tidal pools on the beach. In Victorian times the two pools were strictly segregated, one for men and the other for women. It is still possible today to walk through the tunnels on to what are known as the Tunnel beaches.

Actor PETER SELLERS first trod the stage at Ilfracombe, where his parents managed the Gaiety Theatre. It is still there on the Promenade, sporting its quaint conical tower, but now serves as a gallery and shopping arcade.

Barnstaple

Barnstaple was minting its own coins in the 10th century and received its charter from King Athelstan in AD 930, so vies with Malmesbury in Wiltshire to be BRITAIN'S OLDEST BOROUGH. It was an important port in the Middle Ages and a major textile and pottery centre, but as the River Taw silted up, so the port declined. The town remains an important agricultural and market centre.

Although there has been much rebuilding, the antiquity of Barnstaple is reflected in its medieval street pattern and there are a number of attractive old buildings. Castle Mound, a steep, flat-topped hillock that rises out of the old cattle market, was the motte of Barnstaple's Norman motte and bailey castle. William the Conqueror had the motte raised and a wooden fort erected on the top in 1068 to enforce Norman rule over the Saxon burghers of Barnstaple. A stone castle was built later but was never much used, and after being abandoned in the 14th century it finally fell down altogether during a storm in 1601.

Barnstaple's pride is the 522 foot (159 m) LONG BRIDGE, whose 16 arches have straddled the River Taw since the early 13th century. One of the longest medieval bridges in Britain, it has been refurbished and widened over the years and is still in use for traffic although most vehicles now use the modern bridge upstream.

The twisted lead broach spire of 13th-century St Peter's Church, warped by a lightning strike in 1810 but still regarded as the best spire of its kind in England, rises out of a jumble of narrow, winding shopping streets in the town centre, while beside it is St Anne's Chapel, built as a chantry chapel in the early 14th century and then converted into a school. Barnstaple-born JOHN GAY (1685–1732), author of *The Beggar's Opera*, was a pupil there. The building is now used as a museum. There are two delightful sets of almshouses: Penrose's Almshouses, with a splendid colonnaded front, were built in 1627 in memory of a former Mayor of Barnstaple; and the cream-painted Horwood Almshouses, by the church, were endowed in 1659.

Down on the quayside, from where five ships departed in 1588 to fight the Spanish Armada and, in quieter times, Barnstaple cloth and pottery was sent to the New World, is QUEEN ANNE'S WALK, a small colonnade that was constructed in 1713 as a Merchant's Exchange. Here shipowners and merchants would conduct their business and deals would be sealed by touching the Tome Stone, today mounted on a pedestal beneath the huge statue of Queen Anne that stands atop the entrance.

An archway beneath the 19th-century Grecian Guildhall in the High Street leads to Barnstaple's Pannier Market, named for the pannier baskets carried by horse or donkey from which the market traders sold their produce. The market is still held here three days a week in a splendid market hall of glass

and iron latticework built in 1855, although stalls have replaced the panniers.

Butcher's Row, which runs alongside the Pannier Market, is a very pretty arcade of small white- and cream-painted Victorian shops, all with green doors.

Dominating The Square at the Barnstaple end of the Long Bridge is the tall, distinctive clock tower of the Albert Clock, built in 1862 in honour of Prince Albert, who had died the year before.

Barnstaple also played a minor role in the Jeremy Thorpe scandal in the 1970s as the home of Norman Scott, the male model who tried to blackmail Thorpe, leader of the Liberal Party, over their homosexual relationship. Andrew Newton, who was hired by Thorpe's friends to intimidate Scott, misheard his instructions and went to Dunstable in Bedfordshire instead.

Lundy Island

Occupied since prehistoric times, the old pirate hideout of Lundy Island,

which is reached by ferry from Bideford, lies 12 miles off the North Devon coast and at 1,100 acres (445 ha) is the largest island in the Bristol Channel. Because of its unique flora and fauna Lundy was designated as ENGLAND'S FIRST MARINE NATURE RESERVE AND MARINE CONSERVATION ZONE. The name Lundy comes from the Viking word for puffin and the island is still one of the best places in Britain to see puffins. Today Lundy has 23 holiday properties managed by the Landmark Trust and receives up to twenty thousand day-trippers every year. There is a resident population of about 28 who look after the wildlife and the island's many archaeological sites as well as the pub and tourist facilities.

Bideford

Bideford has more than played its part in Britain's seafaring story. Bideford men sailed with the great Elizabethan explorers, Hawkins, Raleigh and Drake, while in the 16th and 17th centuries Bideford was the third largest port in Britain, trading across the world, in particular with Spain, the West Indies and North America, becoming Britain's leading port for the import of tobacco.

This was all thanks in large part to the town's seafaring lords of the manor, the Grenvilles. The most famous of these was Richard Grenville, born in Bideford's manor house in 1542. He sailed from Bideford to explore and colonise the New World, and in 1585 he captained the seven-strong fleet taking English settlers to establish a colony on Roanoke Island sponsored by his cousin Sir Walter Raleigh. On one of his expeditions in 1586 he brought back a Native American

Indian to Bideford and named him Raleigh. The massive Norman font in Bideford's parish church of St Mary where RALEIGH, THE FIRST EVER AMERICAN INDIAN TO SET FOOT IN ENGLAND, was baptised a Christian is still in use. In 1588 Grenville provisioned five ships at Bideford for the fight against the Spanish Armada, and sitting in Victoria Park at the north end of the quayside are eight cannon captured from one of the Spanish ships.

In 1591 Grenville sailed from Bideford in Sir Francis Drake's flagship the *Revenge* to join an English fleet under Admiral Howard hoping to waylay Spanish treasure ships off the Azores. Confronted by a much larger Spanish fleet than expected, Howard retired the fleet but Grenville, as John Milton wrote later, 'utterly refused to turn from the enimie ... he would rather chose to die than to dishonour himselfe'. The *Revenge* stood alone in the face of 53 Spanish ships and fought them for 12 hours, badly damaging five galleons before Grenville collapsed from his wounds and his crew surrendered. Grenville died a prisoner a few days later and the *Revenge* sank not long afterwards in a storm, along with 15 warships of the Spanish fleet. Grenville's exploits were later glorified in a poem by Alfred, Lord Tennyson.

Bideford's lovely tree-lined quay still bustles today but only with local vessels such as the ferry to Lundy Island. From the quayside there is a splendid view of Bideford' s impressive LONG BRIDGE, built in 1535 on top of an earlier stone bridge that in turn replaced a 13th-century wooden bridge. At 677 feet (206 m) long it is the second longest surviving medieval bridge in England after Swarkestone

Bridge in Derbyshire. Intriguingly, each of the 24 arches has a different span, possibly because each arch was funded by an individual business or patron.

At the north end of the quay is a statue of CHARLES KINGSLEY, who was living in Bideford when he wrote his novel *Westward Ho!* – set in North Devon during the era of the buccaneering Elizabethan explorers like Richard Grenville. In 1925 it became THE FIRST NOVEL TO BE ADAPTED FOR RADIO BY THE BBC. The Victorian resort of WESTWARD HO! on the coast a mile north of Bideford took its name from the novel, THE ONLY TOWN IN BRITAIN TO BE NAMED AFTER A BOOK. It is also THE ONLY TOWN IN BRITAIN TO HAVE AN EXCLAMATION MARK AFTER ITS NAME. Another writer, RUDYARD KIPLING, spent his schooldays in Westward Ho! and set his novel *Stalky & Co* on the hill south of the village where Kipling and his friends used to bunk off and smoke cigars. The hill is now known as Kipling Tors. Westward Ho! has a huge sandy beach, some fine hotels, lots of bungalows and one of the oldest and most famous golf courses in Britain.

Clovelly

Clovelly's whitewashed, flower-bedecked cottages cascade down to the sea in a tumble of loveliness. The cobbled High Street, known as 'Up-along' or 'Down-along' depending on which way you are going, is so steep that villagers step out of their front door on to their neighbour's roof. Falling over 400 feet (122 m) in just half a mile, the street is far too precipitous for cars, meaning that Clovelly is THE ONLY VILLAGE IN ENGLAND WHOSE MAIN STREET IS ENTIRELY TRAFFIC FREE. Instead residents and visitors must go by foot, while essential supplies such as furniture and groceries are hauled by sledge. Both people and supplies were once carried up and down by labouring donkeys but, as at

Lynmouth further up the coast, the Victorians considered this practice to be cruel and put a stop to it, although donkeys are still employed to give rides to children and pose for photographs.

Clovelly was a fishing village as far back as Domesday or before, while the harbour, with its bollards made from captured Spanish cannon, dates from the 16th century when the village began to grow prosperous on herring. It was discovered as a tourist attraction in the mid 19th century thanks to the writings of Charles Dickens in *A Message from the Sea*, and more particularly Charles Kingsley, who spent his childhood in Clovelly where his father was the rector. He returned to Clovelly to write *The Water Babies* while staying in a cottage on the High Street now called Kingsley's Cottage.

Clovelly has managed to preserve its ancient beauty, partly because the nature of the site means there is no room for modern intrusions, but also in large part thanks to CHRISTINE HAMLYN, who owned the village from 1884 to 1936 and made it her life's work to protect and restore Clovelly's charming old buildings. Many of the cottages, some of which date from Tudor times, bear her initials.

The Hamlyn family acquired Clovelly in 1738, when locally born lawyer Zachary Hamlyn bought it off the Cary family who had been lords of the manor since the 14th century. The village is today managed by a descendant of the Hamlyns, JOHN ROUS, great-grandson of Christine Hamlyn and Prime Minister H.H. Asquith. He lives in CLOVELLY COURT, the much restored 18th-century great house at the top of the village. Nearby is the Norman All Saints Church, approached by a long yew avenue and filled with elaborate monuments to the Cary lords of the manor.

Clovelly still fishes but its main income today comes from tourism. Boat trips from the harbour take visitors out into Bideford Bay and along the coast, while the Red Lion Hotel, overlooking the harbour, provides food and accommodation. Also overlooking the harbour is CRAZY KATE'S COTTAGE, a long narrow house with a verandah which belonged to KATE LYALL, who went mad after watching from that very verandah as her fisherman beau drowned outside the harbour. She died in 1736.

The best way to approach Clovelly is from the east via the 3 mile long HOBBY DRIVE, constructed for James Hamlyn-Williams on the cliff top during the Napoleonic Wars by French prisoners of war and afterwards by unemployed English soldiers returning from the war.

St Nectan's, Hartland

Inland from Hartland Quay can be seen the 128 foot (39 m) high tower of St Nectan's Church in Hartland, known as the Cathedral of North Devon. The tower, which was built in 1420, is the second tallest church tower in Devon, and was made so high as a landmark for sailors. The church, begun in 1170 and completed in 1360, possesses a

Norman font, a fabulous painted wagon roof and the biggest and most complete medieval rood screen in Devon. Created in 1450 it has 11 bays, each one unique, and is 45 feet (14 m) long and 12 feet (3.6 m) high with a top as wide as the Devon lane running past outside. In the chancel is an altar tomb thought to have held the relics of St Nectan, a 5th-century saint of Irish descent who came to Devon from Wales. Also in the chancel is a chair in which the Ethiopian EMPEROR HAILE SELASSIE sat when opening the church fête in 1938. Buried in the churchyard is SIR ALLEN LANE, founder of Penguin Books, the man who published the unexpurgated version of D.H. Lawrence's *Lady Chatterley's Lover* in 1959 (which led to a famous obscenity trial) and the original publisher of the incomparable Pevsner Architectural Guides. Also buried there is children's writer MARY NORTON, author of *The Borrowers* and *Bed Knobs and Broomsticks*.

The church is the work of the monks from nearby Hartland Abbey, the last abbey in England to be dissolved by Henry VIII. The abbey was gifted to the Keeper of the King's Wine Cellar and the estate still remains in the same family. The present house is largely mid-18th-century Strawberry Hill Gothick.

Well, I never knew this
about
THE NORTH DEVON COAST

Three miles west of Lynton a steep track leads down to the rocks and sand of WOODY BAY, named for the dense oak woods that sweep down to the bay and once earmarked for development in a scheme that bankrupted the owner in the 1890s. It is now owned by the National Trust. WOODY BAY STATION, about 2 miles inland, is the modern-day base for the LYNTON AND BARNSTAPLE RAILWAY, built in 1898 by SIR GEORGE NEWNES. The railway never made a profit, largely because of the steep inclines it had to negotiate, and it closed in 1935 but was rescued and part reopened between Woody Bay and Killington Lane in 2004. At 964 feet (294 m) above sea level, Woody Bay station is THE HIGHEST RAILWAY STATION IN SOUTHERN ENGLAND.

Hidden away in a secluded valley just outside Ilfracombe, CHAMBERCOMBE MANOR dates from the 11th century and is ONE OF THE OLDEST OCCU-PIED HOUSES IN BRITAIN. Mentioned in the Domesday Book, it was owned by the Champernon family until the 15th century and eventually passed into the hands of the Duke of Suffolk, father of the ten-day queen Lady Jane Grey, who stayed many times in what is now the Lady Jane Grey room. Not surprisingly considering its age, the manor is said to be ONE OF THE MOST HAUNTED HOUSES IN THE COUNTRY. Today the house is open to the public both to visit and to stay in, and there are rooms on show dating from the Elizabethan to the Victorian periods.

The art deco Saunton Sands Hotel overlooks SAUNTON SANDS, which stretch for 3½ miles south to Crow Point at the mouth of the River Taw and are much favoured by surfers. The beach is backed by BRAUNTON BURROWS, THE LARGEST AREA OF SAND DUNES IN ENGLAND, and is sometimes closed so that military aircraft can practise short take-offs and landings. In 1944 the beach was used by American assault troops to practise the D-Day landings.

Between Saunton Sands and Braunton village, which claims to be THE LARGEST VILLAGE IN ENGLAND, lies the GREAT FIELD, BRITAIN'S LARGEST REMAINING AREA OF STRIP FARMING. Just to the south, BRAUNTON MARSH was in 1992 designated BRITAIN'S FIRST BIOSPHERE RESERVE, an area managed so as to maintain a balance between population and environment.

THE TARKA TRAIL, which follows the path taken by Henry Williamson's Tarka the Otter, is a figure-of-eight route centred on Barnstaple. The northern loop goes up the coast to Lynton and back, while the southern loop goes through Bideford to Dartmoor and back and is THE LONGEST CONTINUOUS OFF-ROAD CYCLE PATH IN BRITAIN.

The NORTH DEVON CREMATORIUM in Bickington, across the river from Barnstaple, is THE LARGEST CREMATORIUM IN ENGLAND.

SIR FRANCIS CHICHESTER (1901–1972), THE FIRST MAN TO SAIL SINGLE-HANDED AROUND THE WORLD, was born in Barnstaple, as were theatre director RICHARD EYRE, in 1943, TV antiques expert TIM WONNACOTT, in 1951, and TV presenter DERMOT MURNAGHAN, in 1957.

A mile south of Hartland Quay is BLACKPOOL MILL COTTAGE, perched above a stream just back from the sea and frequently used as a film location, most notably for the BBC adaptation of *Sense and Sensibility*, the TV film of Rosamunde Pilcher's *The Shell Seekers*, the BBC drama *The Night Manager* and the 2017 film *The Guernsey Literary and Potato Peel Pie Society*.

CHAPTER SIX

CORNWALL NORTH COAST

Morwenstow to Land's End
92 miles

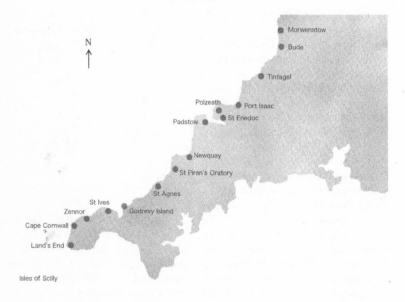

Highlights along Cornwall's north coast include the National Trust's smallest property, the first permanent structure in the world to be built on shifting sands, the longest tub-boat canal ever built, the birthplace of King Arthur, the surfing capital of Britain, the oldest known Christian church in Britain, the last tin production centre in Britain, the world's oldest Cornish beam engine, England's only cape and the most southwesterly point of mainland Britain.

Hawker's Hut

About a mile into Cornwall from the Devon border is HENNA CLIFF, at 472 feet (144 m) the second highest sheer cliff in Cornwall. Half-way down the cliff, reached via a steep, bramble-strewn path, is MORWENNA'S WELL, a small stone dwelling where St Morwenna, one of 24 children of the 6th-century Welsh king Brychan, lived in perfect isolation.

A little further on is VICARAGE CLIFF, almost as high. From here 17 steps lead down to Hawker's Hut, a sturdy wooden shed fashioned out of driftwood and built into the cliff face in the mid 19th century by the local parson the REVD ROBERT STEPHEN

HAWKER (1803–1875). Hawker would come here to smoke his opium pipe, write poetry and entertain guests such as Alfred, Lord Tennyson and Charles Kingsley. He was the author of the unofficial Cornish anthem 'Trelawny', which includes the famous lines:

> *And shall Trelawny die?*
> *Here's twenty thousand Cornish men*
> *Will know the reason why!*

Hawker's Hut is now run as the National Trust's smallest property.

Morwenstow

Ten minutes' walk inland from the hut is the hamlet of Morwenstow, with its Norman church dedicated to St Morwenna, where Hawker was parson from 1835 to 1874. The church is renowned for the Norman sculptures on its interior arches and south doorway.

Hawker was something of an eccentric, known for talking to the birds, for sometimes dressing up as a mermaid with seaweed for hair, and for bringing his nine cats to church – even excommunicating one of them for catching a mouse on a Sunday.

In the autumn of 1843 Hawker inaugurated the modern Harvest Festival here when he invited his parishioners to decorate the church with their home-grown produce for a special Thanksgiving service.

The churchyard is filled with the graves of some 40 seamen shipwrecked on the storm-lashed coast. During his incumbency Hawker not only put a stop to the smugglers and wreckers who frequented the area, but made sure that any bodies washed up on the rocky shore were retrieved and given a proper Christian burial.

Glimpsed through the trees is the vicarage that Hawker built for himself, with chimneys modelled on the towers of the churches where he had served. The big kitchen chimney is said to resemble his mother's tomb.

Bude

Bude is a largely Victorian resort based around the golden sands of Summerleaze Beach which, in common with so many of the beaches of North Cornwall, is pounded by white-tipped Atlantic rollers, once the bane of sailors but popular nowadays with surfers.

Overlooking the beach, atop its own sand dune, is BUDE CASTLE, constructed in 1830 and THE FIRST PERMANENT STRUCTURE IN THE WORLD TO BE BUILT ON SHIFTING SANDS. It was the work of the Cornish scientist and inventor SIR GOLDSWORTHY GURNEY (1793–1875), who overcame the unstable nature of the ground by laying a deep concrete

platform into the sand as a base for the foundations. The technique is still widely used in the modern construction industry, an example being what were once the world's tallest buildings, the Petronas Towers in Kuala Lumpur, Malaysia, which were built on soft wet limestone using Gurney's method.

Bude Castle was lit by another of Gurney's inventions, 'Bude Light', created by forcing a mixture of oxygen and hydrogen through a blowpipe to create an intensely hot flame and adding lime to create a bright light – to all intents and purposes Gurney had invented limelight. He was able to illuminate the whole castle with just one light by using a series of mirrors to reflect the light into different rooms. Gurney's 'Bude Light' was used to light the Houses of Parliament for 50 years, MPs thus becoming the first people to 'hog the limelight'.

Inspired by his fellow Cornishman Richard Trevithick, Gurney also invented a steam carriage which, in 1829, he drove from London to Bath at an average speed of 15 mph, THE FIRST LONG JOURNEY AT SUSTAINED SPEED EVER ACHIEVED BY A SELF-PROPELLED VEHICLE. His story is told in Bude Castle's Heritage Centre.

Below the castle a sea lock, one of the last working locks of its kind in Britain, guards the entrance to the BUDE CANAL, which was built in 1823 to transport sand to Launceston, 35

miles away. The first part of the canal rose 350 feet (107 m) in 6 miles using inclined ramps up which wheeled tub boats were hauled on metal rails. The tubs were hooked on to a long chain driven by a waterwheel. The Bude Canal is THE LONGEST TUB-BOAT CANAL EVER BUILT.

Tintagel

The North Cornish coast is at its most romantic at Tintagel, a long straggling village set on the cliff tops 300 feet (90 m) above the sea and linked to a rocky headland by a thin strip of wave-lashed causeway. An ancient place dripping in mist and legend, the village sprang to fame in the 19th century thanks to Alfred, Lord Tennyson's *Idylls of the King*, which re-affirmed Tintagel's links to King Arthur first put forward in Geoffrey of Monmouth's imaginative *History of the Kings of Britain*, written in the 12th century.

While there is no proof that Tintagel was the birthplace of King Arthur, the dramatic scenery and atmospheric ruins powerfully suggest that it could have been. A footpath leads from the village to the ruins of Tintagel Castle, which was built in the 13th century for Richard Earl of Cornwall, brother of Henry III. The castle is split asunder by a deep crevice that separates the mainland from the island where the bulk of the castle lies. The original land bridge across the gap was washed away in the 15th century and for a long time visitors had to descend a steep staircase to a short bridge across the gap and then climb more steps through the castle ruins to reach the top of the island, where there are the scant remains of a 6th-century Celtic monastery. The new bridge opened in 2019 and runs at the same height as the original crossing, thus avoiding the steps.

You can still follow the old steps down to the pebbly beach, known as the Haven, and explore Merlin's Cave, where Arthur first met Merlin the Wizard.

North across the Haven from the island is the headland of BARRAS NOSE, which came to the National Trust in 1897 as the Trust's first English coastal acquisition. Looming just back from the headland and looking like Dracula's castle is a huge Victorian hotel called the Camelot, built in the late 19th century by the London and South Western Railway to accommodate passengers arriving in search of King Arthur.

The highlight of the village itself is the OLD POST OFFICE, a gloriously crumpled and weather-beaten 14th-century manor house which became a post office in the 19th century and is now owned by the National Trust.

Polzeath

A stone plaque on the cliffs above Polzeath, between Pentire Point and Rumps Point, commemorates the spot where some of the most moving lines of all time were penned.

They shall grow not old, as we that are left grow old:
Age shall not weary them, nor the years condemn.
At the going down of the sun and in the morning
We will remember them.

The words are from the poem 'For the Fallen', written in 1914 by LAURENCE BINYON (1869–1943), a poet and playwright who worked at the British Museum as an expert in Oriental art and literature. They were composed in honour of the British soldiers who died in the Battle of Mons and the Battle of the Marne at the beginning of the Great War, but have since been adopted as a tribute to all casualties of war and have become an integral part of the Remembrance Day Service.

St Enedoc Church

'So grows the tinny tenor faint or loud
All all things draw toward St Enedoc'
Sir John Betjemen

Plugged in the middle of a bunker on St Enodoc Golf Course at Trebetherick

is the 12th-century church of St Enodoc, its stubby and bent stone spire peeking arthritically above the dunes that protect it from the sea. Not too long ago the church was full of sand, and the vicar and congregation had to be lowered in through the roof to attend services. It seems only fitting that the man who did more than most to celebrate and save the country churches of England should be buried here in one of the loveliest churchyards of them all. SIR JOHN BETJEMEN spent many happy holidays in Trebetherick as a boy and returned in later life to buy a home here, where he died in 1984 aged 77. He was buried in the churchyard of his favourite church St Enodoc, in a grave by the path near the lychgate. His mother lies nearby and there is a memorial to his father inside the church.

Also in the churchyard is a memorial tablet to FLEUR LOMBARD (1974–1996), the first female firefighter to die in action in Britain, and to JOHN MABLY and his daughter ALICE who died within days of each other in 1687. Theirs is THE LAST SLAB INCISED WITH EFFIGIES FOUND IN ENGLAND.

Padstow

Once the most thriving port on Cornwall's north coast, Padstow saw its importance decline as the entrance to the River Camel became blocked by the DOOM BAR, a large shifting sandbank that made the channel too shallow for larger boats and caused many shipwrecks. Doom Bar has become famous as the name of the flagship ale of the local Sharp's Brewery, founded across the Camel at Rock in 1994. It is now sold across the world. In 2008 Doom Bar became the FIRST EVER OFFICIAL BEER SPONSOR OF THE BOAT RACE – and

Prideaux Place

is the favourite drink of J.K. Rowling's private detective, Cornishman Cormoran Strike, because it tastes of 'home, peace and long-gone security'.

Today Padstow, with its narrow streets and old weathered houses tumbling down to the harbour, retains the allure of a traditional fishing village, and is prospering as a tourist destination, with many visitors attracted by the restaurants and cafés of TV chef RICK STEIN – to such a degree that Padstow is often referred to as 'Padstein'.

The village is overlooked by PRIDEAUX PLACE, an Elizabethan house that has been owned by the Prideaux family since it was built in 1592. The Great Chamber has what is considered one of the finest Elizabethan plastered ceilings in England, while in the Armoury is ENGLAND'S OLDEST CAST-IRON CANNON, dating from the middle of the 16th century. The deer park is home to one of the oldest herds of deer in England, and legend has it that if the deer die out then so do the Prideaux family.

Prideaux Place appears frequently in the Poldark books of Winston Graham, who was a great friend of the Prideaux family and wrote much of his 12th

and last Poldark novel *Bella Poldark* while staying at Prideaux Place. A serious fire broke out in the house while he was there, but fortunately Graham's hand-written manuscript was rescued from the flames.

Newquay

The 'new' quay that Cornwall's biggest resort sprang from dates from the 17th century, while the town that built up around it became rich on pilchards. A symbol of those days is the quaint, crooked, white-painted building that looks like a mini fort perched on the cliffs above the harbour. This is the unique 'HUER'S HUT' from which a 'huer' would scan the bay for the tell-tale signs of shoals of pilchards and upon spotting them would alert fishermen by crying 'Heva, heva!' Once the fishing boats were launched, the huer would direct the boats to the location of the shoals by means of semaphore signals, using 'bushes', furze bushes covered with some kind of cloth, visible from the sea.

The Huer's Hut stands on the site of a hermitage dating from the 14th century. The hermit was responsible for keeping alight a beacon for guiding shipping in the bay.

During the 19th century, as the pilchards moved away, so the tourists moved in, attracted by Newquay's nine sandy beaches and transported by the railway which arrived there in the 1870s. High on Towan Head, overlooking Fistral Beach, is one of the hotels built to cater for those tourists, the grand, monumental Victorian Headland Hotel, built in 1900 and similar in its Gothic institutional appearance to the Camelot at Tintagel. This was the location for the film of Roald Dahl's *The Witches* and featured in Rosamunde Pilcher's *The Shell Seekers*.

For those who want particularly exclusive accommodation there is THE HOUSE IN THE SEA, a hideaway cottage perched on top of Towan Island, an 80 foot (24 m) high rocky outcrop on Tolcarne Beach cut off at high tide and reached only by a gated suspension bridge. It was built originally as a Victorian tea-room but converted to a three-bedroom house in the 1930s, and was once owned by SIR OLIVER LODGE (1851–1940), the pioneer of electromagnetic waves and inventor of the spark plug. It is today available for holiday lets at up to £6,000 a week.

Newquay today is renowned as the surfing capital of Britain and hosts the annual National Surfing Championships, on Fistral Beach.

St Piran's Oratory

The walls of St Piran's Oratory, THE OLDEST CHRISTIAN CHURCH IN ENGLAND, lie half buried in the sands of Penhale Beach, north of Perranporth. The chapel was built by St Piran some time in the 6th century in thanks for his survival after he was exiled from Ireland. Apparently, having angered an Irish chieftain he was thrown off a high cliff tied to a millstone, but instead of drowning he floated across the sea to Cornwall and landed at the spot now named Perranporth (Piran's port). His first Cornish convert was a badger, but he soon progressed to Cornish men and women who were impressed not just by his inspirational preaching but also by his prodigious ability to drink, a virtue that enabled him to live to the age of 206. He became the patron saint of Cornwall and especially of tin miners, and the Cornish flag is taken from St Piran's white cross on a black background.

By the 10th century St Piran's Oratory had been engulfed by sand and a new church was built a little way further inland. This too was lost to the sand and abandoned in 1804. Both have now been partially excavated and can be visited.

St Agnes

Bonfires were lit on St Agnes Beacon, 629 feet (192 m) high, to warn of the approach of the Spanish Armada in 1588, and again in 1977, 2002 and 2012 to celebrate Elizabeth II's Silver, Golden and Diamond Jubilees. From here you can see 32 churches. Below the Beacon is the village of St Agnes, which was at the centre of Cornwall's tin mining industry. In the early 19th century the local Polperro mine employed more than five hundred people and produced more tin than anywhere else in Britain and possibly the world – from Roman times until the 20th century Cornwall was the biggest producer of tin in Europe. Today, however, the Blue Hills mine in St Agnes is THE LAST TIN PRODUCTION CENTRE IN BRITAIN.

The landscape around St Agnes is dotted with evocative ruins of engine houses and chimneys. Tumbled blocks of granite are all that remain of the harbour down in Trevaunance Cove from where the tin was shipped. The streets of the village are lined with 18th-century houses of granite and slate, and marching down the valley is a steep stepped terrace of miner's cottages called Stippy Stappy, which features in the Poldark novels of Winston Graham – St Agnes becomes St Ann's in the stories.

St Ives

St Ives was founded in the 6th century by St Ia, an Irish princess who is said to have floated across from Ireland on a leaf and built an oratory where now stands St Ia's parish church, dating from Henry V's reign and pretty much unchanged since. Old St Ives lies sand-wiched between two wide sandy beaches and so has had no room to expand and be spoilt, thus retaining its ancient allure and its picturesque maze of colourful, sea-blown cobbled streets. This colour and charm along with the Cornish sea light has, since as long ago as the 1880s, attracted artists like James McNeill Whistler and Walter Sickert.

Although it looks like a film set, St Ives was in reality a tough, rugged fishing port forever battling with the sea and the storms. The combination of its glorious position and the work of many artists has softened and colour washed the hard edges, but a certain hardiness is still required just to fight one's way along the heaving narrow streets and alleyways at the height of summer.

Sculptor BARBARA HEPWORTH moved to St Ives from her native Yorkshire in 1939 and created her studio in a lovely house on a hill behind the parish church. She was tragically killed here in a fire in 1975, but the studio has been open as a museum since 1976. Barbara drew her inspiration from the stark Cornish landscape and many of her favourite pieces can be seen amongst the flowers and palms in the garden. I am not always a fan of modern sculpture but there is one piece in the garden that frames a view of the town and the sea beyond that is the most beautiful thing I have ever seen. I hope they never move it.

The Barbara Hepworth Museum has been managed since 1980 by the Tate, who opened their own gallery in St Ives in 1993 to showcase local artists.

There is a promontory called the Island, at the north end of the town, from which there are panoramic views, and where there is a battery built to defend the town from Napoleon and a simple 14th-century chapel dedicated to the patron saint of sailors, St Nicholas. During the 18th century excisemen would hide in the chapel waiting to spring out on any passing smugglers, but they never had much success – perhaps because the suspected leader of the smugglers was an eccentric fellow called JOHN KNILL who also happened to be the local customs collector and Mayor of St Ives.

Knill clearly collected a lot of customs because he had his own 50

St Nicholas's Chapel

foot (15 m) high monument, a granite obelisk resembling a church steeple, built on a hill overlooking St Ives. Intended as a mausoleum, the KNILL STEEPLE was designed for him by John Wood the Younger, the architect of the Royal Crescent in Bath. Knill also set aside funds for a ceremony to be held every five years on the Day of St James the Apostle in which the Mayor of St Ives, a custom's officer and a vicar, accompanied by a fiddler playing the Furry Dance and ten young dancing girls dressed in white from the 'families of fishermen', set off from the Guildhall and dance through the streets of St Ives to the Knill Steeple. Although it was meant to commemorate him after his death, John Knill lived another ten years and attended the first ceremony in person. And he never got to take up residence in his mausoleum, instead being buried in London in St Andrew's, Holborn. Nevertheless, the Knill Steeple provides a handy navigational aid for shipping. Knill's ceremony is still held every five years to this day.

Zennor

At the end of the alphabet and at the end of the world, storm-lashed Zennor sits 300 feet (90 m) above the sea in a bleak and extraordinarily beautiful landscape of small rock-strewn fields separated by thick granite walls. It is all too easy in this mysterious place to believe the story illustrated on the MERMAID CHAIR, a carved medieval wooden chair that stands by the altar in St Senara's Church. The carving shows a mermaid holding a mirror and a comb. Smitten by the pure singing voice of a choir boy called Matthew Trewhella, Morveren the mermaid lured him down to the sea at Pendour Cove under the high cliffs of Zennor Head and the two of them were never seen again. Although sometimes, on warm summer nights, they can be heard singing together from beneath the waves.

D.H. LAWRENCE wrote much of *Women in Love* while living in Zennor during the Second World War. He was forced to leave eventually because he and his German wife Frieda were suspected of being pro-German.

On moorland above the village is ZENNOR QUOIT, dating from the Bronze Age and THE LARGEST SURVIVING CHAMBERED TOMB IN BRITAIN.

Tin Mining

On the coast between Pendeen and Trewellard and the sea are a number of old tin mines that make up part of the CORNISH MINING WORLD HERITAGE SITE. The Tin Mining Museum is on the site of the Geevor Mine, which closed in 1990 after three centuries of working, the last but one Cornish tin mine to close. It is THE LARGEST PRESERVED MINE SITE IN BRITAIN.

The BOTALLACK MINE is a picturesque grouping of old mine buildings perched on the edge of the cliff that is often used for filming. Both of the *Poldark*

BBC television series were filmed here. The site is owned by the National Trust.

Also owned by the National Trust is the LEVANT MINE, where you can see THE ONLY WORKING STEAM-POWERED CORNISH BEAM ENGINE IN SITU IN THE WORLD. It was built in 1840. In 1919 the mine, whose main shaft was 2,000 feet (610 m) deep, with levels reaching out more than a mile under the Atlantic Ocean, was the scene of a devastating accident when the mine's 'man-engine' broke and 31 miners died falling down the shaft. A man engine was an early kind of lift consisting of a series of stepped wooden rods which were moved up and down between platforms fixed to the wall of the mine shaft. The miner would step off a platform on to a moving rod, get off at the next platform and wait for the next rod and so on. The whole caboosh was powered in the early days by a water-wheel and later by a steam engine, and although slow it was safer and less exhausting than climbing ladders. At the Levant Mine it took about 30 minutes to descend the main shaft via 130 platforms. The idea for man engines came from Germany and the first one in Britain was installed at the Tresavean Mine at Gwennap, near Redruth, in 1842. It was designed by a Cornish engineer called MICHAEL LOAM (1798–1871) and powered by a water-wheel.

Cape Cornwall

Cape Cornwall is ENGLAND'S ONLY CAPE. A cape is a promontory or headland that juts out into the sea where two bodies of water meet, and until the Ordnance Survey began accurate mapping in the early 19th century it was thought that Cape Cornwall was the most westerly point in England and therefore where the Atlantic and the English Channel met. However, the Ordnance Survey proved that Land's End was, in fact, slightly further west.

Land's End

Land's End is England's far west, THE MOST WESTERLY AND SOUTHWESTERLY POINT ON THE ENGLISH MAINLAND. It is 838 miles from the northwesternmost point of Britain at John O' Groats in Scotland, and 556 miles from the northernmost point of England on the Northumberland coast north near Berwick-on-Tweed. On a clear day it is possible from on top of the 200 foot (60 m) cliffs to see the Isles of Scilly, 28 miles away.

Isles of Scilly

The Scilly Isles, considered a part of Cornwall, are said to be all that is left of the lost kingdom of Lyonesse and the burial place of King Arthur. The first English land to taste the Atlantic breakers, the islands nonetheless bask in the warm currents of the Gulf Stream and grow fruit and flowers earlier and for longer than the rest of Britain.

The jagged rocks off the Scilly Isles have caused many a shipwreck, especially in the days before any accurate means of navigation were invented. In 1707 the flagship of ADMIRAL SIR CLOWDISLEY SHOVELL, the *Association*,

leading the fleet returning from the siege of Toulon, in thick fog, hit the rocks west of Scilly and sank. The Admiral, barely alive, was washed ashore on St Mary's Island, where he was found by a poor island woman who suffocated him by pushing his face into the sand, then buried him and made off with his emerald ring. Thirty years later she confessed on her deathbed, gave up the ring and revealed where the Admiral's body was buried, and he was taken away to be reburied in Westminster Abbey. The site of Sir Clowdisley Shovell's temporary grave, at Porth Hellick, is now marked by a quartz block. The loss of the *Association* prompted the government to offer a huge prize for anyone who could devise a means of determining longitude and it was won, in 1761, by John Harrison, who invented the marine chronometer.

It was also off the Scilly Isles that the world's first supertanker disaster occurred in 1967 when the *Torrey Canyon* hit the Seven Stones Reef, 7 miles offshore, and sank, spilling 120,000 tons of oil. At the time this was THE BIGGEST SHIP EVER TO BE WRECKED AND THE WORLD'S MOST EXPENSIVE SHIPWRECK, and it remains the worst ever oil spill off the coast of England.

In 1834 the Duchy of Cornwall leased the Scilly Isles to philanthropist AUGUSTUS SMITH, who became Lord Proprietor. He built himself a house called The Abbey on the second largest island, TRESCO, and laid out a beautiful sub-tropical garden around the ruins of St Nicholas Priory, which became world famous and attracted much-needed tourism to the Scilly Isles. He also introduced THE FIRST COMPULSORY EDUCATION IN BRITAIN for the children of Tresco, 30 years before it was introduced on the mainland. His descendants, the

Dorien-Smiths, retain the lease to Tresco to this day.

Prime Minister HAROLD WILSON famously spent his summer holidays on the island of Samson.

ST AGNES, the southernmost Scilly Isle, is THE SOUTHERNMOST POINT OF BOTH ENGLAND AND THE UNITED KINGDOM.

Well, I never knew this
about
THE NORTH CORNISH COAST

Just outside Bude is EBBINGFORD MANOR, a private home dating back some 850 years and said to have THE SMALLEST PRIVATE CHAPEL IN ENGLAND, and then 2 miles further on is WIDEMOUTH BAY, where the 'hotline' between No. 10 Downing Street in London and the White House in Washington DC comes ashore.

HIGH CLIFF, 8 miles (13 km) south of Bude beyond Crackington Haven, rises sheer from the sea for 735 feet (224 m), Cornwall's highest cliff and THE HIGHEST SHEER CLIFF IN SOUTHERN ENGLAND.

THE MUSEUM OF WITCHCRAFT AND MAGIC, moved to Boscastle from the Isle of Man in 1960, is said to contain THE LARGEST COLLECTION OF OBJECTS DEVOTED TO MAGIC AND WITCHCRAFT IN THE WORLD.

PORT ISAAC is one of the few working fishing villages on Cornwall's north coast and basks in new-found fame as the setting for the popular ITV series *Doc Martin*. It is a beautiful, almost

unspoiled Cornish village of white-washed, overhanging 18th-century fisherman's cottages bedecked with flowers, and streets so narrow that two people can scarcely pass without breathing in. SQUEEZE-EE-BELLY ALLEY, impassable to those who have just indulged in a Cornish cream tea, is said to be THE NARROWEST THOROUGHFARE IN ENGLAND.

The lighthouse on GODREVY ISLAND off Godrevy Point was the inspiration for Virginia Woolf's novel *To the Lighthouse*. The lighthouse was put there in 1859 after the foundering five years earlier of the steamship SS *Nile*, which hit the Stones, a submerged reef beyond the island, and sank with the loss of all 40 passengers and crew. In 1649 a ship called the *Garland* went down off Godrevy while carrying the wardrobe and personal effects of the recently executed Charles I and his family to safety in France.

ST JUST, 1 mile east of Cape Cornwall, is MAINLAND ENGLAND'S MOST WESTERLY TOWN.

CHAPTER SEVEN
CORNWALL SOUTH COAST

Land's End to Saltash
80 miles

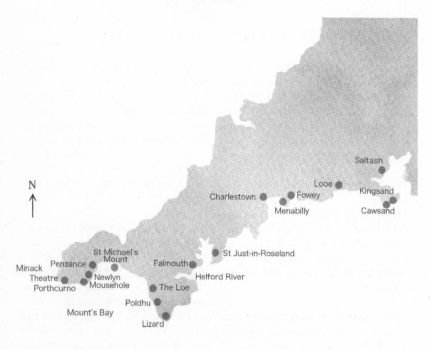

Highlights of Cornwall's south coast include the centre of the universe, a unique theatre, the largest fishing port in England, point zero for Ordnance Survey maps, the birthplace of the Radio Age, British mainland's most southerly point, Britain's largest seal sanctuary, the deepest natural harbour in Western Europe, Manderley from Daphne du Maurier's *Rebecca*, Toad Hall and the largest collection of magnolias in England.

Porthcurno

Porthcurno Cove, 3 miles east of Land's End, was once known as 'the centre of the universe', for here came ashore the submarine telegraph cables connecting Britain to its empire and the rest of world along THE WORLD'S FIRST INTERNATIONAL TELEGRAPH SYSTEM. The first cable, the link to India, was landed here in 1870 and for the next hundred years the Porthcurno Cable Office was at the centre of Britain's international cable network. Between the world wars Porthcurno was THE LARGEST SUBMARINE CABLE STATION IN THE WORLD, operating 14 international cables. In the Second World War tunnels were dug into the granite hillside to house the sensitive telegraphy equipment and protect it from bomb attack, and these tunnels can now be visited as part of the Porthcurno Telegraph Museum housed in the former cable office, which ceased operation in 1970.

Carved out of the granite cliffs high above Porthcurno Cove and set against a sublime backdrop of turquoise sea is the MINACK THEATRE, internationally famous as one of the world's most spectacular open-air theatres.

The Minack was built by hand by ROWENA CADE at the bottom of her garden, with the help of her gardener Billy Rawlings and local craftsman Charles Angove, and over the winter of 1931 they fashioned out of the rock a stage and a rough terrace of seating to create a venue for local drama enthusiasts. The new theatre opened in 1932 with a performance of *The Tempest*, with stage lighting provided by batteries and car headlights.

Rowena Cade continued to build up and improve the theatre every winter until her death in 1983, even constructing a

dressing room out of wooden beams she personally removed one by one from a Spanish ship wrecked on the beach at Porthcurno. She was never charged with theft because the police refused to believe that such a slender soul could have carried the beams up the cliffs on her own.

Today performances at the theatre are attended by up to 100,000 people every year and to watch a play here on a warm summer's evening, with the wind and waves setting the mood, the moon and stars the lighting, the ocean as the backdrop, sometimes with dolphins or basking sharks as extras, is one of life's great experiences. Just one warning – no umbrellas are allowed and it takes a truly horrendous storm to stop a performance, so come prepared...

Mount's Bay

Mount's Bay stretches from Lizard Point to Gwennap Head, south of Land's End, and is Cornwall's biggest bay, with a coastline of some 40 miles in length. It takes its name from St Michael's Mount in the north of the bay.

Mousehole

Mousehole, said the poet DYLAN THOMAS, is 'the loveliest village in England'. He spent his honeymoon in Mowzull, as it is pronounced, in the Lobster Pot Inn, with his new wife Caitlin after they had got married at Penzance Register Office in 1937. The picturesque narrow streets and stone cottages are no older than 17th century, for in 1595 the Spanish sailed into Mount's Bay and sacked Mousehole, along with Newlyn and Penzance, leaving only one building intact, the Keigwin Arms, now a private house.

DOLLY PENTREATH, the last known person to have spoken only Cornish, lies in the churchyard at PAUL, a village in the hills above Mousehole. She died in 1777, possibly at the age of 102, and in 1860 a monument was erected there in her honour by the Emperor Napoleon's nephew Lucien Bonaparte, who grew up in England and had a love for languages.

Newlyn

Newlyn, THE LARGEST FISHING PORT IN ENGLAND, was so pretty that in the 1880s it began to attract its own colony of artists, the Newlyn School, drawn by the natural light and the opportunity to paint outdoors (*plein air*). In 1937 the planners demolished much of the old fishing quarter that had appealed to the artists and they began to drift away, to St Ives or Lamorna Cove, a few miles west, but their legacy lived on and in 2011 the Newlyn School of Art was formed to provide art courses given by established artists living in Cornwall.

On 16 August 1620 the *Mayflower* stopped off at Newlyn to take on water, making Newlyn the Pilgrim ship's last port of call in England.

And Newlyn has a special significance to those of us who love maps – the heights on all Ordnance Survey maps are calculated from the Mean Sea Level observed at Newlyn between 1915 and 1921.

Since 1983 Newlyn has been the home of the Penlee Lifeboat Station, which before that was situated south of the town at Penlee Point. On the evening of 19 December 1981, in one of the worst lifeboat disasters of modern times, the entire eight-man crew of the lifeboat *Solomon Browne* were lost while trying to rescue the crew of the vessel

Union Star, adrift in Mount's Bay in heavy seas after its engines had failed. There were no survivors from either vessel, and altogether 16 men perished. The pilot of the rescue helicopter overhead described the actions of the *Solomon Browne*'s crew that night as 'the greatest act of courage I have ever seen ...'

Penzance

Penzance, Cornwall's first resort town and the only Cornish town to have a promenade, is as far west as the railway dares to go nowadays. A ferry takes you

further west to the Scilly Isles, as does a scheduled helicopter service. Dominating the centre of town is the be-domed Market Hall, now Lloyds Bank but built in 1838 to house the town market and guildhall. Outside is a statue of the town's most famous son, SIR HUMPHRY DAVY, born in Penzance in 1778. He is depicted holding the miner's safety lamp he invented in 1815, which saved the lives of countless Cornish miners. Penzance was also the birthplace, in 1783, of MARIA BRANWELL, mother of the Brontë sisters.

In Chapel Street, which winds its way up into the town from the harbour, is the colourful EGYPTIAN HOUSE, one of only two in Britain, which was built by John Foulton for a local businessman in 1835 at a time when Egypt was being opened up by European explorers and all things Egyptian were the rage. Originally the subject of some derision, the house is now a much-loved symbol of Penzance. It is owned by the Landmark Trust and used for holiday lets.

St Michael's Mount

St Michael's Mount was granted to the Benedictine monks of Mont Saint-Michel, an almost identical island off

the coast of Normandy in France, by Edward the Confessor in the 11th century. They built a priory and church there to which was added a castle in the 14th century. It was on the top of the church tower that the first beacon was lit to warn of the approach of the Spanish Armada in 1588. In 1659 the island was bought by the St Aubyn family, who have lived there ever since, today under a 999-year lease from the National Trust. Queen Victoria visited the island in 1846 and a brass inlay of her footstep is at the top of the landing stage. It is also possible to see the remnants of a railway built in 1900 to carry goods up the steep hill to the castle in place of the pack horses used before. The castle and priory church are open to the public and can be reached along a causeway from Marazion at low tide or by boat at high tide.

The Lizard

The southernmost part of the British mainland, the Lizard gets its name from the Cornish 'lis' meaning palace and 'ard' meaning high. There have been more shipwrecks off the rockbound Lizard shores than anywhere else on the Cornish coastline. Cornwall's first lighthouse was built on Lizard Point in 1619, much to the annoyance of the local populace who made a hearty living from 'wrecking', or helping themselves to the cargoes of the many ships wrecked on the Lizard's treacherous rocks. The present lighthouse dates from 1751.

Between Helston and the sea on the Lizard's west coast is THE LOE, the largest freshwater lake in Cornwall, a mile long and cut off from the sea by a long shingle bank called Loe Bar.

According to Alfred, Lord Tennyson, the Loe is the lake into which King Arthur's sword Excalibur was thrown by Sir Bedivere, to be caught by the hand of the Lady of the Lake and taken down into the depths.

In 1807 a frigate called the *Anson* was driven on to the bar and more than a hundred men lost their lives within sight of the shore. One of those watching helplessly as the tragedy unfolded was HENRY TRENGROUSE (1772–1854), who was so affected that he went away and, inspired by watching a fireworks display in Helston to celebrate the birthday of George III, devised a rocket system for carrying a lifeline out to a ship in distress. His device, now known as a breeches buoy, is still used today, albeit with some improvements. Trengrouse also invented an early form of life-jacket, and over the years his inventions have saved many thousands of lives. He lived in Helston all his life and is buried in the churchyard of St Michael's Church.

A stone monument on the bare cliffs above POLDHU, west of Mullion, marks the very spot where the age of radio began, for it was from here that THE WORLD'S FIRST HIGH-POWERED RADIO TRANSMITTER SENT THE FIRST TRANSATLANTIC RADIO SIGNAL 3,000 miles to Newfoundland, where it was received by the man whose invention had made it all possible, the 'Father of Radio', GUGLIELMO MARCONI. A permanent radio station was later set up at Poldhu, where ship to shore radio communications were pioneered. In 1912 the station at Poldhu was the first to receive the news about the sinking of the *Titanic*. Nothing is left of the original radio station save for the foundations, but along with the memorial there is a museum where the story of

Poldhu's significance to the world of communications, television and the internet is told. A little way inland is THE GOONHILLY EARTH SATELLITE STATION, WHERE THE FIRST INTERCONTINENTAL PICTURE TRANSMISSIONS WERE RECEIVED from the United States via satellite in 1962.

Marconi Memorial

Lizard Point is THE SOUTHERNMOST POINT OF MAINLAND BRITAIN and Lizard village the most southerly settlement, THE ONLY VILLAGE IN MAINLAND BRITAIN TO LIE SOUTH OF THE 50TH PARALLEL. East of the point is Pen Olver, the cliff from which the Spanish Armada was first sighted in 1588.

A little way east of the village, at Church Cove, is MAINLAND BRITAIN'S MOST SOUTHERLY CHURCH, dedicated to St Winwaloe, a Celtic saint of Cornish ancestry. A wooden church was established here in AD 600, and the present stone church was begun by the Normans and enlarged in the 13th century. The lovely old tower is an irregular patchwork of granite and rough-hewn grey, blue and dark green serpentine, a local stone found only on the Lizard. The whole is flecked with golden lichen and shimmers in the salty air. It is said that the last sermon spoken in the Cornish tongue was preached here in 1674.

THE HELFORD RIVER on the Lizard's east coast is a beautiful estuary of seven creeks. FRENCHMAN'S CREEK on the south side, overhung with trees and lush vegetation, is a mysterious, silent place that might be a swamp in Louisiana, and was immortalised by Daphne du Maurier

in her novel of the same name. She spent her honeymoon here on her new husband's yacht *Ygdrasil* in 1932.

On the north side Porth Navas is the site of the Duchy of Cornwall's oyster beds and at one time produced a quarter of Britain's oysters. Unlike today, oysters were once considered just as food for the poor. As Sam Weller remarked in Charles Dickens's *Pickwick Papers*, 'poverty and oysters always seem to go together'. Not these days.

GWEEK, at the head of the estuary, is home to BRITAIN'S LARGEST SEAL SANCTUARY.

Carrick Roads

Falmouth

Falmouth is Cornwall's largest town and harbour and sits at the entrance to the Carrick Roads, which forms THE DEEPEST NATURAL HARBOUR IN WESTERN EUROPE and the third deepest in the world. Four hundred years ago there was just one modest manor house here, ARWENACK HOUSE, home of the Killigrews, which still stands at the heart of the town it spawned, and PENDENNIS CASTLE, built by Henry VIII in 1540 to defend the Carrick Roads and its two original ports, Penrhyn and Truro. Pendennis Castle was the last Royalist stronghold to surrender to Oliver Cromwell during the Civil War, after withstanding a six-month siege in 1646. At the Restoration Sir Peter Killigrew built a parish church for the rapidly growing new town of Falmouth and dedicated it to King Charles the Martyr. In 1688 Falmouth became the communication centre for the growing British Empire when it was chosen to be the Royal Mail's first packet station, from where mail was sent out across the world by fast, lightly armed Falmouth 'packets'. When ships arrived in England from anywhere in the world they would 'report to Falmouth for orders'. It took far less time to send dispatches to London overland by horse from Falmouth than by ship beating up the Channel against the wind – indeed, Falmouth was the first

Pendennis Castle

place in England to learn of Nelson's victory at the Battle of Trafalgar in 1805.

THE PANDORA INN on beautiful Restronguet Creek, on the west coast of the Carrick Roads, dates from the 13th century and is CORNWALL'S OLDEST INN. It is named after HMS *Pandora*, the ship that was sent to find the mutineers of the *Bounty*, who set their captain, William Bligh, adrift in an open boat in the South Pacific in 1789.

'And did those feet, in ancient time, walk upon England's mountains green …' If they did, they would probably have landed here at ST JUST IN ROSELAND, across Carrick Roads from the Pandora Inn. Once you have experienced the magical atmosphere of the lovely 13th-century church of St Just in Roseland, enveloped in sub-tropical gardens beside a dazzling blue creek, you may well find yourself open to the idea that Jesus did indeed set foot on England's pleasant pastures here while accompanying Joseph of Arimathea in search of Cornish tin – pastures don't come more pleasant. Indeed, there is a stone down by the water on to which Jesus is said to have stepped while coming ashore. I defy anyone not to feel a frisson …

Charlestown

Charlestown, further up the coast, is a virtually unchanged Georgian harbour designed at the end of the 18th century

by the harbour engineer John Smeaton for CHARLES RASHLEIGH, a local mine owner. The harbour operated as a port for St Austell and was used for the export of copper and china clay, Cornwall's 'white gold', but by the mid 20th century, because of its tortuous entrance, the harbour had grown unsuitable for larger vessels. St Austell's trade shifted to deeper ports such as Par and Fowey, and Charlestown was left frozen in time. Today the harbour is owned by Square Sail, a company that manages a fleet of tall ships, one or two of which can normally be seen anchored at Charlestown, adding to the harbour's old-world charm. As THE BEST PRESERVED GEORGIAN HARBOUR IN ENGLAND, Charlestown's film set quality has proved an irresistible draw for any number of film and television companies seeking an authentic 18th-century maritime backdrop, the most recent example being the BBC's current *Poldark* series.

Menabilly

'Last night I dreamt I went to Manderley again. It seemed to me I stood by the iron gate leading to the drive …' These lines from Daphne du Maurier's *Rebecca* are amongst the most famous and evocative opening lines in English literature. Anyone can go to Manderley today but only as far as the iron gate, for Manderley is Menabilly, a small, early Georgian house surrounded by woodland and set in glorious countryside above the Gribbin cliffs of East St Austell Bay, not far from Fowey. Menabilly has been the seat of the powerful Rashleigh family since the 16th century and the present house incorporates parts of the original Elizabethan house. Charles Rashleigh was the builder of Charlestown and during the late Victorian era the Rashleighs were the biggest landowners in Cornwall.

Daphne du Maurier discovered Menabilly in 1927, when it had been neglected for a number of years and was in a parlous state, and used it in her 1938 novel *Rebecca* as the model for Manderley. Menabilly even has its own small beach, as featured in the novel. In 1943, using the proceeds from the success of *Rebecca*, du Maurier leased Menabilly off the Rashleighs and restored it, living there for 25 years before handing it back to them in 1969. After her death, du Maurier's ashes were scattered on the cliffs near Menabilly. Today Menabilly is the home of Sir Richard Rashleigh, 6th Baronet, and his family.

Fowey

Described by the poet Robert Bridges as 'the most poetic-looking place in England', Fowey is one of the oldest towns in Cornwall with 'the narrowest streets I ever saw in England' tumbling down 'perpendicular hills' into the river, according to Queen Victoria. The Fowey estuary provides a deep safe harbour and Fowey has thrived on fishing and trade, particularly china clay, as attested to by the many fine houses in the town.

Fowey also has an unsurpassed literary heritage. SIR ARTHUR QUILLER-COUCH, professor, critic and editor of *The Oxford Book of English Verse*, who wrote under the pseudonym 'Q', lived in the Haven, a fine house on the Esplanade, from 1892 until his death in 1944. Q was a great friend of author KENNETH GRAHAME, who got married in Fowey parish church while staying at the Haven and also honeymooned in Fowey. Q was the inspiration for the talkative 'Ratty' in Grahame's *The Wind in the Willows*, while the Victorian FOWEY HALL, a splendid pile built above the town for politician Sir Charles Hanson in 1899, is said to have inspired Toad Hall.

Grahame inscribed a first edition of *The Wind in the Willows* to Q's daughter Foy Quiller-Couch. Foy meanwhile became great friends with Daphne du Maurier, whose parents had a house at nearby Boddinick, and when the two

Fowey Hall

of them went riding on Bodmin Moor du Maurier got the idea for her novel *Jamaica Inn*.

Another writer who honeymooned in Fowey thanks to his friendship with Q was the playwright J.M. BARRIE. Q is buried in the churchyard of the parish church of St Fimbarrus and there is a granite memorial to him overlooking Fowey harbour.

Rame Peninsula

Known as 'Cornwall's Forgotten Corner', the Rame Peninsula is often bypassed by those on their way in or out of Cornwall across the Tamar Bridge further to the north; and, indeed, a part of it was actually in Devon until the 19th century.

RAME HEAD, at the southernmost tip of the peninsula, is crowned by the 14th-century chapel of St Michael, which used to show a beacon to guide ships into Plymouth Harbour. This job is now done by the Eddystone Lighthouse.

The twin smuggling villages of KINGSAND and CAWSAND are attractive to artists as less crowded versions of St Ives. Kingsand, which is known for its clock tower erected to celebrate

the Coronation of George V, was in Devon until boundary changes in 1844. Cawsand, to the south, was always in Cornwall, and the old county boundary is marked by a house called Devon Corn, on which there is a plaque. Kingsand was the home of JOHN POLLARD RN, the man who shot the French sniper who killed Lord Nelson at the Battle of Trafalgar, and of Arthur Ransome's daughter TABITHA, and ANN DAVISON, the first woman to sail single-handed across the Atlantic, in 1953.

Both villages are in the MOUNT EDGCUMBE NATIONAL PARK, the oldest landscaped gardens in Cornwall, consisting of 885 acres (358 ha) of gardens and woodland created by the Edgcumbe family in the 18th century. The park includes England's National Camellia Collection. At the centre of the park stands Mount Edgcumbe House, rebuilt in its original Tudor style after being bombed in 1941. Since 1987 the house and park have been publicly owned and are open to visitors.

The village of CREMYLL sits at the gates to the park, and from here there is a foot passenger ferry to Stonehouse in Plymouth that has been run since the 11th century.

Mount Edgcume House

ANTONY HOUSE, by the Lynher River, was built in 1724 for Sir William Carew, whose family have owned the estate since the 16th century. The grounds were landscaped by Humphry Repton and include the National Collection of Day Lilies. Antony is famous for its portraits, including several by Sir Joshua Reynolds and a portrait of Rachel Carew that inspired Daphne du Maurier's *My Cousin Rachel*. The Carews still live at Antony, although the house and gardens were given over to the National Trust in 1961 and are open to the public during the summer months.

Well, I never knew this about

THE SOUTH CORNISH COAST

THE TATER-DU LIGHTHOUSE, 3 miles east of Porthcurno near Lamorna Cove, became operational in 1965 and is Cornwall's newest lighthouse as well as being BRITAIN'S FIRST FULLY AUTOMATIC LIGHTHOUSE.

ST MAWES CASTLE was built to guard the eastern approach to Carrick Roads at the same time as Pendennis Castle was built at the western approach. Unlike Pendennis, the garrison of St Mawes capitulated to Cromwell's forces in 1646 without a shot being fired – because all the guns faced out to sea.

The two ancient towns of EAST AND WEST LOOE are separate but linked by a Victorian seven-arched bridge, which replaced a medieval bridge that had 13 arches and, in the middle, a small chapel dedicated to St Anne. A little further along the coast is the MONKEY SANCTUARY which was set up in 1964 by Len Williams, father of guitarist John Williams, to rescue woolly monkeys from the pet trade. It was the first centre in the world to successfully breed woolly monkeys.

CHAPTER EIGHT
DEVON SOUTH COAST

Plymouth to Axmouth
125 miles

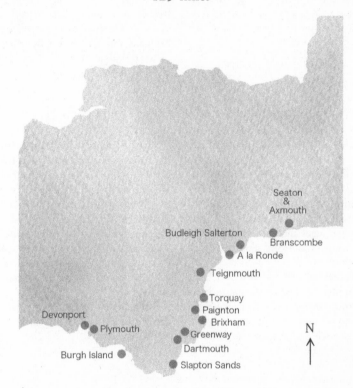

Seaton
&
Axmouth

Budleigh Salterton

Branscombe

A la Ronde

Teignmouth

Torquay

Paignton

Devonport

Brixham

Plymouth

Greenway

Dartmouth

Burgh Island

Slapton Sands

N
↑

Highlights of the Devon south coast include the largest naval base in western Europe, the last piece of England where the Pilgrim Fathers ever stood, the cliff top from where the British Empire sprang, the site of a secret Second World War disaster, the first castles designed for artillery, Britain's highest and lowest lighthouse, the English Riviera, a unique round house, a long stretch of Jurassic Coast, and the southernmost chalk headland in England.

Royal Albert Bridge

The River Tamar forms the border between Devon and Cornwall for all but 4 miles in the north, as it has since the 10th century when it was declared to be the border by the Saxon King Athelstan. The most spectacular crossing of the Tamar is the distinctive Royal Albert Bridge, which carries the Cornish Main Line in and out of Cornwall. It is one of the world's great railway bridges and an iconic image of the transition from England into Cornwall.

The bridge was designed and built by Isambard Kingdom Brunel and was the third major wrought-iron bridge ever to be built. Its unique design, a mix of arch and suspension, is based on the two previous ones, the High Level Bridge across the River Tyne in Newcastle and the Britannia Bridge across the Menai Straits to Anglesey, both by Robert Stephenson. The Royal Albert Bridge is a little over 2,000 feet (610 m) long and 172 feet (52 m) high, with the deck being 100 feet (30 m) above the river. It was opened by Prince Albert himself in 1859, but Brunel was too ill to attend the opening. He died later that year, and his name was inscribed in huge letters on the portals at each end of the bridge as a memorial.

Plymouth

Modern Plymouth, enfolded between the arms of the Plym and Tamar rivers, is made up of three towns, Devonport, Stonehouse and Old Plymouth. In 1439 Old Plymouth became the first city in England to be incorporated by Parliament rather than by the monarch. Since many British explorers sailed from Plymouth there are more than 40 places named Plymouth around the world.

South of the Tamar Bridge and the Royal Albert Bridge the Tamar is joined by the Lynher River and the estuary

formed by the two rivers is known as the Hamoaze.

Devonport

The east bank of the Hamoaze is lined with the docks of DEVONPORT NAVAL BASE, established in the late 17th century as a royal dockyard called Plymouth Dock and now THE LARGEST NAVAL BASE IN WESTERN EUROPE. In 1768 Captain Cook set out from Plymouth Dock on his voyage to Australia.

By the early 19th century Plymouth Dock had become the biggest town in Devon and Cornwall and in 1823 was renamed Devonport to distinguish it from neighbouring Plymouth. In celebration architect John Foulson designed and built the splendid DEVONPORT GUILDHALL and next to it the equally splendid DEVONPORT COLUMN, 124 feet (38 m) high with a viewing platform at the top reached by a climb of 137 steps. Completing what is the finest surviving collection of Regency architecture in Plymouth is the extraordinary ODD FELLOWS HALL, one of only two 'Egyptian' houses in Britain, the other being in Penzance.

Antarctic explorer ROBERT FALCON SCOTT (1868–1912) was born in Devonport and is remembered with a monument on Mount Wise, a viewpoint just east of the Devonport docks.

Stonehouse

Stonehouse is home to THE OLDEST BARRACKS IN BRITAIN, the ROYAL MARINE BARRACKS, a superb complex of Georgian buildings built in the mid 18th century and known as the spiritual home of the Royal Marines. In 1831 the racquets court of the barracks was converted into a theatre, the Globe, which survives as a rare example of a Regency theatre. Its future is, alas, uncertain as the barracks are due to be sold off in 2023.

Stonehouse is also the site of Plymouth's cathedral, the Roman Catholic Cathedral Church of St Mary and St Boniface, seat of the Bishop of Plymouth. It was designed and built in the 1850s by Joseph Hansom, creator of the Hansom cab, and his brother Charles.

Plymouth Hoe

The Promenade and wide lawns of Plymouth Hoe ('hoe' meaning high ridge), were laid out in the 1880s on top of limestone cliffs that rise 100 feet (30 m) above the waters of Plymouth

Sound. The landward side of the Hoe is dominated by the Plymouth Naval Memorial, commemorating the 23,000 naval personnel lost or buried at sea. It was designed in 1924 by Sir Robert Lorimer and is one of three naval memorials in the country, the others being at Portsmouth and Chatham. After the Second World War the memorial was extended by Sir Edward Maufe.

The views along the coast and out to sea from the Hoe are stupendous. DRAKE'S ISLAND, in the foreground, was once fortified to defend the deep-water channel into Devonport and also served as a prison. It is now privately owned and is possibly to be developed as a luxury hotel complex.

Plymouth Breakwater

Three miles out, at the entrance to the Sound, is the Plymouth breakwater, nearly 1 mile long and made from some four million tons of stone. It was one of the first breakwaters to be built anywhere in the world and, at the time, was THE LARGEST FREE-STANDING BREAKWATER EVER ATTEMPTED. Constructed to protect naval vessels entering and leaving Devonport from the treacherous southerly gales, it has a lighthouse at the western end and a beacon at the eastern end, along with a special cage designed to provide a place of safety for shipwrecked sailors. The breakwater was begun in 1812 by John Rennie and completed in 1841 by his son Sir John Rennie. To celebrate the lighthouse becoming operational in 1844 a horse-drawn carriage full of passengers was driven from east to west along the top of the breakwater to the accompaniment of a military band. Just inside the breakwater is the BREAKWATER FORT, an oval sea fort built in 1865 to help defend Plymouth Sound.

Smeaton's Tower

On clear day it is possible from the Hoe to see the Eddystone Lighthouse, perched on the Eddystone Rocks 14 miles out to sea. The present lighthouse is the fourth to be built on the site, and the best view of it is to be had from the lantern of its predecessor, the third lighthouse, known as Smeaton's Tower, the upper portion of which was dismantled and rebuilt on the Hoe in 1884.

Originally built in 1759 by engineer JOHN SMEATON, Smeaton's Tower was of pioneering design and was modelled on the shape of the trunk of an oak tree, tapering upwards from a broad base. Smeaton was the first modern engineer to employ a type of lime mortar or concrete once used by the Romans which can set underwater, and this proved so durable that the lighthouse continued in operation for 120 years and was taken down, not because the structure failed, but because the rock beneath it began to erode. The base of the tower proved impossible to break and is still there next to the new lighthouse.

Smeaton's Tower has become a much-loved landmark on the Hoe and the view from the lantern room, reached by a climb of 93 steps, is sublime.

The Citadel

At the eastern end of the Hoe is the vast complex of the Royal Citadel. This was built in 1665 on the orders of Charles II to protect Plymouth from the Dutch during the Anglo-Dutch Wars, and incorporates a previous fortress built by Sir Francis Drake in 1590. The guns of the Royal Citadel face inland as well as out to sea, a message from the King to the people of Plymouth who had supported Parliament during the Civil War. For

Bowls

It could be argued that Plymouth Hoe is the birthplace of Britain as a world power, for it was from the Hoe that SIR FRANCIS DRAKE departed in 1588 to defeat the Spanish Armada and make England mistress of the seas. The story goes that Drake was playing bowls on the Hoe when he was informed of the approach of the Armada. Well aware that the state of the wind and tide meant the English fleet could not set sail for a few hours, Drake is alleged to have said, 'Time enough to play the game and thrash the Spaniards afterwards.' You can still play bowls on the very Hoe where this momentous story was set and there is a statue of Drake, a former Mayor of Plymouth, nearby on the Promenade. It is by Sir Joseph Boehm and was unveiled in 1884 by a descendant of Drake's brother Thomas, Lady Fuller Drake.

over a hundred years the Citadel was the biggest and most important of England's coastal defences and is still in use by the military today, although guided tours are available.

The Barbican

The Royal Citadel overlooks Sutton Pool, Plymouth's original harbour, named after the little fishing village of Sutton from which Plymouth developed. The area around the harbour is called the Barbican and forms the historic heart of Plymouth. One of the few areas of city to survive the Plymouth Blitz in the Second World War, the Barbican can boast a fine collection of more than two hundred listed buildings, many of them Tudor or Jacobean, and also has THE HIGHEST CONCENTRATION OF COBBLED STREETS IN BRITAIN.

Sutton Pool has been the scene of many pivotal moments in England's history. Here, in 1445, came Margaret of Anjou to meet her future husband Henry VI; and here, in 1501, came Catherine of Aragon, on her way to marry Prince Arthur, eldest son of Henry VII. King Philip of Spain stopped off here in 1554 on his way to Southampton and then Winchester to marry Queen Mary, little knowing that a little over 30 years later a man playing bowls on the Hoe above would be instrumental in the defeat of his mighty Armada.

Martin Frobisher sailed from here in 1578 to search for the Northwest Passage, while the Devon men who helped open up the New World also sailed from Sutton Pool, Humphrey Gilbert for Newfoundland in 1583, Richard Grenville for Virginia in 1585, Walter Raleigh for Guiana in 1594.

In 1838 the pardoned Tolpuddle Martyrs came ashore here on their return from deportation to Australia.

And in 1966 Francis Chichester sailed away from Plymouth in *Gypsy Moth IV* to become the first man ever to sail around the world single-handed.

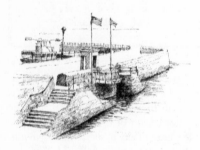

At the entrance to the inner harbour, the MAYFLOWER STEPS commemorate the departure from Plymouth on 6 September 1620 of the *Mayflower*, carrying 102 English Puritan pilgrims to the New World, where they founded a country that four hundred years later has become the most powerful in the world. Plymouth was the last place in the country of their birth that these remarkable men and women ever set foot and they named after it their first landfall in America, Plymouth Rock, and their first settlement, Plymouth, now known as 'America's Hometown'. The actual site from where the *Mayflower* cast off is thought to be where the Victorian Admiral Macbride pub now stands.

Overlooking the inner harbour is Island House, where a number of the *Mayflower* pilgrims were entertained before they left – this could be the last house in England they ever knew. Tucked away down narrow Southside is JACKA BAKERY, THE OLDEST WORKING COMMERCIAL BAKERY IN BRITAIN, which has been making bread since the time of the Armada and baked the ship's biscuits for the *Mayflower*.

Plymouth Gin

Further down Southside is the BLACK FRIAR'S DISTILLERY, THE OLDEST WORKING GIN DISTILLERY IN ENGLAND, where they have been making Plymouth Gin, the official gin of the Royal Navy, since 1793. The ship depicted on the label of a bottle of Plymouth Gin is the *Mayflower*, recalling the fact that some of the pilgrims who sailed on her stayed at the Black Friars Monastery now occupied by the distillery.

St Andrew's Church

Not far away, next to the grand Victorian Gothic Guildhall of 1875, is St Andrew's Church, the largest parish church in Devon. Dating mainly from the 15th century, it sits on the site of the original Saxon church of Sutton and is much restored after being heavily bombed in the Second World War. Catherine of Aragon came to St Andrew's to give thanks for her safe journey to England from Spain, Sir Francis Drake worshipped in the church, and he and the other victorious commanders of the English fleet came here to give thanks for their victory over the Spanish Armada in 1588. Lying beneath a simple stone in front of the chancel steps is the heart of ADMIRAL ROBERT BLAKE (1598–1657), commander of Oliver Cromwell's navy during the Commonwealth and known as 'Father of the Royal Navy' for his success in consolidating the Royal Navy's supremacy on the seas. Next to him is the heart of the explorer MARTIN FROBISHER, who put many new names on the map of the world and was one of Drake's companions in the defeat of the Armada. Captain Bligh of the *Bounty* was baptised here in 1754.

The Door of Unity

Beside St Andrew's is PYMOUTH'S OLDEST BUILDING, the PRYSTEN HOUSE, a courtyard house built in 1498 for merchant Thomas Yogge and now used as a museum. Built into the north wall of the house is a tombstone with the words 'Here lie the brave' inscribed on it. This is a tribute to two American naval officers who were killed in 1813 during a battle between the American brig *Argus* and the English ship *Pelican* in the British American War of 1812. Their bodies were brought to Plymouth for burial in St Andrew's churchyard and in 1930, in a special ceremony organised by the National Society United States Daughters of 1812, their headstone was placed next to the door from The Prysten House into the churchyard. The door was dedicated the 'Door of Unity' as a show of friendship between the peoples of America and Plymouth, from where so many of the first European Americans came.

Burgh Island

Burgh Island is separated from Bigbury-on-Sea on the mainland by South Devon's largest sandy beach, 750 feet (230 m) of firm sand which is covered at high tide. When the island is cut off by the sea, which rushes in from both sides of the beach, access to it is by sea tractor, an ungainly looking machine

with huge wheels and an elevated deck that keeps driver and passengers clear of the water. It is an exhilarating way to arrive at the island's elegant, white-painted art deco hotel, which was built in 1929 by film-maker ARCHIBALD NETTLEFOLD, heir to the Guest, Keen and Nettlefold (GKN) company, and is considered one of the finest examples of art deco design in Britain. In the 1930s the captain's cabin of Britain's last wooden flagship HMS *Ganges* was reconstructed inside the hotel for use as a dining room.

During its heyday in the 1930s the BURGH ISLAND HOTEL attracted many rich and famous guests including Lord Mountbatten, last Viceroy of India, Edward VIII and Mrs Simpson, Winston Churchill, actress Gertrude Lawrence, aviator Amy Johnson, and R.J. Mitchell, designer of the Spitfire. Noël Coward visited, intending to stay for three days, and ended up staying for three weeks; and later, in 1963, the Beatles stayed there while appearing in Plymouth.

Agatha Christie loved Burgh Island and wrote two books while in residence at the hotel. In *And Then There Were None*, THE WORLD'S BEST-SELLING MYSTERY and sixth best-selling novel of all time, Burgh Island appears as Soldier Island, home of the mysterious millionaire who lures a variety of guests

on to the island and kills them off one by one. In *Evil Under the Sun* Hercule Poirot has to solve a murder case while holidaying at a secluded Devon hotel, based on the Burgh Island Hotel.

A small ruined chapel at the island's summit was once used as a huer's hut, where, as at Newquay in Cornwall, observers would make a 'hue and cry' to alert fishermen when they spotted a shoal of pilchards. Pilchard fishing is recalled by the presence on the island of the 14th-century PILCHARD INN, one of Britain's oldest pubs.

Slapton Sands

Slapton Sands should perhaps be called Slapton Shingles since it is a 3 mile long shingle bar that runs north–south between Torcross at the southern end and Strete at the northern end. Enclosed inland by the bar is SLAPTON LEY, at 1½ miles long the largest freshwater lake in the southwest. The lake sits at the centre of a nature reserve and is home to a huge variety of wildfowl. It is also the only place in Britain where the flowering plant strapwort grows.

On a fine day, when the sun shines and the sea is blue, Slapton Sands is a calm and beautiful place to be, but a rusty Sherman tank retrieved from the sea in 1984 and now standing in the car park at Torcross stands monument to one of the most tragic events of the Second World War.

On the night of 28 April 1944, eight landing craft full of American soldiers and equipment left Plymouth to rendezvous in Lyme Bay prior to storming Slapton Sands as part of Exercise Tiger, a rehearsal for the D-Day landing on Utah Beach in Normandy. Nine German torpedo boats attacked the landing craft and sank two of them, pitching hundreds of men into the sea. The other landing craft scattered, leaving the men floating in the cold water and many of them drowned, weighed down by their heavy kit. The disaster was caused by a simple administrative error. Orders given to the landing craft contained a typing error which meant that the American craft and the British Naval HQ on shore were on different radio frequencies. The German boats were spotted on radar by a British destroyer but because of the radio mix-up the British were unable to warn the landing craft and up to a thousand men died, with bodies being washed up on the shores of Lyme Bay for days afterwards. More men lost their lives that night than died during the actual storming of Utah Beach on D-Day.

River Dart

Greenway

A journey up the River Dart makes a delightful detour, the river passing through glorious scenery as it winds its way from Totnes to the coast. High up on the east bank, about a mile upriver from Dartmouth, is Greenway, the home of crime writer AGATHA CHRISTIE for nearly 40 years. The late

Georgian house featured in many of her novels under a variety of guises. It stands above the crossing point to the village of Dittisham on the west bank.

The original Greenway house was a Tudor mansion built in the late 16th century by the seafaring Gilbert family. SIR HUMPHREY GILBERT, the man who took possession of Newfoundland for Elizabeth I in 1583, was born there in 1539 and grew up there, and his half-brother SIR WALTER RALEIGH also lived there for a while. Greenway is said to be the place where a servant threw a bucket of water over Raleigh, thinking his master was on fire, when all Raleigh was doing was trying to have a quiet smoke – the servant had never seen tobacco before! The present gardens are thought to have been laid out by Humphry Repton in the 18th century, but they were originally created with the help of prisoners of war from a warship of the Spanish Armada, captured by Sir Francis Drake and moored off Dartmouth, who were put to work by the Gilberts on levelling the ground at Greenway.

Dartmouth Castle

Guarding the entrance to the Dart estuary, and to Dartmouth's fine natural harbour, are two artillery forts,

Dartmouth Castle on the west bank and Kingswear Castle on the east bank. They were both built at the end of the 15th century, during the reign of Henry VII, and are THE FIRST CASTLES IN BRITAIN TO BE SPECIFICALLY DESIGNED FOR THE USE OF ARTILLERY. Dartmouth Castle shares its rocky bluff with the oldest of Dartmouth's three churches, St Petrox, whose 12th-century tower used to show a beacon to light the way into the harbour. Castle and church together make a dramatic spectacle. Kingswear Castle is now owned by the Landmark Trust and can be rented for holidays.

Dartmouth

Dartmouth has been an important port since Saxon times, and its original wharf is now a picturesque cobbled waterfront lane called BAYARD'S COVE. This is backed with pretty 17th- and 18th-century cottages and with the remains of a small Tudor fort at its southern end, much used for filming, most prominently for the popular 1970s television series *The Onedin Line*.

Stone stairways climb away from the harbour through the numerous black-and-white houses that overhang the tangle of narrow streets making up the town centre. The oldest building in Dartmouth is the CHERUB INN in Higher Street which dates from 1380. Down by the inner harbour, which is known as the Boat Float and more or less acts as the town square, is the early 17th-century BUTTERWALK, its crooked first-floor wooden façades held up from the pavement by granite columns. Charles II held court in one of the rooms looking down on the street.

The 14th-century church of St Saviour, close by the waterfront, boasts a beautifully painted 15th-century wooden rood screen considered amongst the best in the country and a 15th-century wooden door covered in intricate ironwork of 1631. Buried in the church is its founder JOHN HAWLEY (1350–1408), a merchant and seaman who was 14 times Mayor of Dartmouth and is said to be the inspiration for the Shipman in Chaucer's *Canterbury Tales*.

Dominating the town from the north is the impressive BRITANNIA ROYAL NAVAL COLLEGE, where Royal Navy officers are trained. They have been trained in Dartmouth since 1863 when the hulk of HMS *Britannia*, a wooden ship-of-the-line, was towed from Portsmouth and moored on the Dart to serve as a training base. The present campus building was designed by Sir Aston Webb and opened in 1905. Amongst those who attended the college are George V, George VI, the Duke of Edinburgh, Prince Charles, the Duke of York and Prince William. The Queen and Prince Philip had their first 'significant encounter' at Dartmouth, in 1939, when Prince Philip of Greece, as he was then, was a cadet there.

People of Dartmouth

In the visitor centre in the Royal Avenue Gardens beside the Boat Float you can see The Engine That Changed The World, THE WORLD'S OLDEST WORKING STEAM ENGINE, built by a son of Dartmouth, THOMAS NEWCOMEN, in 1720. Newcomen was born in Dartmouth in 1663 and became an ironmonger and blacksmith. Many of his friends worked in the Devon tin mines, which were constantly under threat from flooding; so, along with his friend and neighbour Thomas Savery (the first man to coin the term 'horse power'), Newcomen devised a steam-driven beam engine to pump the mines clear of water. Although crude and not very efficient, NEWCOMEN'S BEAM ENGINE, THE WORLD'S FIRST WORKING STEAM ENGINE, saved Britain's mining industry and made it possible to retrieve the raw materials that fuelled the Industrial Revolution.

Born in Dartmouth in 1793, PARSON JACK RUSSELL was a flamboyant churchman who loved the chase and developed a strain of terrier adapted for hunting – brave, intelligent and able to go down fox holes. Jack Russell terriers, all of them descended from Parson Russell's white fox terrier called TRUMP, are now popular all over the world, not just for hunting but as pets.

FLORA THOMPSON wrote her best-selling novel *Lark Rise to Candleford* while living in Dartmouth, her home for nearly 20 years from 1927. She is buried in Dartmouth's Longcross Cemetery.

CHRISTOPHER MILNE, son of A.A. Milne and known to the world as Christopher Robin from the Winnie-the-Pooh stories, owned and ran the Harbour Bookshop in Dartmouth for over 40 years.

Torbay

Torbay consists of three resort towns, Brixham, Paighton and Torquay, and the village of Goodrington, all lining the coast of the east-facing Tor Bay. Thanks to mild weather, sandy beaches and a picturesque coastline the area has long been fashioned the English Riviera.

Berry Head

The lighthouse on Berry Head, the headland at the southern end of Tor Bay above Brixham, is THE LOWEST LIGHTHOUSE IN BRITAIN, being just 16 feet (5 m) tall. It is also, thanks to the height of the cliffs on which it stands, THE HIGHEST LIGHTHOUSE IN BRITAIN, being 200 feet (60 m) above sea level.

Brixham

Brixham is the oldest of the three towns lining Tor Bay and in the Middle Ages was one of Britain's most important fishing ports. In the 18th century the fishermen of Brixham developed the trawl net and the Brixham fleet became THE FIRST TRAWLING FLEET IN THE WORLD.

Today, colourful old fisherman's cottages tumble down towards the harbour where there is a life-size replica of the *Golden Hind*, the ship in which Sir Francis Drake became THE FIRST

ENGLISHMAN TO SAIL AROUND THE WORLD from 1577 to 1580. In 1588 Drake sailed into Brixham with the *Capitana*, the first prize he had captured from the Spanish Armada.

One hundred years later in 1688 WILLIAM OF ORANGE landed on Brixham Quay to begin his march to London to take over the throne of England at the start of the Glorious Revolution. As he set foot on English soil he claimed, 'The liberty of England and the Protestant religion I will maintain.' There is a statue of him looking rather cross, or perhaps seasick, on the waterfront where he stepped ashore.

A little way from the harbour is the 19th-century church of All Saints where HENRY FRANCIS LYTE (1793–1847) was minister for 25 years. He lived at Berry Head House, now a hotel, high above the town, and one night in 1847, the last year of his life, when he was dying of tuberculosis, he sat alone and weary in his garden. As he watched the darkness of the evening creeping up towards him from the bay, he found the words of one of the most beloved hymns of all time 'Abide with Me' coming to him and bringing him comfort, just as they have to millions of people all over the world ever since he wrote it. Soldiers

sang 'Abide With Me' in the trenches in the First World War; Nurse Edith Cavell sang it as she faced execution by the Germans as a spy; Gandhi is said to have sung it while incarcerated, and it was played by the band of the *Titanic* as the ship sank beneath the waves.

Paignton

Paignton developed from a small fishing village that grew up around a Saxon church. It also had a palace, holiday home for the Bishop of Exeter. Not much of this remains except a corner tower known as the Miles Coverdale Tower, allegedly because Coverdale, Bishop of Exeter in the 16th century, wrote his translation of the Bible there.

Today Paignton is a holiday town with plenty of Victorian villas, novelty rock shops, a tidy stretch of sandy beach, a bracing promenade and a Victorian pier of 1879.

The town's most exuberant and unlikely attraction is OLDWAY MANSION, built in 1871 by ISAAC SINGER, inventor of the Singer Sewing Machine. Singer, whose wife Isabella was the model for the face of the Statue of Liberty, ended up in Paignton after being hounded out of New York and Paris after a series of scandals,

and lavished much of his fortune on Oldway. Alas, he was only able to enjoy his home for a brief time before he died in 1875, leaving the place to his third son Paris. Between 1905 and 1907 Paris had the house rebuilt in the style of the Palace of Versailles and filled it with beautiful things, including a grand marble staircase, Jacques-Louis David's painting of *The Crowning of Josephine by Napoleon*, a gallery based on the Hall of Mirrors at Versailles and, best of all, his mistress the ballet dancer Isadora Duncan.

Oldway Mansion is today owned by the local council and stands empty awaiting restoration.

Torquay

'The loveliest sea village in England'
Alfred, Lord Tennyson

Orignally the quay for Torre Abbey, Torquay, birthplace in 1890 of Agatha Christie, really got into its stride in the early 19th century, when ships of the Royal Navy were anchored in Tor Bay in readiness for action against Napoleon and the officers would come ashore for supplies and to spend time with their families, who were put up in the local hostelries. The town gained a reputation as a good place to stay for wealthy people unable to travel to the Continent because of the war, and then expanded

rapidly in the Victorian era with the arrival of the railway. Elegant white-painted Victorian terraces and hotels climb the hillside, giving the town a distinctly Mediterranean air.

Torre Abbey

Torre Abbey, west of the town, is the best preserved medieval monastery in the southwest and was founded in 1196 as a Premonstratensian monastery. By the time of the Dissolution of the Monasteries it had become the wealthiest such monastery in England. The church and many of the main buildings were demolished, but a splendid 14th-century gatehouse remains and the south and west ranges were converted into a house which was later remodelled in Georgian style. The house was the home of the Cary family from 1662 until 1930, when it was sold to the council, and is now used as an art gallery and museum. Nearby stands a 700-year-old tithe barn which has been known as the Spanish Barn ever since it was used to hold four hundred prisoners of war from the Spanish Armada.

Kent's Cavern

Kent's Cavern is a cave system that runs under the cliffs to the east of Torquay. A fragment of jawbone was discovered

Torre Abbey

in the cavern in 1927 which in 1989 was radiocarbon-dated to 36,000 years BC, making it the earliest human fossil ever found in northwest Europe, although the findings are controversial. A Scheduled Ancient Monument since 1957, the cavern, which was once used as a workshop for making beach huts, is now open to the public as a tourist attraction.

Teignmouth

Teignmouth is a Saxon fishing village that grew into a small port and holiday town in the early 19th century, and there are many Regency buildings along the waterfront and in the streets behind.

The quay was built in 1830 to handle Dartmoor granite, which was shipped from there to build the old London Bridge that now spans the Colorado River at Lake Havasu in Arizona.

A plaque on No. 20 Northumberland Place, a narrow street of Regency houses just in from the river, informs us that the poet JOHN KEATS lived there in 1818. He was there with his two younger brothers George and Tom, who was dying of tuberculosis, and it was thought the Devon air might help. It is believed that Keats finished *Endymion* while living in Teignmouth – perhaps the idyllic Devon countryside all around inspired the first line, 'A thing of beauty is a joy for ever.'

Atmospherics

The rail journey from Teignmouth to Exeter is one of the most scenic in Britain for it runs right alongside the sea. The line was built by Isambard Kingdon Brunel between 1846 and 1859 and involves five tunnels and a series of cuttings. Two of the tunnels run beneath a pair of sea stacks called the Parson and Clerk, which are said to be the Bishop of Exeter and a local priest set in stone by the Devil. The line is often battered by storms, and in 2014 it was closed for two months when part of the line at Dawlish was washed away.

Brunel had originally intended for the trains on this stretch of line to be propelled by atmospheric power. A pipe was laid along the centre of the track and the air pumped out to create a partial vacuum in front of the train, which was then drawn along by the atmospheric pressure behind the train's piston. However, it transpired that the leather valves running along the top of the pipe were constantly getting soaked with sea spray and quickly degraded, allowing air to leak in and compromise the vacuum. The project swiftly foundered and the line was eventually converted to running conventional steam trains. This turned out to be Brunel's only major engineering failure.

Between the railway and the bow-fronted cottages of the main street in the village of Starcross on the Exe estuary stands a tall tower made from red Devon sandstone. This is the best preserved of the engine houses that stood outside every station along the route and contained the boilers that powered the pumps that created the vacuum that moved the trains.

A La Ronde

Hayes Barton

Branscombe

Set on a hill above Exmouth is the unique A La Ronde, a quirky hexadecagonal (16-sided) 'round' house built in 1796 for reclusive spinsters JANE PARMINTER, daughter of a Barnstaple wine merchant, and her cousin MARY after their return from a Grand Tour of Europe. The design is based on the 6th-century Byzantine Basilica of San Vitale in Ravenna in northern Italy. At the centre of the house is the sea-green Octagon Room with eight doors leading off it and, above it, the incredible Shell Gallery decorated with more than 25,000 sea shells.

Jane and Mary lived a quiet life at A La Ronde until they died, Jane in 1811 and Mary in 1849. They are both buried in a chapel they had built in the grounds called Point-in-View.

A La Ronde, which is now owned by the National Trust, is thought to have been the inspiration for Bill Weasley's Shell Cottage in the film *Harry Potter and the Deathly Hallows*.

Budleigh Salterton

Sedate Budleigh Salterton is the setting for Millais's painting *The Boyhood of Raleigh*, and the sea wall seen in the picture is still there in front of the pink pebbled beach. Raleigh was born in 1552 at a thatched farmhouse nearby called HAYES BARTON, and his family had a pew in All Saints Church in East Budleigh.

The pretty little village of Branscombe boasts THE OLDEST WORKING THATCHED FORGE IN ENGLAND and the only such forge that is still operational. The present forge dates from 1580, but there has been a forge here since Norman times. Just up the road, hidden from the sea and Viking raiders by a ridge of hills, is the Norman church of St Winifred, one of the oldest and best churches in Devon. It has one of only two three-decker pulpits in Devon and a linear scratch dial that is unique in England (the norm is semi-circular), and uses the shadow cast by a buttress to mark the hours, which are shown in Roman numerals. Amongst a number of impressive memorials in the church is the Elizabethan altar tomb of JOAN WADHAM, who died in 1583. She had 14 children by her first husband John Kellawy and six by her second husband Sir John Wadham. One of those six, Nicholas, a lawyer, was the founder of Wadham College, Oxford. Joan features on the memorial twice, kneeling behind a statue of each of her two husbands, A UNIQUE DOUBLE THAT IS FOUND ON NO OTHER FAMILY MONUMENT IN BRITAIN.

At Branscombe beach the cliffs turn starkly from red to white, from Devon red sandstone to chalk, for Branscombe sits at the western extent of the chalk that makes up much of southern England. BEER HEAD, a little further east at the far end of the Hooken Cliffs, is the

SOUTHERNMOST CHALK HEADLAND
IN ENGLAND. In 1790, the Hooken
Cliffs were the scene of a dramatic land-
slide when some 10 acres (4 ha) of cliff
slid 250 feet (76 m) towards the sea,
leaving a spectacular jumble of rock
pinnacles and trees.

Seaton and Axmouth

Seaton and Axmouth face each other
across the River Axe and share a long
history as a flourishing Roman port –
Axmouth stood at the southern end of
Britannia's most important Roman
Road, the Fosse Way, which linked the
southwest to Lincoln. It prospered again
under the Saxons and the Normans,
and by the 14th century the port was
handling some 15 per cent of England's
shipping trade and was the most important port in the southwest of England.
Then the mouth of the River Axe was
choked off by landslides and scree, and
Seaton settled into becoming a Victorian
resort town, while Axmouth retired into
a dignified slumber of thatched cottages
and inns gathered around the ancient
church of St Michael, with its richly
carved Norman doorway and fine medieval wall paintings.

In the 19th century Seaton and
Axmouth were linked by BRITAIN'S
FIRST CONCRETE ROAD BRIDGE, a toll
bridge which was built across the mouth
of the River Axe in 1877. The bridge is
still in use for pedestrians but has now
been bypassed by a modern road bridge.

THE SEATON TRAMWAY, established
in 1970, runs north for 3 miles from
Seaton to Colyford and Colyton along
the route of the former Seaton branch
line, which joined the main Salisbury–
Exeter line 2 miles further north. It is
the only electric tramway in the world
to still use old-style tramcars with open
upper decks.

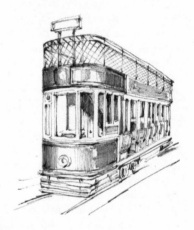

Well, I never *knew this*
about
THE SOUTH DEVON COAST

In 1744 THE WORLD'S FIRST RECORDED
SUBMARINE FATALITY occurred in
Plymouth Sound, just north of Drake's
Island, when a carpenter called JOHN
DAY descended from the sloop *Maria*
in a wooden diving chamber he had
built himself. Weighted down with

some 50 tons of ballast, the chamber
sank out of sight and failed to resurface.
It has never been found.

It is somewhat fitting that Plymouth,
from where Humphrey Gilbert sailed in
1583 to take possession of Newfoundland,

should, over three hundred years later, be the end point for THE FIRST EVER TRANSATLANTIC FLIGHT, from Newfoundland to England. On 31 May 1919 a Curtiss NC-4 seaplane crewed by US Navy aviators landed in Plymouth Sound having crossed the Atlantic, stopping at the Azores for refuelling. Two weeks later Alcock and Brown completed the first ever non-stop transatlantic flight, from Newfoundland to Ireland.

PLYMOUTH SYNAGOGUE, built in 1762, is THE OLDEST ASHKENAZI SYNAGOGUE STILL IN REGULAR USE IN THE ENGLISH-SPEAKING WORLD.

Across the harbour entrance from the Mayflower Steps by Sutton Pool in Plymouth is the NATIONAL MARINE AQUARIUM, THE LARGEST AQUARIUM IN BRITAIN, with THE DEEPEST TANK IN EUROPE, the Atlantic Ocean Tank.

Lying in the 14th-century church at Slapton are SIR RICHARD HAWKINS and his wife LADY JUDITH, lord and lady of the manor of Poole, whose house lay quarter of a mile up the road. Sir Richard was the son of the Elizabethan explorer and privateer Sir John Hawkins. John Hawkins was the first English naval captain to become involved in the slave trade. Richard Hawkins, in sharp contradistinction, was the first naval captain to give his men lemon or lime juice to prevent scurvy. When Richard's wife Lady Judith walked to church from Poole House, two pages would go before her unrolling a red carpet on to the ground to save her shoes from the mud.

CHAPTER NINE
DORSET COAST

Lyme Regis to Christchurch
88 miles

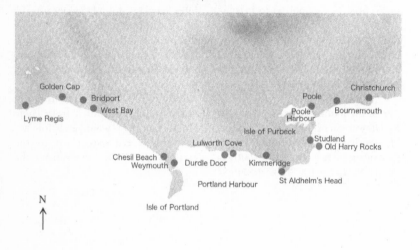

The Dorset coastline has more examples of classic coastal features than any other county's coastline. These include the highest sea cliff on the south coast of England, the longest shingle bar in Europe, an iconic rock arch and an almost perfect crescent bay, a long stretch of England's only natural World Heritage Site, and the second largest natural harbour in the world.

Lyme Regis

'... perched like a herring gull on a ledge suspiciously peering both ways into Devon and Dorset'
John Fowles

The 'Pearl of Dorset', the last or first place in Dorset, Lyme Regis is a delightful old town with narrow hilly streets, palm trees and a busy harbour, no longer commercial but colourful with yachts and small boats, and protected from the sea by a famous harbour wall known as the Cobb.

Monmouth Rebellion

In 1685 the Duke of Monmouth, illegitimate son of Charles II, landed on the beach at Lyme Regis now known as Monmouth Beach, at the start of the Monmouth Rebellion, his doomed campaign to wrest the throne from his uncle James II. At his side was *Robinson Crusoe* author Daniel Defoe. After Monmouth's defeat at the Battle of Sedgemoor, Defoe escaped capture by hiding in a churchyard, where he discovered the name Robinson Crusoe on a tombstone, but others were not so lucky. The king's 'hanging judge' Jeffreys came to the town and oversaw the hanging of 13 men of Lyme Regis.

The Cobb

The Cobb, which dates originally from 1313 but has been rebuilt many times, has featured in two well-known novels, Jane Austen's *Persuasion* and John Fowles's *The French Lieutenant's Woman*, the latter of which was filmed in the town. The most iconic modern image of Lyme Regis is of American actress Meryl Streep standing on the storm-lashed Cobb dressed in a long black cloak and gazing out to sea.

Literary Lyme

JOHN FOWLES lived in Lyme Regis for over half his life, from 1965 until his death in 2005, firstly in a remote farmhouse outside Lyme Regis called Underhill, where he wrote *The French Lieutenant's Woman*, and then at Belmont House, a beautiful two-storey Georgian house at the top of the road leading down to the harbour. This had once been the home of Eleanor Coade, inventor of the hard-wearing Coade stone used for the South Bank Lion, and the front of Belmont House is richly decorated with Coade stone. The house now belongs to the Landmark Trust.

JANE AUSTEN came to Lyme Regis twice, in 1804 and 1805, and stayed at a boarding house in the main street close to the sea. She clearly liked the town and set part of her last completed novel there, including a pivotal scene where one of the characters, Louisa Musgrove, falls off the Cobb and is concussed. A couple of years after Jane Austen's stay the boarding house was transformed with a new bow-windowed Regency façade into the THREE CUPS HOTEL, which became something of a literary retreat, hosting such luminaries as Alfred, Lord Tennyson, Henry Longfellow, Hilaire Belloc, G.K. Chesterton and J.R.R. Tolkien. In 1944 General Eisenhower met Allied commanders in the lounge on the first floor for a briefing prior to D-Day. In 1990 the hotel was closed and has since remained empty while plans for its redevelopment into apartments, shops and offices are discussed

Three Cups Hotel

Jurassic Lyme

In 1811, 12-year-old MARY ANNING discovered the skeleton of THE FIRST ICHTHYOSAURUS, A TYPE OF LIZARD FISH, KNOWN TO SCIENCE, in the cliffs of Black Ven near Charmouth, a mile east of Lyme Regis. Mary was a keen collector of fossils, which she sold to help her family survive after the death of her father, a carpenter, and it took her eight years to completely reveal the skeleton, one of the most important fossils ever found. Mary went on to uncover further

Lassie

THE PILOT BOAT, a pub on the waterfront, was the home of the original Lassie, prototype for the canine star of film and television and the only animal on *Variety*'s list of 100 Icons of the Century. In 1915 the battleship HMS *Formidable* was torpedoed by a German submarine in the English Channel and sank. Later that day a pinnacle from the battleship came ashore at Lyme Regis with 48 survivors and nine dead men aboard. The corpses were laid out in the cellar of the Pilot Boat, whereupon Lassie, the landlord's rough-haired collie, sat down next to one of those assumed dead, Able Seaman John Cowan, and licked his face and hands. She continued to do this for over half an hour and suddenly Cowan stirred and Lassie leaped up with an exultant bark. Cowan was rushed to hospital and made a full recovery, and Lassie stayed by his side throughout his convalescence. The story made headlines all over the world and is thought to have inspired Eric Knight, a young Yorkshire lad living in Canada, who later wrote *Lassie Come Home*, a novel about a faithful collie called Lassie, which was made into a film and inspired a long-running television series.

important specimens, amongst them a marine reptile called a plesiosaurus and a flying reptile called a dimorphodon macronyx. The first known female palaeontologist, Mary was in her way as important to science as Charles Darwin, and her discoveries caused the scientific community to look at the extinction of species in a whole new light. Her work also drew attention to the importance of the coastline of West Dorset and East Devon for fossils, which led eventually to it becoming known as The Jurassic Coast. An intriguing postscript to Mary Anning's story is that she is often said to have inspired the tongue-twisting expression 'She Sells Sea Shells', which was later picked up and turned into a popular music-hall song by the British songwriter Terry Sullivan in 1908.

Bridport

Locally grown flax and hemp introduced by the Romans provided the ingredients for the rope making industry that made Bridport famous. Records go back to King John, who ordered ships' cables from Bridport, and the town became so closely associated with rope making that when someone was hanged they were said to have been 'stabbed by a Bridport dagger'. Bridport's attractive streets, lined with Georgian buildings, were built exceptionally wide to allow for ropes to be laid out and dried. The Old Brewery (now Palmer's Brewery) on the River Brit is THE ONLY THATCHED BREWERY IN BRITAIN.

West Bay

One mile south of Bridport, at the mouth of the River Brit, is West Bay, originally Bridport Harbour, which was built to handle the distribution of the ropes and nets made in Bridport. The harbour marks the western end of the shingle bar of Chesil Beach, and the name was changed to West Bay when the railway arrived, in an effort to promote the place as a resort.

West Bay, with its prominent red cliffs, has proved a popular location for filming. The opening titles of the BBC television series *The Fall and Rise of Reginald Perrin*, where Reggie Perrin, played by Leonard Rossiter, runs along the beach discarding his clothing and then swims out to sea, was filmed at West Bay, as were the TV series *Harbour Lights*, starring Nick Berry, and *Broadchurch*, starring David Tennant and Olivia Colman.

Chesil Beach

Chesil Beach runs for 18 miles from West Bay to the Isle of Portland and is

THE LONGEST SHINGLE SEA BAR IN EUROPE. A unique feature of the beach is the precise way in which the pebbles are graded as they increase in size going from west to east. Local fishermen can tell how far along the beach they are by the size of the pebbles – even at night or in the fog. The eastern section of the beach encloses THE LARGEST LAGOON IN EUROPE, known AS THE FLEET, a brackish, tidal lagoon 8 miles long which provides a haven for the inhabitants of the ABBOTSBURY SWANNERY, EUROPE'S LARGEST SWANNERY – there can be more than six hundred swans there at any one time. The Abbotsbury Swannery is THE ONLY MANAGED COLONY OF NESTING MUTE SWANS IN THE WORLD and was established in the 11th century by the Benedictine monks of St Peter's Monastery, who reared the birds for meat.

The Fleet is a mysterious place, an oasis of calm even when storms are raging on the other side of the bar – in rough weather whole ships have been hurled over the bar into the lagoon, where they become trapped and must be left to rot. *Moonfleet*, J. Meade Falkner's classic novel about smuggling, is set in and around the Fleet.

Isle of Portland

'The Gibraltar of Wessex'
Thomas Hardy

The Isle of Portland is a rocky, almost treeless peninsula, or tied island, that juts out into the English Channel off the coast of Dorset. It stands at the eastern end of Chesil Beach sheltering Portland Harbour in its lee and is about 4 miles long, a mile wide and slopes north to south from 500 feet (152 m) high to 20 feet (32 m) at the southern

tip, Portland Bill. The isle's bare, bleak atmosphere makes it easy to believe that this was the Celtic people's Isle of the Dead, where the insane were sent to eke out a miserable existence in the caves and hollows.

The isle is pockmarked by large open quarries from which the white gold stone of Portland has been taken to beautify the faces of buildings across the world, from St Paul's Cathedral to the UN headquarters in New York. The architect Inigo Jones was the first to recognise the potential of Portland Stone and used it for his ground-breaking Palladian Banqueting Hall in London's Whitehall. The simple but iconic gravestones of British soldiers killed in the two world wars are made from Portland Stone, as is Britain's national memorial, the Cenotaph.

PORTLAND BILL, marked by an obelisk and a lighthouse built in 1906, is the southernmost point of Dorset and the treacherous currents and savage rocks off the bill have claimed many lives, including that of the poet William Wordsworth's brother John, a sea captain who went down with his ship, the *Earl of Abergavenny*, off Portland Bill in 1805.

The campaigner for women's rights MARIE STOPES (1881–1958) frequently came to Portland to study fossils, and after she died her ashes were scattered on the cliffs overlooking Portland Harbour.

Portland Harbour

Protected from the worst of the south-westerly gales by the Isle of Portland and Chesil Beach, the vast sweep of water known as Portland Roads has long been an important strategic anchorage, and was so vital that Henry VIII built two castles to protect it, Portland Castle and Sandsfoot Castle. Despite being so well sheltered the waters could get choppy, and when Queen Victoria and Prince Albert sailed into the bay in 1843 the Queen got terribly seasick and Albert determined that something should be done. Six years later in 1849 he laid the foundation stone of the Royal Portland Breakwater, which would create the first harbour designed specifically for the new steam-powered ships of the Royal Navy. The breakwater was constructed from millions of tons of stone quarried from the Isle of Portland by convicts temporarily stationed on the isle before being transported to the colonies. When completed in 1872 the break-water enclosed 1,300 acres (530 ha) and was THE LARGEST ARTIFICIAL HARBOUR IN THE WORLD. There are now four breakwaters and Portland Harbour is still the third largest artificial harbour in the world. The harbour ceased to be a Royal Naval base in 1995 and is now used for cruise ships, cross channel ferries and water sports of all kinds.

Weymouth

It was in the ancient town of Weymouth, in 1348, that the Black Death first came ashore in England, brought by rats in the cargo unloaded from a foreign merchant ship anchored off the town.

On a slightly lighter note it was also in Weymouth, in 1789, that George III became THE FIRST MONARCH TO USE A BATHING MACHINE. Imagine his surprise when, as he descended the steps and dipped the royal toe into the water, a band hidden in an adjacent machine struck up 'God Save the King!' He so enjoyed Weymouth that he remained there for three months and came back year after year, staying with his brother the Duke of Gloucester in an elegant red-brick terraced house on the seafront. Weymouth became fashionable and Gloucester Lodge, as it is now called, was soon joined by noble terraces of Georgian houses with porticoes and iron balconies lining the esplanade in front of the wide sandy beach, built by wealthy Georgians keen to holiday alongside the Royal Family.

The quiet Georgian architecture is somewhat disgruntled by the intrusion of Victorian exuberance in the guise of the Royal Hotel and Arcade and the Clock Tower of 1887, erected in honour of Queen Victoria's Golden Jubilee.

George III is commemorated by a huge figure of the King wearing a cocked hat and riding a white horse cut

Coastal Icons

Ten miles west of Weymouth the South West Coast Path passes by two of the most iconic features of the Jurassic Coast, geological masterpieces instantly recognisable to any student of geography. The first is DURDLE DOOR, a natural limestone arch carved out by the sea that must have been photographed more times than any other such arch. The word Durdle comes from the Old English 'thirl' meaning to drill or bore, while door is exactly that, hence a doorway drilled through the rock.

A mile or so further on are the turquoise waters of LULWORTH COVE, a small, almost perfectly formed oyster-shaped bay that has appeared in school books the world over as a classic example of the effects of coastal erosion. This length of coast between Weymouth and St Adhelm's Head is considered one of the best places in the world to study geology, since the buckling and twisting rock layers are clearly visible and there are numerous examples of different kinds of geological formations.

into the turf on the downs behind the town. No one is quite sure why he is depicted riding away from the town …

Isle of Purbeck

The Isle of Purbeck is formed by the Purbeck Hills, a ridge of chalk downs extending from Lulworth Cove in the west to Old Harry Rocks, overlooking Poole Bay, in the east.

Purbeck marble, the uppermost layer of stone found across the Purbeck Hills, has been quarried since Roman times and appears in most of the cathedrals of England in the form of pillars and shafts and sometimes flooring.

Kimmeridge

On the western cliffs above Kimmeridge Bay stands a 'nodding donkey' oil pump, which has been pumping oil up from a depth of between 1,200 and 1,800 feet (365–550 m) below the Purbeck Hills since 1959, making it THE OLDEST WORKING OIL PUMP IN BRITAIN. The well is part of BRITAIN'S LARGEST ONSHORE OILFIELD, THE WYTCH FARM OILFIELD, which lies to the south of Poole Harbour with reservoirs stretching east beneath Poole Harbour to the sea off Bournemouth, and still produces about one million gallons of oil a year.

High on the cliffs on the east side of Kimmeridge Bay is the CLAVELL TOWER, built in 1831 as an observatory by amateur astronomer the REVD JOHN CLAVELL of nearby Smedmore House. The tower is round, with the ground floor enclosed in a Tuscan colonnade and a stone parapet on the roof. Thirty-five feet (10.5 m) high and standing on cliffs that rise 330 feet (100 m) above the sea, it provides stupendous all-round views of Dorset and the coastline. It is now owned by the Landmark Trust and in 2006 was moved 80 feet (24 m) inland, to prevent it from falling off the crumbling cliff top into the sea. The Clavell Tower was the inspiration for P.D. James's 1975 novel, *The Black Tower*.

St Aldhelm's Head

St Aldhelm's Head, 350 feet (107 m) high, is the most southerly point of the Isle of Purbeck and is crowned by the tiny 12th-century stone chapel of St Aldhelm, a square building with a pyramidal roof topped by a cross. The interior consists of one room barely lit by one small lancet window and the roof is held up by a sturdy pillar with eight ribs dividing the roof into four beautiful stone vaults. Local legend has it that the chapel was built in 1140 as a memorial and a warning beacon for sailors by a local man who had watched from the cliff top as his daughter and her new husband were drowned after their boat hit rocks and capsized off the headland. It seems likely that the building was used as a lighthouse as well as a chapel, and there are indications that there was a beacon on the roof where there is now a cross.

Studland Bay

OLD HARRY ROCKS, a chalk stack called Old Harry and a stump, the remains of another stack called Old Harry's Wife, stand at the tip of Ballard

Old Marry Rocks

Down, a high headland separating Swanage Bay from Studland Bay, and mark the most easterly point of the Jurassic Coast. The name Harry comes either from the Devil, who was known as 'Old Harry', or from Harry Paye, a pirate who would hide behind the rocks in his ship to ambush passing merchant traffic.

The little village of STUDLAND, which lies at the southern end of Studland Bay, can boast one of the finest Norman churches in Britain. St Nicholas was built around 1080 and contains materials from a previous Saxon church in its walls. Its truncated tower is capped short because the Norman builders could go no higher on shaky foundations, while inside are two plain but beautiful Norman arches, a Saxon font and a sublime chancel beneath the tower, with a vaulted roof divided into four by huge ribs. Beyond that is a vaulted sanctuary. The church is grey and solid against the wind, while from the green churchyard there are glimpses of blue sea and white chalk, coastal England at its loveliest.

From Studland 3 miles of glorious sandy beach lead north to Shell Bay, at the entrance to Poole Harbour. Where the ferry to Sandbanks departs there is

a sculpture marking the end of the 650 mile South West Coast Path from Weston-super-Mare in Somerset.

Poole Harbour

Poole Harbour is THE SECOND LARGEST NATURAL HARBOUR IN THE WORLD after Sydney Harbour, covering an area in excess of 15 square miles. Apart from the main channel, which runs from the harbour entrance to Poole Quay and is regularly dredged to allow access for the cross channel ferry to Cherbourg, the harbour is extremely shallow, with an average depth of only 18 inches (46 cm).

The harbour entrance is just 900 feet (275 m) in width and is crossed by a chain ferry, which carries vehicles between Studland Heath and Sandbanks.

The harbour area has been inhabited for over two thousand years, and in 1964 a logboat dating from around 300 BC was discovered in the harbour during dredging works. At 30 feet (10 m) long the logboat, which is now in Poole Museum, it is THE LARGEST LOGBOAT EVER FOUND IN SOUTHERN ENGLAND.

WAREHAM, at the innermost extremity of the harbour, was an important port for the Anglo-Saxon kingdom of Wessex and suffered a number of Viking raids. In 1015 the Danish King Canute landed in Poole Harbour to begin his invasion of England.

Poole

As ships got larger Wareham's use as a port declined and Poole, originally just a small fishing village, gained in importance. In Tudor times the town established trading links with the North American colonies, particularly with the fisheries of Newfoundland, and by the 18th century there were more ships trading between North America and Poole than any other British port. Fine Georgian buildings around the quayside reflect this era of prosperity. By the 19th century the harbour had become too shallow for modern cargo ships and trade with America moved to the deepwater ports of Southampton and Liverpool. Poole has since become something of a holiday town, providing access to the Isle of Purbeck and the sandy beaches of Studland and Sandbanks, while the harbour is popular for water sports of all kinds.

Sandbanks

Sandbanks, a narrow spit of land projecting across the mouth of Poole Harbour, has the third highest land value by area in the world and the highest house prices in Britain outside central London.

Between 1898 and 1926 the radio pioneer Guglielmo Marconi lived at the HAVEN HOTEL on Sandbanks, close to the entrance to Poole Harbour, and here he established THE WORLD'S FIRST FULLY EQUIPPED RADIO STATION AND THE FIRST RADIO STATION IN THE WORLD TO RECEIVE LONG-DISTANCE MESSAGES. The Haven Hotel radio station sat at the centre of a network of stations based in Bournemouth, the Isle of Wight, Swanage and eventually France, and it was from here that the first radio messages were sent to, and received from, ships at sea. The Haven Hotel is constantly being rebuilt and modernised, but the room where Marconi set up his laboratory is still there and is now called the Marconi Lounge.

Bournemouth

Lying to the east of Poole Harbour, and traditionally in Hampshire, Bournemouth is now the largest town in Dorset, having been unceremoniously moved in 1974.

The growth of Bournemouth has been remarkable, for two hundred years ago there was nothing there except wild heathland and 7 miles of unspoiled sandy beach. Then, in 1811, a Dorset squire called LEWIS TREGONWELL, who was staying along the coast in Mudeford, a pretty fishing village on the edge of Christchurch Harbour where a number of prominent families had holiday homes, went for a walk on the heath beside the River Bourne and liked it so much he decided to build a house there. This was the first house in Bournemouth and it still exists, as a wing of the Royal Exeter Hotel, near the pier.

Squire Tregonwell set a trend and wealthy families began to build themselves large holiday villas along the Bourne valley and the other 'chines' for which Bournmouth is known, coastal valleys planted with trees and shrubs that run inland from the beach. When the railway arrived in 1870, Bournemouth boomed and was soon blessed with all the trappings of a seaside resort. The first entertainment centre, the Winter Gardens, was opened in 1875 and used as a concert hall until 1935, when it was dismantled and replaced with Britain's first indoor bowling green. The new bowling green, however, turned out to have magnificent acoustics and so the bowlers were turfed out and the Bournemouth Symphony Orchestra moved in. In 1979 the orchestra relocated to the Lighthouse Arts Centre in Poole, the largest arts centre in Britain outside London, and the Winter Gardens was demolished in 2006.

The town has two piers, Bournemouth Pier, 838 feet (255 m) long, which was opened in 1880, and Boscombe Pier, 600 feet (180 m) long, opened in 1889. Both piers have been much restored and remodelled ovet the years. In 2009 EUROPE'S FIRST ARTIFICIAL SURFING REEF opened to the east of Boscombe Pier, but it was never very successful for surfing and in 2014 was rebranded as a Coastal Activity Park.

Literary Bournemouth

In 1849 SIR PERCY FLORENCE SHELLEY, the son of poet PERCY BYSSHE SHELLEY and his wife MARY SHELLEY, author of the novel *Frankenstein*, built a house in Bournemouth called BOSCOMBE MANOR so that his wife and ailing mother Mary could benefit from the warm climate and sea air. Mary died in 1851 before the house was finished but had expressed a wish to be buried in Bournemouth along with her parents, the philosophers William Godwin and Mary Wollstonecraft. A family plot was created in St Peter's churchyard and Mary was duly buried there with her parents, who were moved from their original burial place in St Pancras in London. Also there is the heart of Percy Bysshe Shelley, which had been rescued from cremation in Italy, where the poet drowned in 1822.

ROBERT LOUIS STEVENSON lived in Bournemouth from 1884 to 1887, in a house in Alum Chine, west of the Bourne. The house was called Skerryvore after the tallest lighthouse in Scotland, which had been built by his uncle Alan Stevenson. While living there Stevenson wrote *The Strange Case of Dr Jekyll and Mr Hyde* and named Dr Jekyll's butler Mr Poole after the neighbouring town of Poole. Skerryvore was, alas, destroyed during the Second World War.

Lord of the Rings author J.R.R. Tolkien and his wife Edith loved Bournemouth and holidayed there every year for 30 years during the 1940s, 50s and 60s, always staying in Room 205 at the Edwardian Hotel Miramar on Bournemouth's East Cliff. They eventually moved to Bournemouth and lived in a house in Brankscome Chine for the last ten years of his life. Tolkien died there in 1973. He is buried in Oxford.

Christchurch

Another Hampshire town that is now in Dorset, Christchurch dates from Saxon days and still retains its Saxon street layout as well as the remains of a Norman castle and some delightful Tudor and medieval houses. Place Mill on the quayside was mentioned in the Domesday Book. The town stands at the confluence of the Avon and Stour rivers and was originally known as Twynham, 'the place between two waters'. The name was changed to Christchurch when the priory was built in 1094.

At 312 feet (95 m) long, Christchurch Priory is THE LONGEST CHURCH IN ENGLAND and is famous for its carved misericords dating from the 13th and 14th centuries.

Highcliffe Castle

Described as one of the most important surviving examples of Romantic architecture, Highcliffe Castle sits high on the cliffs east of Christchurch. Designed by William Donthorne, it was built between 1831 and 1835 for diplomat Charles Stuart, 1st Baron Stuart Rothesay, on the site of a Georgian house built in 1775 by the baron's grandfather the 3rd Earl of Bute, Prime Minister to George III. The Earl was a keen botanist and died after falling over the cliffs at High Cliff while searching for a rare plant. The remains of his house, two entry lodges, are now the Lord Bute restaurant.

Amongst the guests at Highcliffe were William Gladstone, four times Prime Minister, opera singer Dame Nellie Melba and author Nancy Mitford. In 1907 Kaiser Wilhelm came to stay to recuperate from illness, and the then owner, Major General Edward Stuart-Wortley, would later recall the Kaiser complaining about the British attitude to Germany and that he had been misjudged over German support for the Boers during the Boer War. In an interview with the *Daily Telegraph*, given while staying at Highcliffe, the Kaiser talked about anti-British feeling in Germany, and on a visit to Christchurch Priory commented on the shabby state of the organ saying, 'When I am King of England I will buy you a new one.' A chilling insight into his ambitions, perhaps.

Between 1916 and 1922 Highcliffe Castle was leased by department store owner HARRY SELFRIDGE, who modernised the house, adding new bathrooms, kitchen and central heating. Selfridge, who died broke in 1947, is buried nearby in the churchyard of St Mark's, Highcliffe.

Well, I never *knew this*
about
THE DORSET COAST

At 626 feet (191 m), GOLDEN CAP, mid-way between Charmouth and Bridport, is THE HIGHEST SEA CLIFF ON THE SOUTH COAST OF ENGLAND. The name refers to the colour of the greensand rock at the summit which glows a golden colour in the sun. Golden Cap is one of the few places in England where a tiny white orchid known as Autumn's Lady's-tresses (*Spiranthes spiralis*) – also known as Autumn's Last Hurrah – can be found. The most popular route to the top of Golden Cap is from Seatown, east of the

cliff, where there is a also a well patronised waterfront pub, the Anchor Inn.

LULWORTH CASTLE, 2 miles northeast of Lulworth Cove, was built in 1609 by Thomas Howard, a grandson of the Duke of Norfolk, as a hunting lodge and later passed to the Weld family of London merchants. A small chapel called THE ROTUNDA was built in the park in 1786, THE FIRST ROMAN CATHOLIC CHAPEL TO BE BUILT IN ENGLAND AFTER THE REFORMATION in the 16th century.

BROWNSEA ISLAND, which lies just inside the entrance to Poole Harbour, is 3 miles round and the largest of the islands in the harbour. The Boy Scout movement was born here in August 1907 when Lord Baden-Powell, hero of the Siege of Mafeking in the Boer War and first Chief Scout, brought 20 boys from local Boys' Brigades, along with a few boys from Eton and Harrow, to the island for a camping expedition, where he taught them the practical skills, fair play and good manners for which the Boy Scouts would become known.

CHAPTER TEN
HAMPSHIRE COAST

Lymington to Havant
50 miles

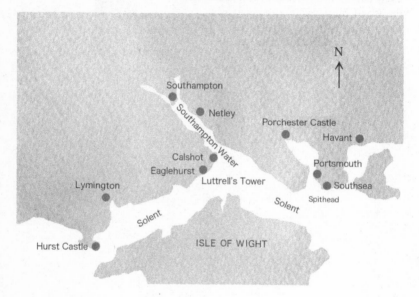

Southampton

Netley

Porchester Castle

Havant

N

Calshot

Eaglehurst

Luttrell's Tower

Portsmouth

Southsea

Lymington

Spithead

Southampton Water

Solent

Solent

Hurst Castle

ISLE OF WIGHT

Highlights of the Hampshire coast include Henry VIII's most powerful coastal fortress, Britain's first stately bungalow, the birthplace of seaplanes and the Spitfire, Britain's busiest cruise port, the longest surviving stretch of medieval walls in England, the site of the world's largest military hospital, the best preserved Roman fort in Europe, Britain's only island city, the home of the Royal Navy and the world's first dry dock.

Hurst Castle

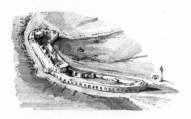

Hurst Castle stands at the end on a 2 mile shingle spit reaching out towards the Isle of Wight and guards the narrow, 1 mile wide Needles Passage which forms the western entrance to THE SOLENT, the body of water that lies between the Isle of Wight and the mainland. The castle, which was built in 1544, has a 12-sided central tower and three bastions in the surrounding curtain wall, and is the most powerful of the forts built by Henry VIII to defend the south coast from invasion by the French. In 1648 Charles I was imprisoned in the Tudor keep overnight when he was taken from Carisbrooke Castle on the Isle of Wight to his trial in London.

During the Second World War the troops occupying the fort built themselves a theatre inside a converted Victorian gun emplacement. Called the Garrison Theatre, it has been restored as a working theatre and is the only surviving Entertainments National Service Association (ENSA) theatre in Britain.

The castle is open to the public and access is via a long, difficult walk along the shingle or, during the summer, by ferry across the marshes from Kenhaven.

The Solent

The Solent is the body of water that lies between the Isle of Wight and the mainland and is Britain's busiest boating and water sports area. The eastern part of the Solent, off Portsmouth, is known as SPITHEAD and this is where the Fleet Review takes place when the monarch reviews the massed ships of the Royal Navy. In 1797, during the fight against Revolutionary France, the Royal Navy's worst mutiny occurred at Spithead when sailors on 16 ships of the Channel Fleet went on strike for more pay and better working conditions.

Luttrell's Tower

Luttrell's Tower is a three-storey Georgian folly with a tall circular stair turret that looks out over the Solent on the western approach to

Southampton Water. It was built in 1780 for the local landowner and MP TEMPLE LUTTRELL and is the only surviving work of THOMAS SANDBY, the first Professor of Architecture at the Royal Academy. Temple Luttrell may, or may not, have been a smuggler but the tower conveniently provides a perfect lookout for anyone wishing to avoid the customs men, and there is a secret passage leading from the beach into the tower's cellar. Luttrell's Tower is now owned by the Landmark Trust.

Eaglehurst

Luttrell's Tower stands in the grounds of Eaglehurst House, which was built in the early 1800s by GENERAL RICHARD LAMBART, 7th Earl of Cavan, Governor of nearby Calshot Castle. Known as THE FIRST STATELY BUNGALOW IN BRITAIN, the house had only one floor, a state of affairs that caused Queen Victoria, who stayed there as a 14-year-old girl, to comment that 'living entirely on the ground floor' was like staying in 'tents'. Victoria so loved the place that she thought about buying it as a holiday home before settling on Osborne House on the Isle of Wight. Radio pioneer GUGLIELMO MARCONI leased Eaglehurst from 1911 to 1916 and used Luttrell's Tower as an experimental radio station for transmitting to the seaplanes being developed at nearby Calshot. In 1912 Marconi and his wife climbed to the top of the tower to wave goodbye to the *Titanic* as she sailed out of Southampton on her fateful maiden voyage across the Atlantic. Later Eaglehurst became the home of architect CLOUGH WILLIAMS-ELLIS, creator of the fairytale Italianate village of Portmeirion in North Wales. It remains a private residence today.

Calshot Spit

Calshot Spit is a 1 mile long sand and shingle bank that lies on the west side of the entrance to Southampton Water. In 495 a Saxon leader called Cerdic landed on the spit in one of the earliest Saxon invasions of post-Roman Britain. In 1540 Henry VIII built an artillery fort called Calshot Castle on the end of the spit as part of his chain of south coast defences.

In 1913, just before the start of the First World War, the Royal Flying Corps established an experimental seaplane base on the spit and Calshot became Britain's leading centre for the development of seaplanes and flying boats through both world wars. The work was sponsored by First Lord of the Admiralty Winston Churchill, who was given his first trip in a seaplane at Calshot. He was piloted by Tommy Sopwith, designer of the first seaplane to be developed at Calshot, the SOPWITH BAT BOAT. Tommy Sopwith later taught Churchill how to fly.

In September 1929 Calshot hosted that year's SCHNEIDER TROPHY, a competition inaugurated in 1912 by wealthy French industrialist Jacques Schneider to encourage the development of seaplanes. The contest involved speed trials over open sea on a 150 mile course and a seaworthiness trial, and it was won by FLIGHT OFFICER HENRY WAGHORN flying a Rolls-Royce engined Southampton Supermarine S6 designed by R.J. Mitchell. Calshot was also the venue for the last Schneider Trophy race ever held, in 1931. The race was won by LT J.N. BOOTHMAN in a Southampton Supermarine S6B and, since this was the third time Britain had won, the Schneider Trophy was awarded to Britain permanently.

It was from the Supermarine that Mitchell developed the Spitfire, the first of which was built in Southampton in 1936.

One of the men who helped to organise both races was T.E. SHAW, Lawrence of Arabia, who was based at Calshot between 1929 and 1931. The older red-brick administration building at Calshot is named Lawrence House in his honour.

During the Second World War, Calshot was the main base for the Short

Sunderland flying boat, a powerful, long-range aircraft which became the workhorse of Coastal Command.

Today Henry VIII's 16th-century castle is dwarfed by a tall Coastguard Tower and a number of vast hangars now used as a base for the RNLI and an activities centre. The Sopwith Hangar was erected in 1913 and is the second oldest aircraft hangar in Britain, after a hangar at Larkhill in Wiltshire.

Fawley

Esso's Fawley Refinery, located on the west bank of Southampton Water, is THE LARGEST OIL REFINERY IN BRITAIN. Although the adjacent Fawley power station was decommissioned in 2013, its 650 foot (198 m) high chimney remains a prominent landmark for ships approaching Southampton.

Southampton

Southampton stands at the head of Southampton Water at the confluence of the rivers Test and Itchen. It was a harbour for the Romans and the Saxons, and in 1016 the Danish King Canute landed here on one of his raids and was offered the Crown of England.

Southampton was the major port linking William the Conqueror's capital of Winchester with his homeland of Normandy, and in 1189 Richard the Lionheart embarked for the Crusades from Southampton.

In 1338, at the start of the Hundred Years War with France, Southampton was sacked by the French who all but destroyed the Norman city walls, which had to be rebuilt by Edward III. Seventy-five years later, in 1415, Henry V and his men sailed from Southampton to gain revenge at the Battle of Agincourt.

In 1620 the *Mayflower* set out from Southampton for America, before being forced to turn back and call into Plymouth. The Mayflower Memorial, crowned with a replica of the ship, stands near the West Gate on Town Quay close to the point of the *Mayflower*'s departure.

Perhaps the most poignant departure from Southampton was the *Titanic*, on 10 April 1912 – four fifths of the crew on board were Southampton men and women, as were a third of those who perished when the ship sank. There are a number of memorials across the city to various crew members such as musicians and postal workers, although the grandest, a bronze tableau on a Portland stone plinth, is in East Park and is dedicated to the ship's engineers, none of whom survived, all 'remaining at their posts'.

In the 20th century Southampton became Britain's leading transatlantic passenger port, headquarters of the great shipping companies such as the White Star Line, P&O and Cunard. OCEAN DOCK, the largest of the Eastern Docks at the very southern tip of Southampton, has been home to all the great transatlantic liners from the *Mauretania* to the *Queen Mary* and *Queen Elizabeth I* and *II*. Cunard's ships are usually christened at Southampton, including the newest cruise liners *Queen Victoria*, by the Duchess of Cornwall in 2007, the *Queen Elizabeth*, by the Queen in 2011, and the *Royal Princess*, by the Duchess of Cambridge in 2013.

The Western Docks along the River Test include the KING GEORGE V GRAVING DOCK which, when it was built in 1933, was THE LARGEST GRAVING DOCK IN THE WORLD.

Old
Southampton

The city was much rebuilt after being badly bombed during the Second World War and looks modern on the surface, but for those who are prepared to explore there are many intriguing remnants of the older Southampton tucked away amongst the tower blocks and shopping centres.

The main towers and more than half of the mighty city walls built by Edward III to replace the Norman walls destroyed by the French and Genoese in 1338 remain, forming THE LONGEST SURVIVING STRETCH OF MEDIEVAL WALLS IN ENGLAND. Incidentally, the sack of Southampton in 1338, one of the opening gambits of the Hundred Years War, was led by CHARLES GRIMALDI and the bounty he acquired during the raid was put towards the founding of the principality of Monaco.

The city's oldest building is St Michael's Church on Castle Way, which has an early Norman tower dating from 1070. The spire above it, 165 feet (50 m) high, was first added in the 15th century, rebuilt in 1732 and then, in 1887, had 9 feet (2.7 m) put on it to make it a more visible landmark for shipping. Indeed, it made such a convenient landmark that German bombers in the Second World War were ordered to leave it alone. Hence, St Michael's avoided any bomb damage.

Behind St Michael's is the handsome TUDOR HOUSE, one of the finest timber-framed town houses in England; it was built in the late 15th century and is now a museum. Close by, integrated into the city walls, are the remains of a big Norman merchant's house called, for reasons that remain obscure, KING JOHN'S PALACE.

High Street

The solid, fortress-like BARGATE, which sits astride the top of the busy High Street, surrounded by shops, was built by the Normans in 1180 as the city's northern and main gate. Much added to over time, the Bargate has been used as the city's Guildhall, Law Courts and as a prison. Marks inside the centre arch were made by trams which, until 1949, ran through the Bargate.

Further south on the High Street is the roofless shell of Holyrood Church, which dates from 1320 but was badly bombed during the war. The tower survived and has been left standing as a memorial to the sailors of the Merchant Navy. On the west face of the tower there is a memorial plaque to CHARLES DIBDIN (1745–1814), composer of rousing sea shanties who was paid by the government to write patriotic songs 'to keep alive the national feelings against the French'. He was responsible for the lines 'In every mess I find a friend, in every port a wife,' which gave rise to the notion of sailors having 'a girl in every port'.

A few doors down the High Street from Holyrood Church is THE RED LION which, it is claimed, dates from 1148 and is THE SECOND OLDEST PUB IN ENGLAND. The pub was sometimes used as a courtroom and here, in 1415, as Henry V's troops were amassing in Southampton before sailing for France, the trial took place of Richard Plantagenet, Earl of Cambridge, and two others who were accused of conspiring to replace Henry on the throne with Edmund Mortimer, the Earl of March. The three men were found guilty and executed outside the Bargate with their severed heads suspended on poles above the gate; and a week later Henry and his 'band of brothers' left Southampton on their way to fight in one of the greatest of all English victories, the Battle of Agincourt – 'and gentlemen in England now a-bed shall think themselves accursed they were not here ...'

Town Quay

The 14th-century WOOL HOUSE on Town Quay, where wool was stored before being exported to Venice and Genoa in Italy, is now a microbrewery and restaraunt. Hidden behind a tall red-brick warehouse on Town Quay are the remains of one of the oldest domestic buildings surviving in England, a large Norman merchant's house, fancifully called CANUTE'S PALACE, although it has nothing to do with King Canute.

Further along Town Quay is the southern tower of the medieval walls, GOD'S HOUSE TOWER, built to guard access to the town from the quayside and named after the next-door God's House Hospital founded in 1168. In the early 15th century the tower was strengthened to accommodate cannon, one of the earliest forts in the country to be designed to carry artillery.

Next to the tower is the Southampton Old Bowling Green, first used in 1299 by the monks of God's House Hospital and THE WORLD'S OLDEST SURVIVING BOWLING GREEN.

Netley

Castle

NETLEY CASTLE, a riotous medley of turrets, battlements and gables, rises out the trees just back from the beach on the east bank of Southampton Water, a mile below of the mouth of the River

Itchen. The original castle was built in 1544 by Henry VIII as part of his 'Device forts' programme to fortify the south coast of England against attack by the French and Spanish. After the Civil War the castle fell into disrepair, and then in the 19th century it was built up little by little into a Gothic-style country home. For much of the 20th century the castle was run as a nursing home and in 1998 it was converted into nine private residences.

Abbey

Lying in a dip behind the castle are the extensive ruins of NETLEY ABBEY, today hidden from the sea by trees. In medieval times, however, the monks would light a lamp at the top of the church tower to act as a landmark and beacon for ships in Southampton Water. The abbey was established by the Bishop of Winchester in 1239 for Cistercian monks from nearby Beaulieu, and benefited much from the patronage of Henry III with the result that the abbey church became far larger and more magnificent than was usual for a Cistercian church. Inscriptions to Henry can be found at the base of the great piers of the transept crossing.

When another Henry, Henry VIII, dissolved the abbey in 1536, he made the gatehouse into a fortress (now Netley Castle) and gave the rest to his Lord Treasurer, Sir William Paulet, who converted the abbey buildings into a Tudor mansion. In the late 17th century the property was sold to a local builder who intended to pull down the church and use the materials for other building works. However, when he set about demolishing the delicate west window he was crushed to death by falling masonry, which was taken as a sign that the abbey should be left as it was, and for the next two hundred years it remained untouched. The romantic, overgrown ruins were painted by John Constable, eulogised in poetry by Thomas Gray and provided Jane Austen with the inspiration for *Northanger Abbey*.

In the early 20th century the site was tidied up and is now under the stewardship of English Heritage, who look after what is one of the loveliest and best preserved medieval Cistercian monasteries in the country.

Royal Victoria Country Park

Set on a rise south of Netley village the green-domed Netley hospital chapel is all that remains of what was then THE LARGEST MILITARY HOSPITAL IN THE WORLD, THE ROYAL VICTORIA MILITARY HOSPITAL. Built in 1856 for injured soldiers returning to Southampton from the Crimean War and other conflicts around the British Empire, the hospital had 138 wards, a thousand beds, its own gasworks, school, bakery and prison and was THE BIGGEST AND LONGEST BUILDING IN BRITAIN, covering 200 acres (80 ha) and with a frontage facing the water a quarter of a mile long. Even so, the hospital was unable to cope with

the slaughter of the First World War and a huge new hospital of wooden huts had to be constructed on the terraces behind the main building. THE WORLD'S FIRST PURPOSE-BUILT MILITARY ASYLUM was built at Netley to treat men traumatised by the horrors of the war, amongst them the poet WILFRED OWEN, who came here from France in 1917 suffering from shell-shock.

The hospital was finally demolished in 1966, with the exception of the chapel which now houses a heritage centre, and the grounds were transformed into the Royal Victoria Country Park.

Portsmouth Harbour

The entrance to Portsmouth Harbour, known as the SALLY PORT, as it is the gap through which navy vessels sally forth, is little over 200 yards (180 m) wide, making the harbour almost impregnable. On the west side of the entrance is FORT BLOCKHOUSE, first fortified in 1431 during the reign of Henry VI and one of the earliest permanently fortified sites in Britain. Until 1998 this was the home of HMS *Dolphin*, the Royal Navy Submarine base, and the Royal Navy Submarine Museum now occupies part of the site. Here you can see THE ROYAL NAVY'S FIRST EVER SUBMARINE, *HMS Holland I*, which was designed by Irishman John Holland and launched at Barrow-in-Furness in 1901 before arriving in Portsmouth in 1902.

Beyond the spit on which Fort Blockhouse is set is Gosport, a former fishing village which became the Royal Navy's victualling yard. Gosport was badly bombed in the Second World War but still possesses a number of forts from differing eras including Fort Brockhurst, one of the inner Palmerston Forts commissioned by Lord Palmerston in 1859 to defend the harbour. One of Gosport's finest older buildings is the railway terminus of 1841, an elegant colonnaded affair designed by William Tite, architect of the Royal Exchange in the City of London. In 1844 the railway line was extended from the main station to Royal Clarence Yard on the waterfront where a private station, the Royal Victoria station, was built for the Royal Family to use when they visited Osborne House, Queen Victoria's holiday home on the Isle of Wight. The last time the station was used was in 1901, when Queen Victoria's body was brought back to the mainland from Osborne, where she had died. Gosport's main railway station closed in 1953, leaving Gosport as the largest town in England without a railway station, and the complex is now used as offices.

Portchester Castle

Portchester Castle, which sits in a commanding position at the head of Portsmouth Harbour, is enclosed within the walls of THE MOST COMPLETE SURVIVING ROMAN FORT IN EUROPE, and the only one where the entire circuit of defensive walls have survived intact. The fort was built in the 3rd century as the most westerly component of the Romans' 'Saxon Shore' defences running along the coast from here to Suffolk. The Roman walls, complete with 14 of the original 20 bastions, are up to 20 feet (6 m) high in places and enclose 9 acres (3.6 ha). It was occupied until the Romans left Britain in AD 370 and then served as a Saxon camp. In the 12th century Henry I built a powerful castle keep, with walls 12 feet (3.6 m) thick, in the northwest corner of the fort, which was added to in the 14th century to create a palace for Richard II. The view from the castle roof commands the whole of Portsmouth Harbour. In 1415 Henry V massed his troops and his fleet here before marching them to Southampton from where they sailed to France and the Battle of Agincourt. And during the Napoleonic Wars some eight thousand French prisoners of war were held at Porchester.

The beautiful Norman church of St Mary, which sits in the southeast corner of the Roman fort, was built to serve a small Augustinian priory established by Henry I at the same time as the castle. The rest of the priory buildings have disappeared, but the church is largely intact and unaltered and has some glorious Norman architecture, particularly the west front with its beautifully decorated doorway and the wide tower arches.

Portchester Castle is now managed by English Heritage.

Portsmouth

Portsmouth, which occupies the western two thirds of Portsea Island, is BRITAIN'S ONLY ISLAND CITY and the second most densely populated place in Britain after Central London. It has been ENGLAND'S MOST IMPORTANT NAVAL BASE since the time of the Tudors, thanks to its impregnable position beside the narrow entrance to Portsmouth Harbour, itself protected by the Isle of Wight.

The Romans had perhaps their most important port here; Richard the Lionheart built the first dock here in 1194; and then in 1415 Henry V gathered his troops at Porchester Castle while awaiting the arrival of the fleet he had commandeered from ports along the south coast – the first 'royal' navy. At the same time he ordered the building of a wooden round tower to guard the harbour entrance. An iron chain that could be raised against incoming enemy ships was thrown across the harbour between the round tower and a corresponding tower on the Gosport side. In 1495 Henry VII fortified Portsmouth dock, rebuilding Henry V's wooden round tower in stone, and constructed THE WORLD'S FIRST DRY DOCK behind the walls, declaring Portsmouth THE FIRST ROYAL DOCKYARD. Charles II strengthened the forts either side of the Sally Port and Portsmouth became the most strongly fortified town in Britain, a fitting home for what over the course of the next two hundred years would become the world's most powerful navy.

In 1787 HMS *Bounty*, under the command of Captain Bligh, set sail from Portsmouth on its fateful voyage for Tahiti which ended in the most famous mutiny in history. In 1805 Admiral Lord Nelson sailed from Portsmouth to fight the Battle of Trafalgar, Britain's greatest naval victory, which assured Britain's naval supremacy for the next hundred years, although at the cost of Nelson's life. Today Portsmouth is home to over two thirds of the Royal Navy's surface fleet.

Historic Dockyard

Portsmouth's Historic Dockyard is home to some of the world's most famous naval vessels. *Mary Rose*, launched in 1511, was Henry VIII's flagship. It was THE LARGEST SHIP THAT HAD EVER BEEN BUILT FOR THE ENGLISH NAVY and the first to be purpose-built as a warship, armed with heavy guns that could be fired through gun-ports. After refurbishment in 1536 during which gun-ports were built along both sides of the ship she became THE FIRST WARSHIP ABLE TO FIRE BROADSIDES. It is thought that the weight of the heavy guns made the *Mary Rose* unstable and may have contributed to the ship sinking while leading an attack on French galleons during the Battle of the Solent in 1545. Caught by a sudden gust of wind the ship suddenly listed heavily to starboard and water rushed in through the open gun-ports, causing her to sink rapidly with the loss of some four hundred lives. The wreck of the *Mary Rose* was discovered in 1971 and raised in 1982. The hull and the many artefacts recovered with it are now on display in the Mary Rose Museum, housed in a futuristic hall opened in 2016. THE MARY ROSE IS THE ONLY SURVIVING

16TH-CENTURY WARSHIP ON DISPLAY
ANYWHERE IN THE WORLD.

HMS *Victory* was launched at Chatham in 1765. She saw service in the American War of Independence, the French Revolutionary War and the Napoleonic Wars, but her most notable claim to fame was as Nelson's flagship at the Battle of Trafalgar in 1805. She was put in dry dock at Portsmouth in 1922 as a museum ship and a plaque marks the spot where Nelson fell, shot by a French marksman as he stood on the quarterdeck in full uniform to inspire his men. As flagship of the First Sea Lord HMS *Victory* is THE OLDEST COMMISSIONED WARSHIP IN THE WORLD.

Launched at Blackwall on the Thames in 1860, HMS *Warrior* was THE WORLD'S FIRST ARMOUR-PLATED IRON-HULLED WARSHIP and remained THE LARGEST AND MOST POWERFUL WARSHIP IN THE WORLD for the next ten years. She was built in response to the launch in France in 1859 of the world's first iron-clad warship, *La Gloire*, and HMS *Warrior* proved so intimidating that the French navy never

left port, so she never had to fire a shot in anger. By 1871, however, this highly effective deterrent had already become obsolete and was decommissioned in 1883, eventually becoming a floating oil jetty at Pembroke Dock in Wales. She was rescued from there in 1979 by the Maritime Trust, a body established in 1969 by the Duke of Edinburgh and MP Sir John Smith, founder of the Landmark Trust, and towed to Hartlepool, where she was restored as THE LARGEST MARITIME RESTORATION PROJECT EVER UNDERTAKEN. In 1987, fifty-eight years after she had left Portsmouth as a hulk, HMS *Warrior* returned and has been docked in Portsmouth's Historic Dockyard as a museum ship ever since.

Old Portsmouth

High Street, the heart of Old Portsmouth, was laid waste by bombing in the Second World War but some older buildings survived. Portsmouth Grammar School lies behind the long Georgian façade of a former barracks at the eastern end of High Street, while two doors down is Buckingham House, once YE SPOTTED DOGGE INNE, where James I's favourite, the unpopular Lord High Admiral of the Fleet GEORGE VILLIERS, Duke of Buckingham, was stabbed in the heart by JOHN FELTON, a disgruntled naval officer passed over for promotion and owed substantial back pay. The house was sold in 2017 complete with the knife used for the murder. Opposite, a plaque on the Unitarian Chapel records the burial here of shoemaker JOHN POUNDS (1766–1839), who gave local children free reading and arithmetic lessons and was the inspiration for the Ragged School Movement for free education.

The entrails of the murdered Duke of Buckingham are buried a little further down High Street in PORTS-MOUTH CATHEDRAL – the rest of him lies in Westminster Abbey. The cathedral has been built up around the chancel and transepts of the church of St Thomas, built in 1188. The tower was added in the 17th century and the cupola and lantern, for guiding shipping into the harbour, in 1703. The Byzantine-style nave and aisles were begun by Sir Charles Nicholson in 1935 and finally completed, to a smaller scale than originally envisaged, in 1991.

South of High Street are the roofless remains of the early 13th-century ROYAL GARRISON CHURCH where Charles II and Catherine of Braganza were married in 1662. The church was left in ruins by bombing in the Second World War.

At the seaward end of High Street is the SQUARE TOWER, part of the fortifications built by Henry VII in 1494. There is a bust of Charles I set in a niche in the wall of the tower which was presented to the town by the King in 1623 in thanks for his safe arrival in Portsmouth after foreign travels, and it was a long-held belief amongst the people of Portsmouth that if the bust was removed great misfortune would come to the city. In 1937 the bust was removed and loaned to the Royal Academy for an exhibition, and four years later the city was reduced to rubble by German bombs. The bust now on the tower is a copy, the original kept in Portsmouth Museum.

In front of the Square Tower is a sculpture of a chain link which commemorates the departure from here in 1787 of the 'First Fleet' of convict ships to Australia.

Spice Island

The Square Tower lies at the foot of Spice Island, a spit of land that runs northward along the east side of the entrance to Portsmouth Harbour. Spice Island, whose name is derived from the area's nickname 'the Spice of Life', based on its reputation as a somewhat disreputable area of seedy inns and brothels, retains much of the atmosphere of Old Portsmouth. A section of fortified walls links the Square Tower to Henry V's Round Tower and bow-windowed Georgian houses line the cobbled streets.

At the northern tip of Spice Island is PORTSMOUTH POINT, from where there are panoramic views of the harbour and dockyards. Two old inns, the Spice Island Inn and the Still and West, provide refreshment while one watches the busy comings and goings of Britain's busiest naval port. The Point also provides a splendid view of Portsmouth's newest attraction, the 560 foot (170 m) high SPINNAKER TOWER, an observation tower designed to resemble a spinnaker sail. The tower, which opened in 2005, has three observation decks, the top one open to the elements and the bottom one with a glass floor.

Southsea

SOUTHSEA CASTLE stands on the southernmost point of Portsea Island and was built by Henry VIII in 1544 as one of his south coast Device forts. The castle has a magnificent view over Spithead and Henry watched from here as his flagship the *Mary Rose* sank in 1545. The king was so fat by then he could hardly walk and had to be hoisted on to the castle walls in his chair. Southsea Castle gave its name to the surrounding area which, during the Victorian era, developed as Portsmouth's seaside resort.

Comedian PETER SELLERS was born in Southsea in 1925, and SIR ARTHUR CONAN DOYLE practised as a doctor in Southsea in the 1880s while he wrote his first Sherlock Holmes novel, *A Study in Scarlet*.

The hovercraft service between Southsea and Ryde run since 1965 by Hovertravel, the world's oldest hovercraft operator, is THE LAST REMAINING COMMERCIAL HOVERCRAFT SERVICE IN THE WORLD.

Well, I never knew this about
THE HAMPSHIRE COAST

HYTHE'S slender iron pier, which opened in 1881, is 2,100 feet (640 m) long and runs east from the centre of Hythe out to the deep-water channel of Southampton Water, providing a docking station for ferries running between Hythe on the west bank to Southampton on the east bank. The narrow-gauge electric railway that carries passengers along the pier is THE OLDEST CONTINUOUSLY OPERATING PUBLIC PIER TRAIN IN THE WORLD.

THE DOUBLE ROPE HOUSE in Portsmouth's Historic Dockyard is 1,095 feet (334 m) long and, when it was constructed in 1776, was THE LONGEST BUILDING IN THE WORLD. It was the first building in which the majority of the processes carried out in rope making could all take place under the same roof.

PORTSMOUTH FOOTBALL CLUB (known as Pompey) took part in the first official Football League match ever to be played under floodlights. The game was played at Fratton Park, Portsmouth's home ground, on 22 February 1956 against Newcastle. Portsmouth lost 2–0.

PORTSMOUTH is the birthplace of several notable figures including, in 1712, JONAS HANWAY, who introduced the umbrella into Britain from Persia; in 1806, the engineer ISAMBARD KINGDOM BRUNEL; and in 1812 the novelist CHARLES DICKENS, whose birthplace in Old Commercial Road, near the old dockyard, is now a museum in his memory.

CHAPTER ELEVEN
ISLE OF WIGHT COAST

West Cowes to East Cowes
57 miles

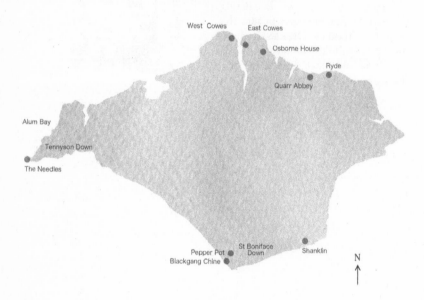

The Isle of Wight, an England in miniature, is the largest island off the coast of England and covers an area of some 150 square miles. It has a varied coastline of 57 miles and highlights include the home of the world's oldest and largest regatta, the most famous chalk stacks in Britain, a haunt of poets, the oldest amusement park in Britain, Britain's only surviving medieval lighthouse, the first radar station in Britain to be bombed, the oldest seaside pier in Britain and a startling modern Byzantine abbey.

Cowes

Cowes Castle, home of the world's most prestigious yacht club, the ROYAL YACHT SQUADRON, welcomes visitors arriving from Southampton into the world's most famous yachting harbour. The Royal Yacht Squadron was founded in 1815 as The Yacht Club for 'gentlemen interested in saltwater yachting'. The Prince Regent was interested in saltwater yachting so he joined in 1817 and when he became King George IV in 1820 he made it The Royal Yacht Club. In 1833 William IV, the 'Sailor King', commanded that it should become The Royal Yacht Squadron.

The RYS has always had a close connection with the Royal Navy and members are allowed the fly the Royal Navy's White Ensign from their yachts. Admiral Thomas Hardy, captain of the *Victory*, Nelson's flagship at the Battle of Trafalgar, was amongst the early Honorary Naval members.

In 1826, as part of the annual regatta at Cowes the RYS began to organise and lay down rules for yacht racing, including the rule requiring a yacht on the port tack to give way to another on starboard. This was the start of Cowes Week, THE OLDEST AND LARGEST REGATTA IN THE WORLD, which is held at the beginning of August after Glorious Goodwood.

In 1851, the year of the Great Exhibition, Queen Victoria and Prince Albert watched as the schooner *America* of the New York Yacht Club won the Royal Yacht Squadron's £100 Cup race around the Isle of Wight. The race was renamed and the America's Cup is THE OLDEST INTERNATIONAL SPORTING TROPHY IN THE WORLD.

The biennial Fastnet Race, although not run by the RYS, starts from Cowes.

Cowes Castle was built in 1539 as one of Henry VIII's Device forts to defend the important anchorage on the River

Medina from his European enemies. The Royal Yacht Squadron leased the castle in 1855 and hired the architect Anthony Salvin to remodel and enlarge it to how we see it today. The RYS bought it outright in 1917.

East Cowes and West Cowes are linked across the River Medina by a chain ferry called the Cowes Floating Bridge.

Alum Bay

Named after the alum that was mined here in the 16th century, Alum Bay is backed by multi-coloured cliffs of white quartz, red iron oxide and yellow limonite. The effect is startling and the best way to see the cliffs is from the chair lift that runs from the pleasure park at the top down to the pebble beach. Jars or vials of the coloured sands make a popular souvenir.

A monument on the cliff top commemorates the pioneering radio station set up here by Guglielmo Marconi in 1897. From here he experimented with sending radio signals over water to Bournemouth and Poole and a number of ships at sea. Lord Kelvin sent the first paid-for radio telegram from here on 3 June 1898.

The Needles is the name given to the three 100 foot (30 m) high chalk stacks off the western tip of the Isle of Wight, remnants of the chalk ridge that once joined the island to the mainland at Studland, where their equivalent is the Old Harry Rocks. The formation takes its name from a fourth, needle-shaped pillar called Lot's Wife which collapsed during a storm in 1764 leaving a wide, tooth-like gap. The Old Battery on the headland overlooking the Needles is a restored Victorian fort.

The chalk cliffs of Tennyson Down, which rise 480 feet (146 m) above the sea near the Needles, are crowned with a monument to the poet Alfred, Lord Tennyson, who lived nearby at Farringdon House for almost 40 years. He walked on the down every day taking in the sea air, which he said was worth 'sixpence a pint'.

Shanklin

The old fishing village of Shanklin is a chocolate box scene of thatched pubs and tea shops at the top of the biggest chine, or coastal ravine, on the Isle of Wight. Inscribed above the water fountain outside The Crab Inn is a poem by the American poet Henry Wadsworth Longfellow, who stayed at The Crab in 1868, describing it to a friend as 'a lovely little thatched-roof inn, all covered with ivy'.

The larger part of Shanklin is Victorian, and it is the island's most popular resort. A lift carries visitors between the esplanade and Keats Green on the cliff top. Keats stayed in Shanklin in 1819, at Eglantine Cottage on the High Street, and completed the first book of *Lamia* while he was there.

Part of the D-Day operation's PLUTO pipeline, which carried fuel under the Channel to Allied forces in France, can still be seen in Shanklin Chine.

Ryde

If you have a 'Ticket to Ride', as the Beatles did in the 1960s, the chances are that you will arrive on the ferry from Portsmouth at the head of Ryde's famous pier. Britain's fourth longest pier at half a mile long, Ryde pier was opened in 1814 and is THE OLDEST SEASIDE PIER IN BRITAIN. The trains that run from the pier head and down the island's east coast to Sandown and Shanklin used to run along the Piccadilly Line in London and date from 1938, THE OLDEST PASSENGER TRAINS STILL IN USE IN BRITAIN. THE WORLD'S ONLY REGULAR PASSENGER HOVERCRAFT SERVICE runs from Ryde Esplanade to Southsea in Portsmouth.

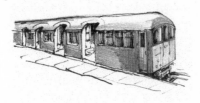

Osborne House

When Queen Victoria first saw Osborne House she declared it was 'impossible to imagine a prettier spot' and bought it, along with 342 acres (139 ha) of land, in 1845. The Georgian house already there was far too small to accommodate the burgeoning Royal Family, so it was pulled down and replaced with a vast Italian Renaissance-style villa, designed by Prince Albert to complement the view, which reminded him of the Bay of Naples. The builder was THOMAS CUBITT, who was responsible for the famous façade of Buckingham Palace, and the house was completed in 1851, with much of the cost being met by

the sale of the Prince Regent's Royal Pavilion in Brighton.

The house consisted of two main wings connected by a Grand Corridor, which was lined with a parade of statues and made a fine undercover promenade in bad weather. The whole house was filled with gifts presented to the Queen from around the world, along with exhibits from the Great Exhibition. A particular feature were the newfangled flushing lavatories, amongst the first in England, which were installed in the royal quarters.

The gardens were laid out in terraces, also in Italian style, and included THE FIRST PALM TREE PLANTED IN A PRIVATE GARDEN IN ENGLAND, a gift from the King of Portugal.

On 26 May 1857 Queen Victoria and her family posed at Osborne for THE FIRST EVER OFFICIAL PHOTOGRAPH OF THE ROYAL FAMILY.

After Prince Albert died in 1861, Victoria kept Osborne House as a shrine to his memory and spent much of her long period of mourning there. Affairs of state still had to be attended to, however, and in 1890 a new wing was added, with a huge banqueting hall called the Durbar Room designed and decorated by LOCKWOOD KIPLING, father of Rudyard Kipling, in Indian style to reflect Victoria's position as Empress of India.

Queen Victoria died at Osborne in 1901 and her successor Edward VII presented the house to the nation. For a while it was used as a Royal Naval college and then, during the First World War, as a convalescent home for officers. Poet ROBERT GRAVES and *Winnie-the-Pooh* author A.A. MILNE were amongst the patients.

Osborne House is now in the care of English Heritage and the house and garden have been restored as closely as possible to how they were in Queen Victoria's time.

Well, I never *knew this* *about*

THE ISLE OF WIGHT COAST

Named after the collapsed chine, or coastal ravine, upon which it sits, BLACKGANG CHINE opened in 1842 and is THE OLDEST AMUSEMENT PARK IN BRITAIN. Its star feature is Britain's biggest and best preserved whale skeleton, 75 feet (23 m) long, which washed up on a beach near the Needles in 1842.

Standing behind Blackgang Chine, on the summit of St Catherine's Hill, 780 feet (236 m) high, is an octagonal tower known as THE PEPPER POT, the remains of BRITAIN'S ONLY SURVIVING MEDIEVAL LIGHTHOUSE. It was built in 1320 by local landowner Sir Walter de Godeton, Lord of Chale, as a penance for receiving wine plundered from the wreck of a French ship in Chale Bay.

When it was built in the 12th century, ST LAWRENCE OLD CHURCH west of Ventnor was the smallest church in England, 20 feet (6.1 m) long and 12 feet (3.6 m) wide. It lost its title when a 10 foot (3 m) chancel was added in 1842.

Behind Ventnor is ST BONIFACE DOWN, at 791 feet (241 m) high THE HIGHEST POINT ON THE ISLE OF WIGHT. In 1940, at the beginning of the Second World War, the radar station on the hill was the first radar station in Britain to be bombed, on this occasion by Stuka dive bombers, an event that was reconstructed in the 1969 film *Battle of Britain*.

A mile or so to the west of Ryde is the extraordinary Byzantine-style red-brick QUARR ABBEY, designed and built by exiled French Benedictine monks in 1914.

CHAPTER TWELVE
SUSSEX COAST

Chichester Horbour to Rye
90 miles

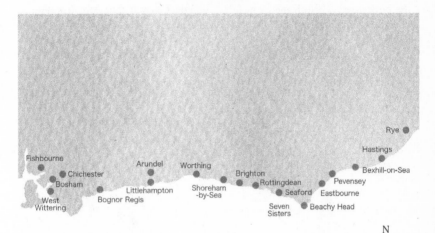

Highlights of the Sussex coast include the village where King Canute attempted to hold back the tide, Britain's first royal palace, a famous sleepy lagoon, Britain's second largest inhabited castle and oldest airport, the largest college chapel in the world, the first official nudist beach, Britain's most spectacular Bed and Breakfast, the place where William the Conqueror landed, the birthplace of British motor racing and the steepest funicular railway in Britain.

Chichester Harbour

Chichester Harbour, in the far west of Sussex, is one of the few wild and undeveloped areas on the south coast, 10,000 acres (4,000 ha) of tidal flats, mudflats and salt marsh, home to thousands of sea bird and waders. There are three main channels, the Thorney, Bosham

and Chichester, each with its own atmosphere and small harbours, such as WEST ITCHENOR, Birdham, which sits at the end of the CHICHESTER CANAL, opened in 1822 to take large ships into the heart of Chichester, and DELL QUAY, once the main harbour for Chichester and one of the most important ports in England. It is now important as the home of the ancient waterfront pub the CROWN AND ANCHOR. From many parts of the harbour it is possible to see the spire of CHICHESTER CATHEDRAL, THE ONLY MEDIEVAL ENGLISH CATHEDRAL THAT CAN BE SEEN FROM THE SEA.

Bosham

Outstanding amongst the harbour villages is Bosham, a well-known beauty spot, the lure of artists, yachtsmen and wildfowl, a classic English seaside village that sits on its own seaweed-littered inlet off the Bosham Channel. Georgian houses and fishermen's cottages and the ANCHOR BLUE INN raise their skirts above the muddy water while gardens and green lawns are lapped by the sea, and the car park often surrenders to the tide. All is peaceful now, but Bosham has a past that has profoundly shaped our island story. The Romans were here. A legionary commander Vespasian, later Emperor, is believed to have had a base at Bosham for his invasion of the Isle of Wight, and in the early 1800s a colossal stone head, thought to be from a huge statue of Vespasian, was uncovered at Bosham. Now in Chichester Museum, this is THE LARGEST STATUE EVER FOUND IN BRITAIN.

And could Bosham be the place where the divinity of kings was finally disproved? The Danish king CANUTE had a palace at Bosham and it was here that he went down to the water's edge and commanded the tide to turn back, knowing that it would not, so that he could prove to his fawning courtiers that he was not all-powerful. He also met with tragedy at Bosham, for in 1020 his eight-year-old daughter fell into the millstream and drowned. She was buried beneath the stone floor of the church.

The Saxon EARL GODWIN made Bosham his home and it was inherited by his son HAROLD, our last Saxon king. The Saxon chancel in HOLY TRINITY CHURCH is much as Harold would have known it and as it appears in the Bayeux Tapestry, in which Harold is shown at prayer before embarking from Bosham on the voyage that was to seal his fate in 1064. His ship was wrecked on the coast of Normandy and he was taken to Duke William in Rouen, where it is believed he made an agreement to support William's claim to the throne of England on the death of Edward the Confessor. When Harold returned to England and claimed the throne for himself, William felt cheated and came to take his due by force at the Battle of Hastings. Some records state that after Hastings the body of King Harold was brought back to

Bosham for burial, and in the 1950s a tomb was discovered under the floor of the church with the head, right leg and left hand missing, injuries that, according to accounts by the Bishop of Amiens, correspond to those that Harold had sustained at his death. Could the sleepy village of Bosham be the last resting place of Saxon England?

Fishbourne

Lying at the head of the Chichester Channel is Britain's first royal palace, Fishbourne Palace, THE LARGEST RESIDENTIAL ROMAN BUILDING EVER DISCOVERED IN BRITAIN; indeed, at about 500 feet (150 m) square, it is the largest Roman residence known north of the Alps, with a larger footprint than Buckingham Palace. Built in around AD 75 for the British king Cogidubnus of the local Regni tribe as a reward for his loyalty to Rome, it boasts THE EARLIEST GARDENS FOUND IN BRITAIN AND THE LARGEST COLLECTION OF MOSAICS ever found in situ – particularly notable is the mosaic showing Cupid riding a dolphin, thought to have been laid down in about AD 160. The palace, which burned down in about AD 270, was discovered by accident in 1960 by an engineer laying a new water main.

West Wittering

SIR HENRY ROYCE, the engineer behind Rolls-Royce, lived in West Wittering from 1917 until his death in 1933, and the studio where he came up with some of his best designs can still be seen beside the main road through the village. West Wittering has one of the best beaches in Sussex with over a mile of good sand, and it was while walking along the beach here that Royce came up with the design for his world-beating 'R' engine, sketching his initial ideas in the sand. The 'R' engine set all sorts of world air speed records and twice won the Schneider Trophy along the coast at Southampton Water, in 1929 and 1931, in a Supermarine S6 seaplane. The same engine later helped the Supermarine S6 become the first aircraft to fly at over 400 mph. The

first Bentley car produced by Rolls-Royce was brought to West Wittering for Royce's approval and, thinking it was too fast to cope with the old-style suspension, he set about designing a new type of suspension for it. He sketched out his ideas on the back of an envelope as he sat up in bed the night before he died, and when his nurse delivered the plans to the Rolls-Royce engineers at Derby they found that his last act had been to invent the adjustable shock absorber.

Bognor Regis

'Bugger Bognor,' George V is alleged to have said just before he died, in response to his doctor's assurance that he would soon be well enough to holiday at his favourite seaside town. The little fishing village of Bognor was developed into a resort in the 18th century by wealthy hatter and East India Company merchant Sir Richard Hotham. Queen Victoria called it 'dear little Bognor' and George V granted Bognor the title 'Regis' in thanks for its convalescent properties. Today Bognor is the most traditional of English seaside towns, popular for its sandy beach, gardens and amusement arcades.

Arundel

There is a wonderful view of Arundel from Climping Sands, a sand and shingle beach backed by sand dunes that lies a mile south of the village of Climping. The land between the dunes and Arundel is completely flat and the spectacle of the towers and turrets of Arundel Castle rising out of the misty marshes is unforgettable. Indeed, the extraordinary Gothic outline was the

inspiration for the fantastical castle in Mervyn Peake's *Gormenghast*. Home to the Dukes of Norfolk and their ancestors for over 850 years, Arundel Castle vies with the Duke of Northumberland's Alnwick Castle to be the second largest inhabited castle in England after Windsor.

The present castle, grouped around a Norman keep, was restored by Henry, the 15th Duke, who inherited Arundel in the 1860s at the age of 15. Vastly rich, he grew eccentric and would shuffle around the town dressed in shabby clothes and with a long unkempt beard. Once, while he was waiting at the station to greet a friend off the train, an imperious lady summoned him to carry her case, thinking he might be grateful for a tip. 'Here, my man, is a penny for you,' she said pressing a coin into his hand. No doubt it's the first honest penny you've ever earned.' 'Indeed it is,' the Duke murmured in reply.

The 15th Duke, whose family are the leading Roman Catholic family in Britain, was also responsible for the building of Arundel's glorious French Gothic Roman Catholic Cathedral on the other side of the town. Completed in 1868 it was designed by Joseph Hansom, inventor of the Hansom cab, and from a distance its Gothic silhouette neatly complements that of the castle.

Arundel's Early English parish church of St Nicholas is unique in that it contains both Anglican and Catholic chapels. The Duke of Norfolk's private chapel, where many of the family are buried, is Catholic and can only be entered from the castle, although it is part of the parish church. The chapel and the rest of the church are separated by a glass partition.

Shoreham-by-Sea

Shoreham-by-Sea, a Saxon town with Roman origins, is the nearest south coast port to London and still has a working commercial harbour. It sits on the River Adur, which does a sharp eastward turn just before it reaches the sea and separates the town from a thin strip of shingle beach. The beach is accessed from the town by a footbridge.

Shoreham, while outwardly sedate and unassuming, is actually blessed with a remarkable number of extraordinary features. To begin with it has not one but two superb, architecturally important churches. Old Shoreham Church, at the centre of the Saxon town upriver, dates from the 10th century and boasts a huge Norman tower. New Shoreham Church, St Mary de Haura (of the harbour), which sits at the centre of the new town built by the Normans nearer to the sea, dates from 1130 and is colossal, even though reduced to half its original size in the 18th century.

MARLIPINS MUSEUM in the High Street is housed in THE OLDEST COMPLETE SECULAR BUILDING STILL IN ACTIVE USE IN BRITAIN, a 12th-century structure probably built as a hospital with a distinctive chessboard pattern façade of stone and flint.

Crossing the Adur near the Old Church is the OLD SHOREHAM TOLLBRIDGE, THE LAST WOODEN TOLLBRIDGE OF ITS KIND IN BRITAIN, and possibly the world. Opened in 1782, it was rebuilt in 1916, closed to traffic in 1970 and restored in 2008 for use as a footbridge.

Shoreham Airport

At the western end of the old tollbridge is Shoreham Airport. Founded on grazing land in 1910 by Harold Piffard, a former pupil at Lancing College, it is THE OLDEST AIRPORT IN BRITAIN,

THE OLDEST PURPOSE-BUILT COMMERCIAL AIRPORT IN THE WORLD and THE OLDEST CONTINUOUSLY OPERATING AIRPORT IN THE WORLD. In 1911 THE WORLD'S FIRST RECORDED CARGO FLIGHT took off from Shoreham when Horatio Barber, in a Valkyrie monoplane, flew a box of Osram lightbulbs over to Hove. The airport has an exquisite art deco terminal building built in 1936, which is much in demand for filming 1930s scenes including those from the Netflix series *The Crown* and a number of episodes of ITV's *Poirot*, starring David Suchet.

Brighton

If stately Hove is the maiden aunt, then brash Brighton to the east is the rakish uncle, a character it picked up from the Prince Regent who really put Brighton on the map in the 18th century.

Brighton's first brush with Royalty came in October 1651 when Charles II arrived in what was then the little fishing village of Brighthelmstone, one step ahead of Cromwell's soldiers who were hunting for him after his defeat at the Battle of Worcester. The King took rooms at the George Inn while his companions searched for a getaway boat to take them all to France. They eventually found a local sea captain called NICHOLAS TATTERSELL who agreed to transport them across the Channel in his coal brig *Surprise*, and on the morning of 16 October Charles left England for exile in France. When the King returned he lavishly rewarded Tattersell for his help, and with his winnings Tattersell bought the OLD SHIP, Brighton's oldest hotel, first recorded in 1559. Today, to commemorate the exploits of their former owner, the Old Ship organises an annual Royal Escape yacht race from Brighton to Fécamp on the Normandy coast.

Tattersell is buried in Brighton's oldest building, the 13th-century St Nicholas Church, set low on a mound above the town where a Druid temple once stood. Also buried there is PHOEBE HESSELL who, in order to be close to her soldier love, dressed herself as a man and served for 17 years in the British Army. Despite being wounded at the Battle of Fountenoy in 1745 she was never rumbled and returned to Brighton where she lived to be 108.

Dr Brighton and the Royal Pavilion

In 1750 a doctor from Lewes, Dr Richard Russell, published a book about the health-giving effects of the sea air at Brighthelmstone, and in 1783 the Prince of Wales, later Prince Regent and then George IV, who was always in need of reviving, thought he would give Dr Brighton, as it became known, a try and rented a farmhouse there. He enjoyed it so much that he bought the farmhouse and commissioned Henry Holland and later John Nash to convert it into a beach hut fit for a prince.

The result was the Royal Pavilion, all onion domes, minarets, cupolas and pinnacles, an exotic blend of Mogul Indian, Middle Eastern Islamic and Chinese design that is unique in Britain. No expense was spared on the interior, which was filled with the finest furniture, lots of lacquer and gilt, mirrors and crystal chandeliers – the chandelier in the Banqueting Hall had a lotus flower motif and weighed over a ton. The roofs of the Banqueting Hall and Music Room were designed to resemble Saracen tents, while the iron pillars of the Great Kitchen, THE FIRST IRON PILLARS TO BE USED IN THE CONSTRUCTION OF A PRIVATE HOUSE ANYWHERE IN THE WORLD, were made to look like palm trees. Here the prince could escape the confines of the London Court and indulge in the original 'dirty weekend' in Brighton with his mistress Maria Fitzherbert.

Appropriately enough, many years later, in 1979, and very much in the spirit of the Prince Regent, Brighton became THE FIRST SEASIDE RESORT IN BRITAIN TO INTRODUCE AN OFFICIAL NUDIST BEACH.

Piers

Prince George's friends soon followed him to Brighton and put up the glorious Regency terraces for which Brighton is renowned. In 1823 Brighton became home to THE WORLD'S FIRST SEASIDE PLEASURE PIER, THE CHAIN PIER, designed along the lines of a suspension bridge by Sir Samuel Brown, who had built the world's first suspension bridge, the Union Bridge, across the River Tweed in 1820. The pier was described by William IV, who took pleasure in walking up and down it while staying at the Royal Pavilion, as 'the most delightful place in the world'. It also served as a terminus for the cross channel ferry from Dieppe. The pier was destroyed by a storm in 1896 but the two entrance kiosks were saved

The Chain Pier

and now flank the entrance to its replacement, the Palace Pier, a third of a mile long, which opened in 1899.

The Palace Pier is the only one of Brighton's two piers still in operation. Brighton's second pier, the West Pier, designed by the famous pier builder Eugenius Birch, opened in 1866 but over time, and in spite of being the first English pier to be Grade I listed, proved too costly to maintain and was closed in 1975. Now only the gaunt skeleton of the pier survives, standing forlornly out to sea like a diffident crab.

In 2016 the British Airways i360 observation tower, at 531 feet (162 m) high THE TALLEST MOVING OBSERVATION TOWER IN BRITAIN, was erected at the landward end of the former West Pier. Intended to attract people to the site and so promote the rebuilding of the pier, the needle shaped tower was designed as a vertical pier and has a circular viewing platform that ascends to a height of 453 feet (138 m), carrying up to two hundred people.

Madeira Drive, east of the Palace Pier, is the finishing line for THE WORLD'S OLDEST MOTORING EVENT and the world's biggest gathering of veteran cars, the LONDON TO BRIGHTON VETERAN CAR RUN, which takes place annually on the first Sunday in November and is open to cars built before 1905. The first run, the Emancipation Run, took place in 1896 and was held to celebrate the raising of the speed limit from 4 mph to 14 mph and the abolition of the rule that required every mechanised road vehicle to be preceded by a man holding a red flag.

MADEIRA TERRACE, which runs along the beachfront beneath Madeira Drive, is a covered promenade projecting from the cliff wall made up of 151 cast-iron arches on cast-iron columns supporting a cast-iron latticework screen. This remarkable and quite ravishing piece of Victorian engineering was begun in 1890 and completed in 1897, and at 1,300 (396 m) feet long it is THE LONGEST CAST-IRON STRUCTURE IN BRITAIN.

Running along in front of Madeira Terrace on its way from Palace Pier to Black Rock, a distance of 1¼ miles, is BRITAIN'S FIRST PUBLIC ELECTRIC RAILWAY, NOW THE WORLD'S OLDEST OPERATING ELECTRIC RAILWAY, THE VOLKS RAILWAY. It was opened in 1893 by MAGNUS VOLK, a German inventor and Brighton resident who was the first person on the south coast of England to have a telephone and to fit electric lights in his house.

Volks is buried in the churchyard of the early 12th-century St Wulfram's Church in Ovingdean, a small village in the Downs just east of Brighton. Also buried there is the stained glass artist Charles Kempe, whose family developed the Kemptown area of east Brighton. There is only one other church in England dedicated to St Wulfram, a 7th-century French saint, and that is in Grantham, Lincolnshire.

At the end of Madeira Drive, where the chalk cliffs begin, is Brighton Marina, which covers 127 acres (51 ha) and was the largest marina in Europe when it opened in 1978.

Just beyond the marina, looking imperiously down from the clifftop, is Roedean, perhaps Britain's most famous girls' school after St Trinian's. Roedean was founded in Lewes Crescent in Brighton in 1885 by the Misses Dorothy, Millicent and Penelope Lawrence to provide young ladies with an all-round education, and moved into its present imposing premises in 1899.

Rottingdean

Rottingdean's rocky beach occupies a gap in the chalk cliffs while the charming narrow High Street of Old Rottingdean village runs inland along a valley in the downs before opening out on to a green and village pond. Here, between 1897 and 1902, lived the writer RUDYARD KIPLING, THE YOUNGEST PERSON EVER, AND THE FIRST ENGLISHMAN, TO WIN THE NOBEL PRIZE FOR LITERATURE. He and his family rented The Elms, a large house across the road from St Margaret's Church, having initially stayed with his aunt and her husband, the artist EDWARD BURNE-JONES, who had a holiday home in the village, North End House, on the other side of the green. Burne-Jones died the year after Kipling moved to Rottingdean, and is buried in the churchyard. The church itself features a number of stained-glass windows by Burne-Jones commemorating the marriage of his daughter Margaret in the church. Also living in Rottingdean, in The Dene, at the bottom of the green by the village pond, were the in-laws of Kipling's first cousin STANLEY BALDWIN, the future Prime Minister.

While living in Rottingdean Kipling worked on *Stalky & Co* and the *Just So Stories*, and it was here that he fell in love with what he called 'Sussex by the Sea' and wrote his poem 'Sussex' in which he describes 'our blunt, bow-headed, whale-backed Downs ...'

Both the Elms, and the house where Burne-Jones lived, now called Prospect Cottage, are still there. In 1920 ENID BAGNOLD moved into Burne-Jones's old house with her husband SIR RODERICK JONES, chairman of Reuters. While she was there Enid, great-grandmother of former Prime Minister David Cameron's wife Samantha, wrote

---

Daddy Long Legs

Had Kipling wanted to go to Brighton while he was living in Rottingdean he would have been able to take advantage of the short-lived BRIGHTON AND ROTTINGDEAN SEASHORE ELECTRIC RAILWAY, known affectionately as the 'Daddy Long Legs'. This was the brainchild of MAGNUS VOLKS, inventor of the Volks Electric railway, and ran between the eastern end of the Volks Railway in Brighton to a pier on Rottingdean beach. It consisted of a tramcar perched on high stilts that moved along on submerged rails running along the sea bed some 100 yards offshore. Alas, Daddy Long Legs only lasted for about five years, forced to close in 1901 when the Brighton Council decided to build groynes out into the water to protect the coastline from erosion. Lengths of the track can still be seen at low tide, along with the stumps of the posts that carried the power lines high above the water.

---

her well-known play *The Chalk Garden*, inspired by her own garden at Rottingdean, and the novel for which she is best known, *National Velvet*, which was made into a Hollywood film starring a 12-year-old Elizabeth Taylor. Enid Bagnold died in Rottingdean in 1981, aged 91, and is buried in St Margaret's churchyard.

Seaford to Eastbourne

Seaford was once the port for Lewes, but in 1579 a storm diverted the River Ouse a couple of miles to the west where it was decided to build a new

haven called, appropriately enough, Newhaven. On the waterfront in Seaford is Tower No. 74, the western-most of the chain of round Martello Towers built in the early 19th century between Seaford and Aldeburgh in Suffolk to defend the south and east of England from invasion during the Napoleonic Wars. Martello Towers were based on the design of a small 16th-century round defensive fortress at Mortella Point in Corsica, built to defend the coastal villages from North African pirates.

East of Seaford are THE SEVEN SISTERS, a series of undulating chalk cliffs running between Seaford and Eastbourne. Just to be confusing there are eight peaks and seven dips in between them, so perhaps the correct name for the cliffs should be the Eight Brothers, although, of course, sailors tend to give things female names. The cliffs are brilliantly white as they are unprotected from erosion and are often used by film-makers to represent the

less pristine White Cliffs of Dover which, being protected because of the harbour beneath, tend to be streaked green with vegetation.

At the foot of the easternmost peak is BIRLING GAP, another smuggling haunt now served by a café, and up on the cliff beyond that is Britain's most famous inhabited lighthouse BELLE TOUT, a decommissioned lighthouse now used for what is perhaps England's most spectacularly located Bed and Breakfast. The lighthouse was operational from 1834 until 1902, after which it was sold off as a private house. In 1986 Belle Tout starred in the BBC series *The Life and Loves of a She-Devil* and also appeared in the 1987 James Bond film *The Living Daylights*. In 1999, because the foundations were becoming threatened by the erosion of the cliffs the lighthouse was moved bodily 56 feet (17 m) inland, using a pioneering technique involving greased concrete rails.

East of Belle Tout is THE HIGHEST CHALK SEA CLIFF IN BRITAIN and perhaps the most famous chalk headland of them all, BEACHY HEAD, named by the Normans a 'Beau Chef' or beautiful headland. The cliff drops almost sheer 534 feet (163 m) down to the sea, where stands one of England's most photographed lighthouses, the 142 foot (43 m) high red-and-white striped Beachy Head

lighthouse which took over from the Belle Tout lighthouse in 1902.

Pevensey

Pevensey Castle, standing inland now on what was once a peninsula jutting out from the Sussex coast, was England's front door and its weakest link. It was here that William the Conqueror landed on 28 September 1066 at the start of the last successful invasion of England.

In the 3rd century the Romans put a fort here called ANDERIDA, one of their chain of forts built along the south coast to fend off the Saxons, and the remains of the Roman walls enclose 10 acres (4 ha).

When the Normans arrived they erected the first Norman fortification on English soil here, a temporary wooden fort built within the Roman walls to establish a beach-head. This was later turned into a mighty stone castle by the Conqueror's half-brother

Robert de Mortain, who also refurbished the Roman fortifications. The castle was in a strategically vital position, guarding the entrance to Pevensey's natural harbour, and was consequently occupied by subsequent kings who wanted to prevent anyone else with invasion in mind following in the footsteps of the Conqueror.

THE FIRST KNOWN LETTER WRITTEN IN THE ENGLISH LANGUAGE was sent from Pevensey Castle by LADY JOAN PELHAM in 1399, during the reign of Richard II. It was written to her husband Sir John Pelham, Constable of Pevensey, who was in exile with Richard's rival for the throne Henry Bolingbroke (later Henry IV) and had left his wife to defend Pevensey against the King's men while he helped Henry gather his forces to mount a challenge to Richard. In the letter Joan writes to her husband that she hopes he is safe and sings off, 'Written at Pevensey, in the castle ... by your own poor J. Pelham.'

After being fortified against the threat of the Spanish Armada in 1588, Pevensey Castle was neglected for over 350 years but was suddenly reoccupied during the Second World War after the fall of France, because Pevensey was still such an obvious landing place for the invading Germans, despite now being a mile inland.

Today, Pevensey Castle, where England's history was twice written, sleeps once more, this time under the benevolent eye of English Heritage.

The lovely village that grew up beside the castle contains a 13th-century church, a medieval mint house, successor to the mint set up by William the Conqueror, and ENGLAND'S SMALLEST TOWN HALL, THE TUDOR COURT HOUSE.

Bexhill-on-Sea

Few people would credit Bexhill-on-Sea as the BIRTHPLACE OF BRITISH MOTOR RACING, but it is. In 1902 the 8th Earl De La Warr who, along with his father, was responsible for developing Bexhill into a fashionable resort, organised THE FIRST MOTOR RACE EVER SEEN IN BRITAIN, THE GREAT WHITSUNTIDE MOTOR RACE, to be run along Bexhill's Bicycle Boulevard, which he had laid out along the seafront. Since the Earl owned the land it was exempt from the national speed limit of 14 mph and the race was won by Frenchman Léon Serpollet, who reached a speed of 54 mph in his steam car, Easter Egg. Bexhill would go on to host motor races until 1907, when THE WORLD'S FIRST PURPOSE-BUILT MOTOR RACING CIRCUIT was opened at Brooklands in Surrey.

Bexhill already had a racy reputation, since the previous year Bexhill beach had become the first beach in Britain to allow – shock horror – mixed bathing.

De La Warr Pavilion

Bexhill is famous today for one of the best loved and most photographed art deco buildings in the world, the seafront De La Warr Pavilion. Opened in December 1935 it was almost the first major Modernist public building in Britain, pipped only by Hornsey Town Hall which was opened five weeks earlier. The De La Warr Pavilion is often used for filming dramas requiring a 1930s setting such as ITV's *Poirot*, starring David Suchet, and was the scene of reggae singer Bob Marley's first UK appearance – appropriate enough considering that the reggae artist's

great-grandfather, Frederick, was born along the coast in Rye, in 1820.

Although much admired today, the De La Warr Pavilion hasn't always had such good write-ups. This is how comedian Spike Milligan, who served in the Pavilion when it was used by the military during the Second World War, described it in his book *Adolf Hitler: My Part in His Downfall*: '... a fine modern building with absolutely no architectural merit at all. It was opened just in time to be bombed. The plane that dropped it was said to have been chartered by the Royal Institute of British Architects with Hugh Casson at the controls and John Betjemen at the bombsight.'

Hastings

High on a crag above the narrow streets of Hastings's delightful Old Town, full of half-timbered and weather-boarded houses, sits HASTINGS CASTLE, THE FIRST NORMAN CASTLE IN ENGLAND. In 1066 William the Conqueror landed along the coast at Pevensey, established a small wooden fort there and then marched to Hastings, where he built a wooden motte and bailey castle as a base from where to set out for the battle that would win him the throne of England. In 1070 the castle was rebuilt in stone, but from the 13th century on

suffered various mishaps, much of it falling into the sea as the soft sandstone cliffs collapsed, being burned by the French, stripped of its stone during the Dissolution of the Monasteries and bombed during the Second World War. The few fragments that remain are hugely evocative of a pivotal moment in England's history and the site provides spectacular views.

The castle is accessible by the WEST HILL LIFT, a funicular railway 500 feet (152 m) long that runs largely in a tunnel and climbs 170 feet (52 m) to a café near the castle. Further east, on the other side of the Old Town, is the EAST CLIFF LIFT, THE STEEPEST FUNICULAR RAILWAY IN BRITAIN, with a gradient of 78 per cent. The twin towers of the lift's upper station once held water used to operate the cars which originally worked on the water balance principle (*see* Lynton, North Devon).

At the bottom of the East Cliff Lift is THE STADE, a shingle beach where EUROPE'S LARGEST BEACH-LAUNCHED FISHING FLEET is based. Here can be found Hastings's unique net shops, tall, tar-blackened wooden sheds used for storing the fishermen's nets. They are built so tall because the beach used to be much smaller and there was limited space – each shop has two or three floors.

If Bexhill saw the birth of British motor racing then Hastings saw the birth of television. In 1923, in his rooms at 21 Linton Crescent, Scotsman JOHN LOGIE BAIRD succeeded in transmitting shadowy images of a man's hand using a cardboard disc cut out of a hat box, a tin plate, a bicycle lamp lens, sealing wax and some darning needles. Thus were the first television pictures made. The following year, 1924, as his experiments became more sophisticated, Baird moved to the upper floor of 8 Queen's Avenue but was soon asked to leave after an unfortunate incident involving 12,000 volts that flung the budding genius across the room and fused the whole building.

After a scuffle outside on the pavement with his irate and unsympathetic landlord a lightly burned Baird gathered up his stuff and returned in dudgeon to London. In 1941, having given television to the world, he returned to the south coast, to a house by the railway station in Bexhill, where his life flickered out in 1946.

Hastings is the only one of the five original Cinque Ports in Sussex. All the others, New Romney, Hythe, Dover and Sandwich, are in Kent. Cinque ports originated in Saxon times and were basically ports that were given special privileges by the monarch in return for supplying ships and men in times of war.

Well, I never knew this
about
THE SUSSEX COAST

PAGHAM HARBOUR was the 'sleepy lagoon' of composer ERIC COATES's work 'By the Sleepy Lagoon', famous as the signature tune for Radio Four's *Desert Island Discs*. Coates (1886–1957) lived in Selsey and was inspired by the view across the harbour to Bognor Regis.

'Away to sweet FELPHAM, for Heaven is there,' wrote the artist and poet WILLIAM BLAKE, who lived in the village for three years from 1800 to 1803 while illustrating the poems of a local squire called William Hayley. Felpham has now been subsumed by Bognor Regis but still retains a village atmosphere, and the thatched, brick-and-flint cottage where Blake lived and began the poem that would become 'Jerusalem' is still standing, near the Fox Inn.

Composer SIR HUBERT PARRY (1848–1918) lived along the coast in RUSTINGTON from 1881 until his death and there wrote the music for Blake's 'Jerusalem'.

LITTLEHAMPTON can boast THE LONGEST BENCH IN BRITAIN. Made from painted hardwood slats recovered from coastal groynes and other sources, the bench was unveiled in 2010, can seat three hundred people and runs for over 350 yards (324 m) along the Promenade, bending around bins and lamp-posts on the way.

OSCAR WILDE wrote his last and most popular play, *The Importance of Being Earnest*, while staying in WORTHING. The plot was inspired by an article in the *Worthing Gazette* about a baby who had been found in a hamper at King's Cross station. It took him just 21 days to write the play, which he later described as 'the best I have ever written', and he even named his hero Jack Worthing after the town.

Between Worthing and Shoreham-by-Sea, standing on the side of the downs to the north are two of the most remarkable religious buildings in Britain, separated by less than a mile in distance but by almost a thousand years of history. The Saxon ST MARY'S CHURCH AT SOMPTING has a church tower dating from around 1020 topped by a Rhenish Helm roof, similar to towers found in the Rhineland but unique in Britain.

A mile to the east is LANCING COLLEGE CHAPEL, THE LARGEST SCHOOL CHAPEL IN THE WORLD. Ninety feet (27 m) tall, it is also has one of the tallest vaulted interiors of any church in Britain. Work on the chapel began in 1868 and stopped in 1977 with the completion of the rose window, 32 feet (9.8 m) in diameter and THE LARGEST ROSE WINDOW IN ENGLAND. The French Gothic style of the chapel is the same as that of Arundel Cathedral, which had been built along the coast not long before Lancing was started, and the appearance is remarkably similar. The original vision was for a 300 foot (90 m) high tower on the north side but this plan has been quietly dropped.

THE DUKE OF YORK PICTUREHOUSE in Brighton opened in 1910 and is the oldest unaltered purpose-built cinema still in use in Britain.

PEACEHAVEN, a planned seaside town founded in 1915 on the cliffs between Brighton and Newhaven, is where the Greenwich (Prime) Meridian crosses the south coast. Standing on the exact spot on the cliff top is a monument celebrating the Silver Jubilee of George V, who was on the throne when Peacehaven was being built. Inscribed on the monument are the distances from here to some of the major towns and cities of the British Empire.

Standing across the road from the Royal Victoria Hotel in St Leonard's, west of Hastings, is the Conqueror's Stone, said to be the very stone on which William the Conqueror ate his first meal in England, after marching to Hastings from his landing place at Pevensey.

Lancing College Chapel

CHAPTER THIRTEEN
KENT COAST

Romney Marsh to the Isle of Sheppey
100 miles

Highlights of the Kent coast include the largest expanse of shingle in Britain, the home of Dr Syn the Scarecrow, Britain's largest ossuary, the last new pleasure pier to be built in Britain, the tallest surviving Roman building in Britain, Britain's first concentric castle, the landing place of three invasion forces, the world's first international hoverport, the world's first Gothic Revival domestic home, the largest Wetherspoon in Britain, Britain's oldest scenic railway, the world's first purpose-built freestanding clock tower, the oyster capital of Britain and the birth-place of British aviation.

Romney Marsh

'The world is divided into Europe, Asia, Africa, America and Romney Marsh,' wrote the Revd Richard Barham, a local Victorian rector, in *The Ingoldsby Legends*. Romney Marsh is certainly a world apart, some 100 square miles of windswept, low-lying wetland, ditches and dykes, marsh and meadow, much of it reclaimed from the sea and protected by long shingle banks. The ubiquitous Romney Marsh sheep that brought wealth to the Marsh villages are well adapted to the damp ground as their hooves are resistant to foot rot and they thrive in the harsh windy conditions, making them valuable for exporting all over the world. The Marsh was also popular with smugglers, known as 'Owlers' for the eerie call they made when communicating with each other, and many of the churches and inns have secret rooms where contra-band was hidden.

Dungeness

Desolate Dungeness, the southernmost point of Kent and one of the driest places in England, is THE LARGEST EXPANSE OF SHINGLE IN BRITAIN and one of the largest such expanses in the world, some 5,500 acres (2,225 ha). An important nature reserve, it is home to over six hundred types of plant and many types of insect unique to Britain. There has been a lighthouse on the point since 1615 and now there are no fewer than three. The base of the third lighthouse erected on the point, by Samuel Wyatt in 1792, has been turned into accommodation; the fourth light-house, 135 feet (41 m) high and built in 1904, is now a visitor attraction with spectacular views; while the fifth, which was put up in 1961, is still active and can throw its beam 17 miles.

Dungeness is scattered with isolated homes and quirky cottages, some made from old railway carriages, lived in by fishermen and those who want to get away from it all. Perhaps the most famous resident was film director DEREK JARMAN, who lived in PROSPECT COTTAGE, a tiny black clap-board bungalow on the beach, until his death in 1994. Lines from 'The Sun Rising', a poem by John Donne, are embossed on one side of the house, and the director's garden, full of salt-loving plants and features lovingly created out of driftwood and debris from the shore, flourishes all around it on the shingle, preserved just as he left it.

This truly feels like the end of the world, and all of it lives in the menacing shadow of the Dungeness Nuclear Power Station, whose great square blocks loom south of the point. There are two stations, 'A', built in 1965 and closed in 2006, and 'B', opened in 1983 and licensed to operate until 2028.

Lydd

Lydd, on the edge of Dungeness, is the most southerly town in Kent and the proud possessor of the longest church in Kent, All Saints, 200 feet (61 m) long and known as the Cathedral of the Marsh. The 15th-century tower, 132 feet (40 m) high, is one of the tallest in Kent and is a prominent landmark for shipping in the Channel. All Saints stands on an ancient spot, and incorporated into the church is the original 5th-century Romano-British basilica that occupied the site.

Lydd seems an unlikely place to have an international airport but it does. BRITAIN'S FIRST PRIVATE AIRPORT, LYDD AIRPORT, was opened in 1954, the first airport to be built in Britain after the Second World War. By the end of the 1950s, by virtue of being the nearest airport to France, it was one of the busiest airports in the country. While no longer quite such a major hub, the airport operates scheduled services to Le Touquet and is able to handle passenger jets up to the size of a partially loaded Boeing 737 or Airbus A319. A new, longer runway is planned.

New Romney

New Romney, the capital of Romney Marsh, is one of the original five Cinque Ports and used to be a harbour town sitting at the mouth of the River Rother. The sea that once lapped at the feet of the town's glorious Norman church tower is now over a mile away.

The church tower, one of the finest Norman towers in England, is 100 feet (30 m) high and 32 feet (9.8 m) square, is decorated with 50 windows and arches and still has a mooring ring attached.

New Romney's seafront now belongs to the resorts of LITTLESTONE and GREATSTONE, whose names recall the days when vessels would enter Romney Harbour between two shingle beaches with different sized stones – thanks to longshore drift those on the Greatstone (south) side were bigger than those on the Littlestone (north) side. Littlestone Golf Course was a favourite of Denis Thatcher, husband of Prime Minister Margaret Thatcher.

Almost on the beach by the golf course is ROMNEY BAY HOUSE, built in the 1920s by CLOUGH WILLIAMS-ELLIS, creator of Portmeirion in North Wales, as a holiday home for the American actress and journalist HEDDA HOPPER. She holidayed here during her acting years before she became the Queen Bee of Tinseltown, for 30 years writing a syndicated gossip column for the *Los Angeles Times* that could make or break the careers and marriages of Hollywood stars. The house is now a fine hotel.

ST MARY'S BAY, not so long ago the tiny hamlet of Jesson, was the home for many years of children's author EDITH NESBIT, best known for her novel *The Railway Children*. She is buried in the churchyard of ST MARY'S IN THE MARSH, a mile inland. NOËL COWARD, who in his younger days lived in a cottage next to THE STAR INN in St Mary's in the Marsh, and wrote some of his early works there, was a great fan of Edith and the two became good friends. It is even alleged that Coward died with a copy of Edith's *The Enchanted Castle* beside his bed.

Dymchurch

Dymchurch lies 7 feet (2.1 m) below sea level and is protected from the tide by the Dymchurch Wall, an immensely strong sea wall that runs for 4 miles between St Mary's Bay and Hythe. It was begun by the Romans as a shingle barrier which was then reinforced with faggots and clay in the 13th century. In 2011 a completely new wall was built to defend the town and the Marsh against the expected rising sea levels. The complex drainage system of Romney Marsh has been run from Dymchurch from the 13th century until quite recently by a committee known as the Lords of the Level, who sat in the court room in New Hall which stands opposite the Norman church in the north of the village. This lovely old building dates

from 1575 and is now a museum. The Drainage Board is now headquartered in Rye.

Dymchurch has three Martello Towers, Nos 23, 24 and 25. Tower 23 has been converted into a private residence. In 1969 Tower 24 became the first Martello Tower to be opened to the public and is now a museum. Tower 25 is maintained but remains empty, and it was from Tower 25 that the first V1 flying bomb to reach England was spotted by the Observer Corps.

In the 18th and 19th centuries Dymchurch was at the centre of a number of smuggling rings and was redolent with the calls of the Owlers, their exploits immortalised in Russell Thorndike's novels about Dr Syn, who was vicar of Dymchurch by day and 'Scarecrow', leader of a gang of smugglers, by night. The 1964 Disney film of the novels, starring Patrick McGoohan as the Scarecrow, was filmed at Dymchurch and other places on Romney Marsh, with the beautiful isolated church of St Clement at Old Romney doubling as Dr Syn's own church in Dymchurch.

Hythe

Hythe, the Old English for 'haven', was the central one of the Cinque Ports. In fact, there are two Hythes, the Victorian seafront Hythe and the medieval and Georgian Hythe on the hill. Overlooking them both from a commanding position is the magnificent 11th-century parish church of St Leonard. In the vaulted ambulatory below the chancel is a huge ossuary or bone store, adorned with a thousand grinning skulls set on shelves along the walls and a large stack of some eight thousand neatly piled thighbones. They are the mortal remains of people who lived in the period between William the Conqueror and the Tudors and were probably put here when the graveyard was cleared for the various extensions to the church. This is ONE OF ONLY TWO SURVIVING OSSUARIES IN ENGLAND and by far the largest. The other is at Rothwell in Northamptonshire.

At the western end of the High Street on the hill is the old malthouse of the Hythe Brewery, which was founded in 1669. In 1801 the brewery was taken over by the Mackeson family, and in 1907 they began brewing the MACKESON'S MILK STOUT for which the company became known. The first beer to use milk sugar, each pint was said to contain as much energising carbohydrate as ten ounces of full fat milk. Mackeson's Stout is still brewed, but now by Hydes, in Salford, and the Hythe Malthouse has been converted into an antiques centre.

A plaque above a chemist in the High Street marks the birthplace in 1808 of SIR FRANCIS PETTIT SMITH, the inventor of the marine screw propellor which would replace the paddle wheel previously used by steamships. It was the screw propellor that made possible the great transatlantic liners, such as Isambard Kingdom Brunel's SS *GREAT BRITAIN*, THE FIRST IRON STEAMER TO CROSS THE ATLANTIC.

As a boy, Smith experimented with boat propulsion on the ROYAL MILITARY CANAL which runs through Hythe, separating the old town on the hill from the Victorian seafront. The canal was built between 1805 and 1809 and runs from Hastings to Folkestone

along the old cliff line above Romney Marsh and was designed as a means to stop the French using the low-lying marsh as a beach-head from where to launch in invasion during the Napoleonic Wars.

For a long time Hythe was defended by two castles, Saltwood and Lympne, situated on the hills above the town. SALTWOOD CASTLE, essentially a Norman castle that has been expanded over the centuries, was owned by the Archbishops of Canterbury from after the Norman invasion until the time of Henry VIII. The four knights who murdered Thomas Becket in 1170 met at Saltwood Castle before riding to Canterbury Cathedral to carry out their evil deed. Having been allowed to ruin, the castle was restored as a private house in the 19th century by an ancestor of BILL DEEDES, the only person to have been both the editor of a major daily newspaper (the *Daily Telegraph*) and a Member of the Cabinet, who grew up there. It was later bought by the art historian SIR KENNETH CLARK, presenter of the seminal BBC television series *Civilisation*, and passed on to his son the MP and diarist ALAN CLARK. Today it is still the home of his widow Jane.

LYMPNE CASTLE was built in the 11th century for the Archdeacons of Canterbury. It stands on the cliffs above Romney Marsh and during the Second World War served as an invaluable lookout post, as from the castle it was possible to see the explosions as V1 rockets were launched from Calais. The information was relayed to the gunners along Hythe Bay, who were then able to shoot down many of the rockets as they approached the English coast.

Dover

The Gateway to England

Dover, chief of the Cinque Ports, stands where the River Dour breaks through the famous white cliffs that for centuries have symbolised home for returning English folk. This is the end of the North Downs and of the North Downs Way, which starts 153 miles away at Farnham in Surrey. Stone Age men and Iron Age men have all defended this gateway and the Romans built a harbour here. THE PHAROS, a huge 80 foot (24 m) tall octagonal stone tower, much of which still stands on the headland in the grounds of Dover Castle, was their lighthouse. What is left reaches 40 feet (12 m) in height, THE TALLEST SURVIVING ROMAN BUILDING IN ENGLAND. The Romans left us another treasure, too, the magnificent ROMAN PAINTED HOUSE in the town centre, built in the 2nd century with walls covered by THE OLDEST PAINTINGS EVER DISCOVERED IN BRITAIN.

Dover Castle

The Key to England

In the early 11th century the Saxons built a church, ST MARY IN CASTRO, beside the Pharos. Then William the Conqueror built a castle on the same headland, and in 1180 Henry II expanded this into the first concentric castle in England, with at its centre one of the largest and most powerful keeps of any English castle. During the reign of King John a series of tunnels was dug underneath the castle to help defend it against the French, and these were expanded in the early 1800s during the Napoleonic Wars.

The tunnels under Dover Castle were used again the Second World War, in 1940, as the headquarters of Operation Dynamo, the evacuation of Dunkirk.

Also during the Napoleonic Wars a GRAND SHAFT was built into the cliffs of the Western Heights on the other side of the town from the castle. This consisted of two concentric hollow brick cylinders 140 feet (43 m) high sunk into the chalk, with three inter-linked spiral staircases of two hundred steps set between them. The three stair-cases enabled three detachments of soldiers from the barracks at the top of the cliff to get down to the beach swiftly

Dover's Channel Firsts

On the lawn at the eastern end of the Promenade there is a bust of
CAPTAIN MATTHEW WEBB, THE FIRST PERSON TO SWIM THE
CHANNEL. In 1875 he swam from Calais to Dover in a time of 21
hours and 45 minutes.

In the woods on top of the eastern cliffs east of the castle a memorial
in the shape of an aeroplane marks the spot where in 1909 LOUIS
BLÉRIOT crash landed after making THE FIRST FLIGHT ACROSS THE
CHANNEL IN A HEAVIER-THAN-AIR MACHINE. He took 37 minutes in
a Blériot Type XI monoplane he had designed himself – the memorial
is in the shape of that plane.

Back down on the lawn at the eastern end of the Promenade, a couple
of hundred yards west of the Webb bust, is a statue of CHARLES
ROLLS of Rolls-Royce fame, who in 1910 became THE FIRST MAN TO
FLY THE CHANNEL IN BOTH DIRECTIONS NON-STOP.

and simultaneously in the event of an attack. THE GRAND SHAFT, THE ONLY TRIPLE SPIRAL STAIRCASE IN BRITAIN, is open to the public at certain times from March to November.

Walmer Castle

Walmer Castle is the southernmost of three coastal forts built by Henry VIII in the shape of the Tudor Rose. Built to defend the Kentish Downs, it was only used as a fort until the beginning of the 18th century when it was modified for use as the official residence of the Lord Warden of the Cinque Ports, an important post dating from the 12th century that eventually became an honorary title bestowed by the Sovereign on members of the Royal Family or former Prime Ministers. WILLIAM PITT THE YOUNGER held the post from 1792 until 1806 and it was in the drawing room at Walmer that Pitt met Nelson for the first time, in 1801. In October 1805, just before the Battle of Trafalgar, Pitt sat on the terrace of Walmer Castle with the American inventor ROBERT FULTON watching a demonstration of Fulton's new 'torpedo', which Fulton was trying to persuade Pitt to buy for use against Napoleon's navy. Despite the fact that two torpedoes succeeded in blowing up a brig anchored offshore, the victory at Trafalgar a few days later meant that the Royal Navy no longer needed newfangled gadgets and Fulton returned home to concentrate on building America's first successful commercial steamboat.

THE DUKE OF WELLINGTON was Lord Warden of the Cinque Ports from 1829 to 1852 and in fact died at Walmer Castle in 1852. Wellington's apartments have been left much as he would have known them, including not just the room where he died but the camp bed in which he expired. Also to be seen are one of the original pairs of Wellington boots worn by Wellington himself, along with a note to his boot-maker George Hoby on how to cut them correctly.

Other well-known Wardens were SIR WINSTON CHURCHILL, from 1941 to 1965, and the QUEEN MOTHER, from 1978 to 2002. The present incumbent is ADMIRAL OF THE FLEET MICHAEL BOYCE.

Deal

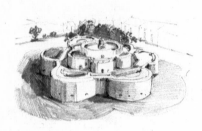

Lacking a sandy beach, Deal never became a resort town and retains a beautiful unspoiled Georgian seafront. It is thought that Julius Caesar landed on the coast somewhere near here when he came and saw and conquered, but the coast has changed much since 55 BC and no one can be sure exactly where. At the southern end of the town is Deal Castle, the largest of Henry VIII's three Tudor Rose castles, which is open to the public as a museum.

Equally intriguing is Deal's TIME BALL TOWER, converted in 1855 from a semaphore tower used for communicating with London or for passing messages along the coast. At a few minutes before 1 p.m. every day the black time ball on top of the tower would be raised to the top of the mast and then dropped, triggered by a signal from the Royal Observatory, at 1 p.m. precisely. The provided an accurate time check for the ships at anchor in the Downs, the stretch of water between Deal and the Goodwin Sands 5 miles offshore. The Tower is now a museum and the time ball is still activated in a regular basis.

Sandwich

Sandwich is the northernmost of the original Cinque Ports but, like New Romney, is no longer by the sea but 2 miles inland. Now a place of eerily timeless medieval streets, it was once a major port on the south bank of the WANTSUM CHANNEL, which cut the Isle of Thanet off from the rest of Kent and was a major shipping route linking the River Thames and the English Channel. When the Wantsum silted up in the 17th century Sandwich was left high and dry – the last ship to dock there was in 1672 – and was never developed as either an industrial town or a resort town, leaving it as ONE OF THE BEST PRESERVED MEDIEVAL TOWNS IN BRITAIN, most of it still contained within its medieval walls.

Sandwich may seem an unobtrusive place, but the name of this 'market town on the sand' is known and used around the world, thanks to the 4TH EARL OF SANDWICH, JOHN MONTAGU, FIRST LORD OF THE ADMIRALTY. There are many stories of how the Earl gave his name to a humble foodstuff beloved everywhere. Depending on who you listen to, he was either gambling at the Shakespeare's Head tavern in Covent Garden or working at his desk in the Admiralty; either way he was too busy to stop for a proper meal, so he asked his servant to 'just bring me a piece of meat between two bits of bread'. Others saw what he was eating and liked the look of it. 'Bring me what Sandwich is having,' they cried, and so the sandwich was born – some have called it Britain's biggest contribution to world gastronomy. The word 'sandwich' has also become part of the English language, meaning to be squeezed in from both sides.

Sandwich is also known internationally for the ROYAL ST GEORGE'S GOLF CLUB, a links course set on the sand dunes between Sandwich and the sea. In 1894 it became the first club outside Scotland to host the Open Championship and today it is the only golf course in Southern England on the rota of Open Championship venues. It has hosted 13 Opens to date. The Royal St George's is the best known of three golf courses located on this stretch of coastline, the others being The Royal Cinque Ports Golf Club and the Prince's Golf Club, both former Open Championship venues.

Isle Of Thanet

The Isle of Thanet, at the southeastern tip of England, was a real island until the late 17th century, separated from mainland Kent by a 2 mile wide stretch of water called the WANTSUM CHANNEL. For the Romans this became an important shipping route and they built a fort at each end to protect it, Richborough at the eastern end and Reculver at the western end. The channel continued to be a major shipping highway into the Middle Ages, providing a safe passage from the River Thames to the English Channel, but by the end of the 17th century the Wantsum had silted up, leaving Thanet no longer an island. The course of the Wantsum Channel is still roughly traced by the River Stour to the south and the River Wantsum, no more than a ditch, to the north.

Richborough Castle

The huge Roman fort of Richborough Castle marks both the beginning and the end of Roman rule in Britain. It was here, on the west bank of the Wentsum Channel, that the Romans landed when they invaded in AD 43. And it was from here that the legions went home again, to protect Rome from the barbarians, early in the 5th century. The invaders of AD 43 established a beach-head at Richborough, which they called Rutupiae, constructing a huge square earthwork, later reinforced in stone. From here they began Watling Street, the road to London, THE FIRST PAVED ROAD EVER SEEN IN BRITAIN. In AD 85 they raised a huge triumphal arch above it, 80 feet (24 m) high and covered in marble, the foundations of which can still be seen amongst the impressive remains of the 3rd-century fort the Romans later built at Richborough as part of the chain of forts raised to defend the Saxon Shore. For four hundred years Richborough was BRITANNIA'S GREATEST PORT, but after the Romans left it sank into oblivion until 1,500 years later, in 1914, the Saxon Shore was threatened once again and a vast secret harbour was constructed at Richborough to handle supplies for Britain's army fighting in France during the Great War. After the war the harbour was dismantled and disappeared completely, leaving just the Roman ruins.

Pegwell Bay

Pegwell Bay, wide and shallow with a flat sandy shoreline, is thought to have been the site of three landings pivotal to England's history.

In 55 BC JULIUS CAESAR landed at what is now the hamlet of EBBSFLEET and established a small defensive fort there. He returned to the fort the following year, 54 BC, and set out from there to confront the armies of defending Britons. Although Caesar left without defeating the Britons he arranged a series of treaties with the leaders of the various British tribes, essentially making them client kings of Rome, and these treaties were exploited almost a century later in AD 43 when the Emperor Claudius sent an invasion force to Britain. Caesar's fort at Ebbsfleet has recently been discovered and the site is undergoing further excavations.

In AD 449, at the behest of King Vortigern of Kent, who needed help fighting the Picts and the Scots, the Germanic chiefs HENGIST and HORSA landed on the shores of Pegwell Bay to begin the Anglo-Saxon invasion of England. On the top of a low cliff at the north end of the bay sits a full-size replica Viking longboat, the *Hugin*, which was sailed across the English Channel by a Danish crew in 1949 to celebrate the 1,500th anniversary of the landing.

In AD 597, ST AUGUSTINE landed at Ebbsfleet at the start of his mission to convert the heathen Saxons to Christianity. This event is marked by a stone cross erected in 1884 a few hundred yards inland on the site of Augustine's Oak, the tree under which Augustine is said to have met King Ethelbert of Kent, and nearby is St Augustine's Well, the stream where St Augustine baptised Ethelbert.

Easily identifiable down on the shore below the Viking longship are the last vestiges of THE WORLD'S FIRST INTERNATIONAL HOVERPORT, which opened in 1969 to handle hovercraft services to Calais. These came to an end in the 1980s and the hoverport was eventually demolished, leaving just the weed-strewn concrete base of the slipway and marshalling yard.

Ramsgate

Ramsgate is the southernmost of the trio of seaside resorts that line the chalk cliffs on the eastern edge of the Isle of Thanet, and the only one that faces south. Fine Georgian, Regency and Victorian terraces form a picturesque backdrop to ENGLAND'S ONLY ROYAL HARBOUR, an accolade bestowed by George IV in 1821 to thank the folk of Ramsgate for their welcome when he passed through the port on his way to and from Hanover. While in Ramsgate the king stayed with his friend SIR WILLIAM CURTIS, a biscuit manufacturer known as Sir Billy Biscuit. Despite his success in baking biscuits Sir Billy was almost illiterate and thought that Reading, Writing and Arithmetic all began with 'R', thus coining the phrase 'the Three Rs'. An obelisk, affectionately known as the Royal Toothpick, was raised in front of the harbour in 1822 to commemorate the King's visit. Ramsgate's Royal Harbour was the main assembly point for the fleet of small boats that helped in the evacuation of Dunkirk in 1940 during the Second World War. The Royal Harbour

The Grange

has now been transformed into one of Britain's largest marinas, while a new harbour built on reclaimed land to the west serves cross channel traffic.

On the cliff above the newer harbour is THE GRANGE, built in 1844 as a family home by AUGUSTUS PUGIN, who pioneered the Gothic Revival style of architecture and was responsible for the design of the clock faces of Big Ben and much of the interior of the Houses of Parliament. The Grange is Victorian Gothic and is an important building as it marked a new style of domestic architecture, away from the prevailing Georgian style, influencing many of the architects of the Victorian era. Pugin died in the house in 1852, aged just 40, and is buried in St Augustine's Church next door, which he built and financed himself. The Grange is now owned by the Landmark Trust and is used for holiday lets.

Broadstairs

The most sedate of Thanet's three resorts, Broadstairs is closely associated with CHARLES DICKENS, who described the town as 'our English watering place'. He often visited Broadstairs in the 1830s and

40s and wrote *David Copperfield* while staying at FORT HOUSE, a large castellated house built in 1801 on the cliff overlooking the sands of the town's main beach. Because of its association with Dickens, the house, which stands on the site of an old battery, became known as Bleak House and the name stuck. Today the house is run as both a wedding venue and a museum. On Victoria Parade, a little further south above the beach, is the DICKENS HOUSE MUSEUM, located in the cottage on which Dickens based the home of Betsey Trotwood in *David Copperfield*.

Margate

An easy day trip from London, Margate is the oldest and most traditional of the three resorts and has been a holiday destination for Londoners since 1753, when the bathing machine was invented by a local Quaker, BENJAMIN BEALE.

Margate has always had 9 miles of sandy beach. It has a Norman church. It did have an original Eugenius Birch pleasure pier built in 1856 but this was destroyed by a storm in 1978. It still has two famous theatres, THE TOM THUMB, which is THE SECOND

SMALLEST THEATRE IN BRITAIN, and the Theatre Royal, which dates from 1787 and is THE SECOND OLDEST THEATRE IN BRITAIN. In 1885 the School of Acting, BRITAIN'S FIRST FORMAL ACTING SCHOOL, was set up at the Theatre Royal by the then manager SARAH THORNE.

The origins of Margate's DREAMLAND amusement park down by the beach go back to 1880 when a carousel was set up on the site. Dreamland's wooden scenic railway was built in 1920 and is now THE OLDEST SCENIC RAILWAY IN BRITAIN, and the second oldest scenic railway in the world.

Like Deal, Margate has a Time Ball Tower. In Margate's case the time ball is located on top of the town's Victorian clock tower, built in 1887 to celebrate Queen Victoria's Golden Jubilee. The Time Ball is dropped at precisely 1 p.m. each day, one of the few remaining active Time Balls in the world.

Margate's newest seafront attraction and a key part of the town's regeneration scheme is the TURNER CONTEMPORARY, an art gallery designed to provide a space for contemporary visual arts. It commemorates Margate's association with the artist J.M.W. Turner, who attended school in Margate and made regular visits throughout his life, claiming that the Isle of Thanet had 'the loveliest skies in Europe'. Margate had another attraction for Turner too – the gallery is built on the site of the boarding house where he used to stay, the Rendezvous guest-house run by his mistress Sophia Booth.

Margate's most mysterious attraction is THE SHELL GROTTO, ten minutes' walk from the beach, at the back of an ordinary souvenir shop. The grotto is a gently descending underground passageway and chamber covered from wall to ceiling with a mosaic of some 4.6 million delicately painted sea shells of every kind, mostly from the local area. The grotto was discovered in 1835 but no one knows when it was built or who built it. Or why.

Reculver

The tall, unusual and remarkably intact twin towers of Reculver's medieval church standing starkly above Herne Bay are a marvellous sight and a useful landmark for shipping. The Romans built a fort here in the 1st century to

guard the western entrance to the Wantsum Channel and strengthened it in the 3rd century as part of their defence of the Saxon Shore. When the Romans left, the Saxons took over the site and in AD 669 King Egbert of Kent built a monastery and a church there, which became so important that King Edbert II of Kent was buried in the church in AD 760. In the 12th century the church was remodelled by the Normans and the twin towers were built, to which spires were added in the 13th century. By the 19th century the church was threatened by coastal erosion and demolished. The towers, however, minus their spires, were saved by Trinity House because they were such an essential navigational aid, and groynes were placed along the beach below to try and mitigate the erosion.

Whitstable

Whitstable is THE OYSTER CAPITAL OF BRITAIN and has been since Roman times. The annual Whitstable oyster festival is amongst the largest in Europe.

Whitstable was also at one end of THE WORLD'S FIRST REGULAR STEAM FREIGHT AND PASSENGER RAILWAY SERVICE, which opened between Canterbury and Whitstable on 3 May 1830. THE CANTERBURY AND WHITSTABLE LINE, which soon became known as the Crab and Winkle Line, was built so that goods and passengers arriving at Whitstable's newly extended harbour from London could be carried on to Canterbury by rail rather than on a slow and expensive turnpike. The line pioneered a number of innovations including THE FIRST PASSENGER RAILWAY TUNNEL, which was run under Tyler's Hill just outside Canterbury, and in 1834 the line

introduced THE WORLD'S FIRST SEASON TICKET for citizens of Canterbury who wanted to go to Whitstable on a regular basis, either for business or for the weekend. The line closed in 1952 and there is no trace of it in Whitstable, but part of the disused trackway has been turned into a footpath and the blocked-up entrances to the Tyler Hill tunnel can still be seen.

Isle of Sheppey

The Isle of Sheppey is where Britain learned to fly. In 1909 the Aero Club of Great Britain, which became the Royal Aero Club, the UK's national co-ordinating body for air sports, built BRITAIN'S FIRST AERODROME on the marshes south of Leysdown on Sea. The land was perfect for experimental flying, being flat, windy, near to London and close to the sea if they needed to make a crash landing. Their clubhouse was an adjacent 16th-century house called MUSSEL MANOR. Amongst the first to use the aerodrome were the three SHORT BROTHERS, HORACE, EUSTACE AND OSWALD, who built THE WORLD'S FIRST AIRCRAFT FACTORY next to the aerodrome, where they could manufacture six Wright flyer aircraft for which they had obtained a licence from the Wright Brothers.

On 2 May 1909, JOHN BRABAZON, who housed his Voisin aircraft in one of Short's hangars, flew it for 1,500 feet (450 m) at a height of 35 feet (11 m) over the Leysdown fields, completing THE FIRST POWERED FLIGHT BY A BRITISH PILOT IN BRITAIN. The following year he would become BRITAIN'S FIRST OFFICIAL PILOT, being awarded Pilot's Licence No 1.

In the same week in 1909 that Brabazon flew the first flight the WRIGHT BROTHERS, ORVILLE AND WILBUR, came to visit the Short factory, being driven down from London in the very first Rolls-Royce Silver Ghost by Charles Rolls. On 4 May 1909 Brabazon, the Short Brothers, the Wright Brothers and Charles Rolls were all photographed together standing outside the Aero Club clubhouse at Mussel Manor – the picture can be seen on the wall at Mussel Manor (now Muswell Manor) which is open to the public as a bar and restaurant and is a fascinating place for anyone interested in the history of aviation.

Short Biplane No. 1 was built for Charles Rolls. Short Biplane No. 2 was built for John Brabazon, and it was in this aircraft that on 30 October 1909 he became the first Englishman to fly a circular mile in a British aircraft, circling for almost 2 miles above Mussel Manor.

In November 1909 the Short Brothers moved their factory to Eastchurch, a couple of miles further inland. These buildings have since become Sheppey Prison.

Well, I never knew this about
THE KENT COAST

In the churchyard of ST LEONARD'S CHURCH in HYTHE is the gravestone of LIONEL LUKIN, who in 1785 converted a Norwegian yawl into THE WORLD'S FIRST 'UNSINKABLE' LIFEBOAT.

Hythe is the southern terminus for the ROMNEY, HYTHE & DYMCHURCH RAILWAY, which runs for 13½ miles between Dungeness and Hythe along a 15-inch (381-mm) gauge track. It was THE SMALLEST PUBLIC RAILWAY IN THE WORLD until 1982, when the Wells and Walsingham Light Railway opened with a 10¼-inch (260-mm) track.

During the Second World War the Romney, Hythe & Dymchurch Railway was requisitioned for the war effort and one of the railway's many duties was to patrol the line in a specially built armoured train – THE ONLY MINIATURE ARMOURED TRAIN IN THE WORLD. The line was reopened after

the war in 1947 in a special ceremony led by legendary duo Laurel and Hardy.

THE CHANNEL TUNNEL, at just over 31 miles long, is the third longest railway tunnel in the world, and has THE LONGEST PORTION UNDERWATER OF ANY TUNNEL IN THE WORLD.

SHAKESPEARE CLIFF, just west of Dover, marks where the Channel Tunnel leaves the English coast. The cliff is so called because it features in Shakespeare's *King Lear* (Act IV, Scene VI) when Edgar is describing the scene to his blind father Gloucester, '... how fearful and dizzy 'tis to cast one's eyes so low ...'

At the foot of the white cliffs of ST MARGARET'S BAY, just north of Dover, is a row of 1930s art-deco houses that were once owned by the playwright NOEL COWARD and his family and friends. The properties are right on the beach with the sea lapping at their walls and Coward bought the end house in 1945 as a quiet retreat from his hectic life in London. He called it WHITE CLIFFS and, in order to preserve his privacy, persuaded his mother and a couple of friends to buy the other houses. Amongst the friends he invited down to stay at White Cliffs were Gertrude Lawrence, Daphne du Maurier, Spencer Tracy and Katharine Hepburn.

In 1951 Coward sold White Cliffs to his friend the author IAN FLEMING, who set his James Bond novel Moonraker in Deal, a little to the north of St Margaret's Bay. Fleming entertained his fellow authors Somerset Maugham and Evelyn Waugh at White Cliffs, and also liked to play golf at ROYAL ST GEORGE'S, up the coast at Sandwich (see Sandwich). Royal St George's becomes Royal St Mark's in the Bond novel Goldfinger and is where the famous golf match between Bond and Goldfinger takes place. In 1964 Fleming was elected captain of Royal St George's but had a heart attack during a committee meeting at the club in August of that year and died the next day in Canterbury.

DEAL PIER, 1,026 feet (31 m) long, was opened in 1957, THE LAST NEW PLEASURE PIER TO BE BUILT IN BRITAIN.

Standing next to the Obelisk between the harbour and the beach in Ramsgate is the ROYAL VICTORIA PAVILION, built in 1904 as a concert hall and assembly rooms, and now transformed into THE LARGEST WETHERSPOON PUB IN BRITAIN.

HERNE BAY'S landmark CLOCK TOWER, designed in the style of a Grecian temple with a clock on top and standing 85 feet (26 m) tall including the weather-vane, was built in 1837, and was THE FIRST PURPOSE-BUILT FREE-STANDING CLOCK TOWER of its kind in the world.

FAVERSHAM is home to BRITAIN'S OLDEST BREWER, SHEPHERD NEAME, which was founded in the town in 1698.

SHEERNESS DOCKYARD was originally constructed in 1655 under the supervision of diarist Samuel Pepys when he was Charles II's Secretary of the Admiralty. Sheerness was the base of the Royal Navy's Nore Command, responsible for protecting the waters of the North Sea, and in 1797 it was the site of the Nore Mutiny when sailors went on strike for better pay and conditions.

CHAPTER FOURTEEN
ESSEX COAST

Southend to Harwich
60 miles

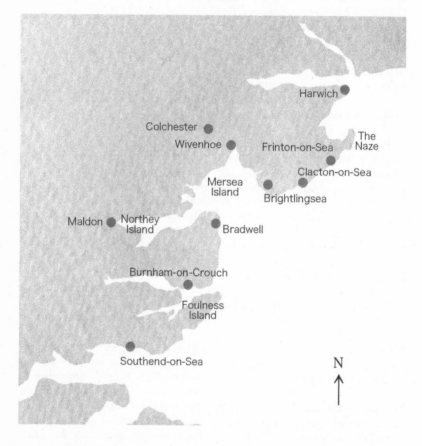

The coastline of Essex, made up of a myriad of inlets, creeks, lagoons, salt marshes, oyster beds, lonely islands and solitary backwaters, all punctuated by busy yachting havens and cheerful, bustling resorts with sandy beaches, is 350 miles long, THE LONGEST COASTLINE OF ANY ENGLISH COUNTY. Much of it is natural, unspoiled and untouched, the haunt of wildfowl and big skies, wind and water, its great allure the contrasts of solitude and exuberance, natural beauty and man-made entertainment. Highlights include the longest pier in the world, the most perilous byway in England, the oldest unrestored church in England, the oldest recorded battlefield in Britain, Britain's only triangular church tower, the grave of George Washington's last English ancestor, the largest surviving Norman keep in Europe, the last town in Britain to have a pub, Britain's only treadwheel crane, the birthplace of modern America and the oldest timber-framed building in England.

We begin with one of Britain's brightest, brashest and most cheerful resorts ...

Southend-on-Sea

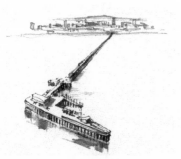

Southend, the nearest seaside resort to London, is actually the south end of Prittlewell, a quiet village that grew up around a Cluniac priory founded in the 12th century. Originally just a few fishermen's huts, Southend started to grow in the 1790s when a terrace of houses and a hotel were put up as the first phase of a new town designed to attract wealthy Londoners looking for sea air. When Caroline of Brunswick, the wife of the Prince Regent, came to stay in 1804, the terrace and hotel were named 'Royal' and fashionable society soon followed. Getting to Southend was difficult, though, and development rather stalled until the railway arrived in 1856, when Victorian houses and hotels were built everywhere, leaving Royal Terrace as the only surviving Georgian terrace in Southend.

Southend now has all the trappings of a proper seaside resort, with funfairs, amusement parks, a bandstand, a cliff railway and, its crowning glory, THE LONGEST PLEASURE PIER IN THE WORLD. One and a half miles long, the pier was begun in 1889 and extended in 1898 to accommodate the steamers bringing day-trippers from London. It was extended to its full record length in 1929 in order to reach water deep enough to take boats that were becoming ever larger – when the tide recedes off Southend it leaves over a mile of mudflats, and if boats could not discharge their passengers at Southend they would continue on to Margate. A small diesel train runs to and from the pier, where there is a lifeboat station and a modern pavilion used for theatre and art exhibitions.

Foulness Island

At just over 9,000 square miles, Foulness Island is the largest island in Essex and the fourth biggest island off the English coast. Since 1911 it has been owned by the Ministry of Defence and is used for weapons testing, hence is closed to the public except on open days, usually the first Sunday of every month between April and October. Even the few residents on the island, around 160 people mostly living in the island's two villages, CHURCHEND and COURTSEND in the north of the island, need a pass to get home. And it's not just the military who test here. The highest point on the island is just 6 feet (1.8 m) above sea level and is topped by the sparse remnants of HILL HOUSE, the first brick building on the island. It was here that former land speed record holder RICHARD NOBLE tested the jet engine of his Thrust II car, which went on to become THE FIRST CAR EVER TO BREAK THE SOUND BARRIER.

The target of most of the military testing is MAPLIN SANDS, a vast area of mudflats off the southeastern coast of Foulness Island. Maplin Sands was the eventual site of THE FIRST SCREW-PILE LIGHTHOUSE ever designed, although it was not the first to be erected; that was the Wyre screw-pile lighthouse off the coast of Fleetwood in Lancashire. In the 1970s there was a plan to build London's third airport on Maplin Sands but this was eventually ruled out because of the threat of bird strikes. The clue is in the name – Foulness comes from the old English 'fulga naess' meaning 'wild bird's nest', and the whole area is one of the most prolific in Europe for migrating and breeding bird life.

Before the military built a bridge to the island the only way of getting there was on foot along one of the oldest paths in Britain, THE BROOMWAY, a 6 mile prehistoric tidal pathway along a ridge of firm sand through Maplin Sands that was once marked out by 'brooms', bundles of twigs and sticks attached to a pole. Since the military bridge requires a permit, the Broomway is still the only way for members of the public to access Foulness Island and it is still a public right of way, although it has been described as 'the most perilous byway in England', as it disappears beneath the water at high tide and the tides come in faster than a man can run. There are also frequent mists, which can be very disorientating, and there have been over a hundred recorded deaths since 1600, and probably many more that no one knows about.

Burnham on Crouch

Burnham on Crouch is the largest settlement on the Dengie Peninsula, which

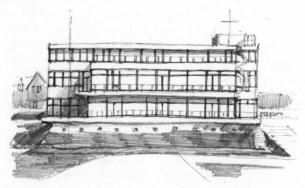

Royal Corinthian Yacht Club

lies between the River Crouch in the south and the Blackwater to the north. It is a former oyster port that has become one of Britain's most popular yachting centres, earning the nickname 'the Cowes of the East Coast', and every August holds an annual regatta known as Burnham Week, which dates back to 1893. The fine Georgian High Street is overlooked by a jolly Victorian octagonal clock tower, erected in 1877, shaped like a lighthouse with a lantern at the top. Down on the quayside is one of the few examples in Britain of the International style of architecture developed in the 1920 and 30s, the clubhouse of the ROYAL CORINTHIAN YACHT CLUB. It was designed by JOSEPH EMBERTON in 1931 and was Britain's contribution to the International Exhibition of Modern Architecture held at the Museum of Modern Art in New York City in 1932. Burnham is renowned for its large number of pubs.

Bradwell

At the northeast tip of the Dengie Peninsula, on the site of the Roman fort of Othona, is ST PETER'S CHAPEL at Bradwell, THE OLDEST UNRESTORED CHURCH IN ENGLAND and one of the oldest 20 intact buildings in the whole country. The chapel sits all on its own on the seashore east of Bradwell-on-Sea and was built to mark the spot where St Cedd landed in AD 654 on his mission to convert the East Angles to Christianity. This was one of the biggest buildings in Britain when it was put up. Using materials from the ruined Roman fort, the Saxons created what was to all intents and purposes a cathedral, 50 feet (15 m) long, 22 feet (7 m) long and 25 feet (8 m) high. The people of this part of Essex worshipped here for six hundred years or more, but so remote was the spot that the congregation dwindled away and the chapel eventually passed out of knowledge – which is probably how it survived untouched. The church ended up serving as a farmer's barn until, in 1920, a passing rambler noticed the noble proportions, the round window high up in the wall, the arches and the gables. He started to look around and realised he was looking at something wondrous. This was sacred ground. The hay bales and the horse carts were removed and St Peter's was revealed and restored to its former purpose. Services are held once a week and for special occasions.

Northey Island

Northey Island sits in the middle of the Blackwater estuary just east of Maldon and now belongs to the National Trust. It has just one permanent resident, a caretaker who looks after a tower house that is available for holiday lets. The island is connected to the mainland by a causeway that disappears beneath the tide twice a day and has a special place in history. In AD 991 a powerful force of some four thousand Danes landed on the island with a mind to plundering Maldon, but when the tide ebbed they found the causeway defended by an Essex nobleman called Earl Byrhtnoth and a small army of Saxons. A bitter fight ensued and both the Earl and the

Norse leader were killed, but it ended in victory for the Danes and the payment of the first Danegeld, a tax levied by King Ethelred the Unready to raise funds for paying off the Norsemen. The site of THE BATTLE OF MALDON, the causeway from Northey Island, is THE OLDEST RECORDED BATTLEFIELD IN BRITAIN.

Maldon

Maldon, from where comes Maldon Sea Salt, is one of only two Saxon towns in Essex, the other being Colchester. It was also the subject of one of the oldest English poems, '*The Battle of Maldon*', which celebrates the heroic death of Earl Byrhtnoth. ALL SAINTS CHURCH, which dates from before 1170, has THE ONLY TRI-ANGULAR CHURCH TOWER IN BRITAIN. It also has a memorial window to George Washington's last English ancestor, LAWRENCE WASHINGTON, who is buried in the churchyard in an unmarked grave. He was the great-great-grandfather of the first President of the United States of America.

In 1696 an energetic non-conformist minister named JOSEPH BILLIO arrived in Maldon and acquired a parcel of land on Market Hill where the United Reform Church now stands. He built a meeting house and here preached fervent, impassioned sermons, full of gusto, to audiences of four hundred or more. Such was his enthusiasm that his name passed into the language, 'like billio' meaning with great zest and energy.

Mersea Island

Mersea Island is BRITAIN'S MOST EAST-ERLY INHABITED ISLAND. It was one of the first ever British holiday resorts, being a playground for Romans living in Colchester, somewhere they could indulge in the local oysters which were considered to be the only good thing to come out of Britannia. There are two communities, built-up WEST MERSEA, which has a Norman church, a jetty and one of Britain's first inshore lifeboat stations, and straggling EAST MERSEA, also with a Norman church. Rector here from 1870 to 1881 was SABINE BARING-GOULD who wrote the hymns 'Onward Christian Soldiers' and 'Now the Day is Over', the latter apparently composed to fit with the chimes of the bells of West Mersea's church, which he could hear drifting over the fields. In the churchyard at East Mersea there is an unusual 'mortsafe' grave, that of SARAH WRENCH, who died when she was 15 years old. A 'mortsafe' grave is one that is covered with a protective cage to guard against grave robbers and such graves are more commonly found in Scotland.

Colchester

Colchester is THE OLDEST RECORDED TOWN IN BRITAIN and, as Camulodunum, was the first Roman town in Britain and its first capital. The Balkerne Gate, through which the

road from Londinium entered the town, was built in AD 70 and was 107 feet (33 m) long and 27 feet (8.2 m) high. It is THE LARGEST AND BEST PRESERVED ROMAN GATEWAY IN BRITAIN. It originally had four arched entrances and was THE ONLY FOUR-ARCHED ROMAN GATEWAY FOUND IN BRITAIN. It was built to keep the town safe after it had been reduced to ashes by Boadicea, although the Roman capital was moved to Londinium.

After the Romans left, the Saxons gave the town its modern name of Colchester, which means 'the Roman fortress on the River Colne', and in the 11th century the Normans constructed COLCHESTER CASTLE on top of the Roman temple of Claudius, with THE LARGEST SURVIVING NORMAN KEEP IN EUROPE. Even having been reduced from four storeys to two the keep is enormous and covers one and a half times the ground space of the White Tower of the Tower of London.

On the south side of the town are the impressive remains of THE FIRST AUGUSTINIAN RELIGIOUS HOUSE IN BRITAIN, ST BOTOLPH'S PRIORY, which was founded in 1100.

And Colchester could be described as the birthplace of electricity. In the heart of the town is the beautiful old half-timbered TYMPERLEYS, built in 1490 by courtier John Tymperley and later the home of WILLIAM GILBERT (1544–1602), scientist and physician to Elizabeth I and inventor of the word 'electricity'.

The Sunshine Coast

The coastline of the Tendring Peninsula, named after the village at its centre, and bounded by the Colne River to the south and the Stour to the north, is known as the Sunshine Coast. The three main resorts of the Sunshine Coast are Clacton-on-Sea, Frinton-on-Sea and Walton-on-the-Naze.

CLACTON-ON-SEA is the biggest and liveliest of the three resorts. CLACTON PIER, although only 1,170 feet (357 m) long, covers an area of some 6½ acres (2.6 ha) and consequently is THE LARGEST PIER IN ENGLAND IN TERMS OF AREA. When it was constructed in 1871 as a landing stage for goods and day-trippers this set in motion a building spree of hotels, boarding houses and amusement parks as the original villages of Little Clacton and Great Clacton spread to the seafront.

Where Clacton is the young Victorian rake, FRINTON-ON-SEA is the Victorian *grande dame*. The cliff-top Greensward is overlooked by sedate Edwardian villas and quite a few surprisingly daring art deco houses, but there are no seafront amusement arcades or candy-floss emporiums or souvenir shops, no pier, no cyclists even. Indeed, Frinton was THE LAST TOWN IN BRITAIN TO HAVE A PUB, and that wasn't until 2000 when the Lock & Barrel opened to much harrumphing and dismay. Frinton, you see, was developed in the 1890s by entrepreneur RICHARD POWELL COOPER, using the proceeds from the world's first effective sheep dip (invented by his family company), as a 'high-class and select watering place'. He was determined that Frinton would not follow the same vulgar, cheap and cheerful 'fish and chip' path as Clacton but would be somewhere that the Quality would wish to visit. In this he was successful. The Prince of Wales (later Edward VII) was a frequent visitor, especially to the golf course, and Connaught Avenue, Frinton's main shopping street, known as 'the Bond Street of East Anglia', was named after another frequent visitor, the Prince's brother The Duke of Connaught.

The most select part of Frinton developed between the sea and the railway, with the manually operated wooden level-crossing gates on the only road into town acting as a dividing line between the Quality and those from the 'wrong side of the tracks'. In 2009 these iconic gates were demolished by Network Rail, overnight and in secret, after a three-year campaign to save them. Despite all the setbacks Frinton still looks and feels very different from its neighbours and has managed somehow to retain its dignified atmosphere.

WALTON-ON-THE-NAZE, a mix of Clacton's brashness and Frinton's decorum, has the third longest pier in Britain, 2,600 feet (790 m) in length. It was opened in 1895 and has been extended a number of times since.

Harwich

Harwich is Britain's second busiest passenger ferry port. The narrow streets of the town were laid out in the 13th century and the old part of the town still retains its medieval grid pattern layout. Harwich provides the only safe anchorage between London and the Humber and has played an important part in England's maritime heritage at least since 1340, when Edward III assembled his fleet here before sailing off to victory against the French at the Battle of Sluys, the first big naval conflict of the Hundred Years War. Frobisher, Drake and Raleigh all sailed from here.

Harwich is as important to the New World as to the old. It was a Harwich man, CHRISTOPHER NEWPORT, christened in St Nicolas Church in 1561, who captained the fleet that established Jamestown, the first permanent European settlement in the New World. And it was a Harwich man, CHRISTOPHER JONES, born in the town in around 1570 and twice married in St Nicholas Church, who captained the *Mayflower*, which carried the 102 pilgrims who established the second permanent European settlement in the New World at Plymouth in what is now Massachusetts in 1620. Christopher Jones, who lived at 21 King's Head Street, in a house that is still there, purchased the *Mayflower* in 1608 and it was while on a trip down the Thames to London in her that he was commissioned to take the pilgrims to America. In fact, the *Mayflower* became the Pilgrim Fathers' first American home, because they lived on the ship for over six months after arriving in America while they built their new settlement. When the *Mayflower* returned to England in April 1621 she was scrapped for timber, some of which was used in the construction of the Mayflower Barn at Jordans in Buckinghamshire, and it was said that the letters of the name Harwich could long be made out on one of the beams.

Harwich became a naval base in the 17th century, with the diarist Samuel Pepys, Secretary of the Admiralty for Charles II, as the town's MP. Recalling those days, down on the green by the harbour is THE ONLY TREADWHEEL CRANE IN BRITAIN, built in 1667. The crane was used for lifting stores and ammunition and was powered by two men walking in the middle of the treadwheel.

To the south of the green is the HARWICH REDOUBT, a circular fort 180 feet (55 m) in diameter, the most formidable fortification on the Essex coast. The redoubt was built in the early 19th century to supply and support the Martello Towers running from Suffolk to Sussex as part of a chain of fortifications to defend the southeastern coast of England against invasion during the Napoleonic Wars. It is the only example of a supply fort open to the public.

Nearby, at either end of the green, are two brick lighthouses built in 1818 by John Rennie the Elder, designer of the London Bridge now in Arizona. The LOW LIGHTHOUSE on the waterfront is 45 feet (13.7 m) high and is now a Maritime Museum, while the HIGH LIGHTHOUSE, just inland and 90 feet (27 m) high, houses a private wireless museum. The two lighthouses worked together as leading lights, one seen above the other from the sea pointing the way into the harbour.

At the end of King's Head Street is the quaint Ha'penny Pier, which used to cost a halfpenny to enter and was where steamships once left for the Continent. The bigger ships now leave from Parkeston, on the Stour to the west, but the ferry to Felixstowe still goes from the Ha'penny Pier.

Well, I never knew this about

THE ESSEX COAST

In 1884 WIVENHOE was at the epicentre of THE WORST EARTHQUAKE EVER RECORDED IN ENGLAND, the 1884 Colchester Earthquake, which damaged over two hundred buildings, including the church, although the church's Norman tower with its quaint 18th-century cupola stood firm.

Surrounded by water on three sides, BRIGHTLINGSEA was an important port in the Middle Ages and the only associate member of the Cinque Ports outside Kent and Sussex. An associate member, sometimes known as a limb, can contribute to the ship quota of a main Cinque Port in return for certain privileges. Brightlingsea is a limb of Sandwich and, in an annual ceremony, the town council still swear allegiance to the Mayor of Sandwich. JACOB'S HALL in Brightlingsea High Street was built in the 14th century and takes its name from the man who built it. It is thought to be THE OLDEST TIMBER-FRAMED BUILDING IN ENGLAND.

THE NAZE is a headland of salt marsh and rapidly eroding cliffs reaching a height of 70 feet (21 m). At the highest point of the Naze is the NAZE TOWER, an 86 foot (26 m) high octagonal tower built

in 1721 by Trinity House as a landmark navigational aid for shipping heading along the flat, featureless coast towards Harwich. During the 18th century the tower was home to a tea house run by actress MARTHA REAY, mistress of the eponymous Earl of Sandwich; it has served as a wartime lookout and as one of the first radar stations in the Second World War. It is now open to the public and has a viewing platform at the top reached by a climb of 111 steps.

ST NICHOLAS CHURCH in HARWICH, where Christopher Jones was twice married, was rebuilt in 1821 with THE FIRST CAST-IRON PILLARS EVER USED IN A CHURCH.

THE ELECTRIC PALACE CINEMA on King's Quay Street in Harwich was built in 1911 and is THE SECOND OLDEST UNALTERED CINEMA IN ENGLAND STILL IN USE, retaining not just its ornamental frontage but its silent screen and original projection room as well.

CHAPTER FIFTEEN
SUFFOLK COAST

Felixstowe to Lowestoft
50 miles

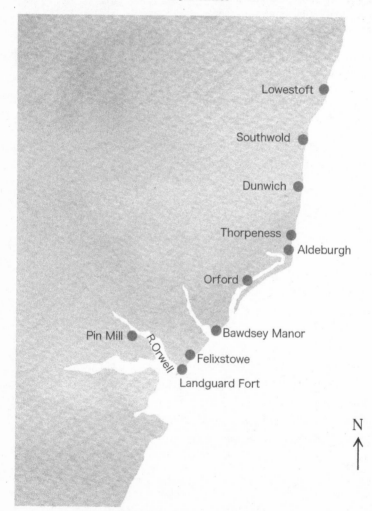

Lowestoft

Southwold

Dunwich

Thorpeness

Aldeburgh

Orford

Pin Mill

Bawdsey Manor

R. Orwell

Felixstowe

Landguard Fort

N

The Suffolk coastline suffers from the highest rate of erosion of any county coastline. Highlights include Britain's largest container port, the site of the first land battle fought by the Royal Marines, the first fully operational radar station in the world, a unique polygonal castle keep, the largest and most northerly Martello Tower, a House in the Clouds, the Atlantis of England, the finest medieval church of any seaside town in England and Britain's easternmost point.

Felixstowe

Felixstowe began life as a small village standing on the site of the 11th-century Benedictine priory of St Felix and developed into a resort at the beginning of the 20th century. The seafront is largely Edwardian. The pier was built in 1905 and at 2,640 feet (805 m) long was one of the longest piers in Britain. It was shortened during the Second World War and then rebuilt at the shore end in 2017 to become Britain's newest pier.

In 1882 a harbour was constructed west of Felixstowe town on the north bank of the River Orwell and this has grown into BRITAIN'S LARGEST CONTAINER PORT handling cargoes from more than four hundred ports around the world.

South of the container port, on the spit of land at the mouth of the Orwell across from Harwich, is the LANDGUARD FORT, built on the orders of James I to defend the Harwich approach. In what would turn out to be the last seaborne invasion of England the fort was attacked by the Dutch in 1667 in an attempt to clear the way for an attack on Harwich, the nearest safe anchorage on the east coast to London, which the Dutch were already blockading. The attack on the fort was repulsed by men of the Duke of York and Albany's Maritime Regiment of Foot, later known as the Admiral's Regiment, who had been formed three years earlier in 1664 as the first official unit of English naval infantry, making THE BATTLE OF LANDGUARD THE FIRST LAND BATTLE TO BE FOUGHT BY THE ROYAL MARINES. The current fort dates from the 18th century, with additions of the 19th and 20th centuries, and was continuously occupied through both world wars and until 1956, when it was disarmed and closed.

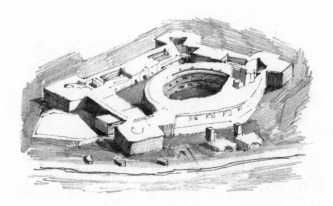

South of the fort at Landguard Point is a nature reserve, and a ferry runs from View Point, near the fort, to the Ha'penny Pier in Harwich during the summer months.

North of Felixstowe is the FELIXSTOWE FERRY GOLF CLUB, founded in 1880 and the fifth oldest golf club in England. Captain in the early days was ARTHUR BALFOUR, Prime Minister from 1902 to 1905. During the Second World War the golf course was used as a launch site for Operation Outward, when thousands of balloons carrying incendiary devices or trailing wires designed to cause short circuits in power lines were released into the air to be carried to Germany by the prevailing winds.

Bawdsey Manor

Bawdsey Manor, a vast Victorian redbrick confection of Elizabethan-style turrets and towers and gables set almost on the beach on the north bank of the River Deben, across from Felixstowe Ferry, was the unlikely home of THE FIRST FULLY OPERATIONAL RADAR STATION IN THE WORLD.

The house was built in 1885 by SIR WILLIAM CUTHBERT QUILTER a stockbroker, MP and co-founder of the National Telephone Company. In 1936 Bawdsey was bought by the Air Ministry and turned into a top secret research station where a team led by Scottish physicist ROBIN WATSON-WATT, a descendant of James Watt, inventor of the steam engine, worked on developing the new RADAR technology. The stables and outbuildings were converted into workshops and 360 foot (110 m) tall steel transmitter towers were erected along with 240 foot (73 m) tall wooden receiver towers. In 1937 Bawdsey began operation as the first station in the network of coastal early warning radar stations known as CHAIN HOME, THE WORLD'S FIRST OPERATIONAL RADAR SYSTEM.

At the outbreak of the war Bawdsey was considered vulnerable and the scientific team was moved to Dundee in Scotland, but the manor was retained as an RAF base, latterly as a Bloodhound surface-to-air missile base, until 1991 when it was a closed. It became a school and it now provides school activity courses.

Orford

Orford, today not much more than a small village of attractive houses grouped around a square, was once an important port, second only to Ipswich in Suffolk. It was slowly cut off from the sea by the gradual build-up of Orford Ness, THE LARGEST VEGETATED SHINGLE SPIT IN EUROPE, now 10 miles in length and 13 feet (4 m) high, which diverted the River Ore southwards.

Orford Castle was built by Henry II between 1165 and 1173 and is the oldest castle in Britain for which documentary evidence exists. It was the first royal castle in Suffolk and was intended to consolidate his dominion over the powerful East Anglian nobles such as Hugh Bigod, Earl of Norfolk. The Bigods, described by Suffolk writer Julian Tennyson as 'about the roughest brood ever hatched in England', came across with William the Conqueror and saw themselves as kings of East Anglia, in constant conflict with the monarch of the day. Their name has passed into the language as 'bigot' meaning a 'person intolerant to any views other than his own'.

England on account of its design, which consists of a 90 foot (27 m) high circular central tower buttressed by three slightly taller rectangular towers and a lower integral gatehouse. The keep sits on a low mound within the scant remains of a curtain wall and outer defences.

From the rooftop of the castle it is possible to see the 'pagodas' out on Orford Ness where BRITAIN'S FIRST NUCLEAR WEAPON, BLUE DANUBE, was developed and tested in the 1950s. Orford Ness has a long history of top secret military use. From 1915 onwards it was used to test aviation weaponry from bombs to fighter machine-guns and night flying techniques. Then in 1935 it was used for early radar experiments before the team moved south to Bawdsey Manor. In the 1960s missile warheads were tested at Orford, but in 1971 atomic weapons research was moved to Aldermaston in Berkshire and the area was decommissioned and cleared of munitions before being acquired by the National Trust in 1993.

Aldeburgh

The remarkably intact polygonal keep of ORFORD CASTLE is unique in

A prosperous port and fishing village since the Domesday Book, Aldeburgh is now more famous for its annual Music Festival founded by BENJAMIN BRITTEN in 1948 and held in the

SNAPE MALTINGS, 5 miles to the west on the River Alde.

The town's oldest building is the wonderfully quaint half-timbered Tudor MOOT HALL on the seafront. When it was built in 1520 it was in the centre of the town, but much of the old Aldeburgh that surrounded it has been washed away by the sea.

South of the town on the shingle isthmus between the River Orde and the sea is the northernmost of the 103 Martello Towers that stretch around the southeast coast from Seaford in Sussex to Aldeburgh. The Aldeburgh Martello is the largest Martello Tower and the only one to be designed as a quatrefoil. It is also the only surviving building from the village of Slaughden, which was washed away by the North Sea. It is now owned by the Landmark Trust and available for holiday lets.

On the beach at the north end of the town is *Scallop*, a sculpture by MAGGIE HAMBLING unveiled in 2003 that resembles two men in a sailing boat, one man in a sailing boat, a sea bird or a scallop, depending on where you are looking from. The sailing boats evoke an incident from Benjamin Britten's opera *Peter Grimes* based on a poem by local poet GEORGE CRABBE, which details the harrowing story of a Suffolk fisherman of that name.

ALDE HOUSE, a Georgian house opposite the church in Aldeburgh, was the home of NEWSON GARRETT, a Victorian businessman who built the Snape Maltings where the Aldeburgh Musical Festival now takes place. He became Mayor of Aldeburgh, and 15 years later his eldest daughter, ELIZABETH GARRETT ANDERSON, also became Mayor of Aldeburgh and THE FIRST WOMAN MAYOR AND MAGISTRATE IN BRITISH HISTORY.

She was also THE FIRST WOMAN IN BRITAIN TO QUALIFY AS A DOCTOR, and co-founded the Elizabeth Garrett Anderson Hospital in London, the first woman's hospital staffed by women. Garrett's younger daughter MILLICENT married HENRY FAWCETT, the blind Postmaster General who introduced the post office savings bank, sixpenny telegrams, postal orders and the parcel post. Both daughters were great campaigners for women's suffrage.

On the northwest outskirts of Aldeburgh is the RED HOUSE, where Benjamin Britten lived with PETER PEARS from 1957 until the composer's death in 1976. He enjoyed the quiet location away from the seafront and wrote much of his music here. The Steinway piano on which he practised can be seen in his studio.

Elizabeth Garrett Anderson and Benjamin Britten are both buried in the churchyard of Aldeburgh's St Peter and St Paul Church.

Thorpeness

In 1910 Scottish railway baron Glencairn STUART OGILVIE bought the tiny fishing hamlet of Thorpeness and transformed it into a fairytale holiday village of pretty mock-Tudor and Jacobean houses set around the Mere, a shallow boating lake created out of the hamlet's silted-up harbour. In 1923 a 70 foot (21 m) high water-tower was built to supply water to the village and, to disguise its rather mundane appearance, the tower was clad with weatherboarding and made to look from afar like a cottage; it became known as THE HOUSE IN THE CLOUDS. In 1979, once the water-tower was no longer needed, the building was converted into a proper home which is now available for holiday lets.

Next to it stands a post windmill that was built in the next-door village of Aldringham in 1803 and was then moved to Thorpeness in the 1920s to pump the water to the House in the Clouds. Fully refurbished, the windmill is now in private hands.

Dunwich

For those who dream of lost cities, Dunwich is the Atlantis of England, recorded in the Domesday Book as one of the ten largest cities in England, capital of East Anglia, the seat of bishops and a port to rival London. Today it lies beneath the waves of the North Sea, THE LARGEST MEDIEVAL UNDERWATER 'LOST' CITY IN THE WORLD. It had 11 churches, including a round church similar to the Temple church in London – one of only four surviving round churches in England. St Peter's Dunwich was the biggest church in Suffolk. All were doomed by a terrible storm in 1286. The melancholy ruins of the 'new' Greyfriars

friary, built in 1290 after the first storm, stand stark in a field as a reminder of how Dunwich fought back. But in vain. Four more terrible storms over the next hundred years took away the defences and mighty Dunwich surrendered to the sea. Houses and churches and towers all crumbled. The Blackfriars Dominican priory succumbed in 1717.

The last church to be lost to the sea was All Saints, which finally disappeared altogether in 1922, leaving behind just a forlorn gravestone on the cliff edge – 'In memory of Jacob Forster who departed this life on March 12th 1796 aged 38 years.' A section of buttress from the church was rescued and placed beside the Victorian church of St James as a memento.

Dunwich today is a timeless place with a good inn, THE SHIP. While dining there you might perhaps fancy, just before the wind blows, that you can hear the bells of old Dunwich ringing out a ghostly warning.

Southwold

The Domesday Book records Southwold as a prosperous fishing village, but a shingle bar that built up across the harbour mouth prevented the town from developing into a major port. The elegant Georgian town of today has grown up around seven small greens which mark the site of buildings that were burned down in a bad fire in 1659 and were never rebuilt so as to provide firebreaks. Since Southwold is surrounded by water on three sides growth has been restricted and the town retains a dignified air that attracts the Quality – it is estimated that 50 per cent of the houses in Southwold are second or holiday homes.

Southwold is instantly recognisable by its iconic white-painted lighthouse, a prominent landmark surrounded by houses and right in the centre of the town. It is 101 feet (31 m) high, stands 121 feet (37 m) above sea level and its beam can be seen from 20 miles away. A rich, malty smell mingling with the salty breezes draws attention to another Southwold icon across the green, ADNAMS BREWERY, standing on a town centre site where beer has been brewed since at least 1345. George and Ernest Adnams bought what was then the Sole Bay Brewery in 1872 and the business has remained in the family ever since. Until 2006, casks of Adnams Ale were delivered to pubs around the town by horse and dray, a heart-warming sight that, alas, is seen no more since a new distribution centre was opened a few miles away.

One of the trademarks of Adnams is SOUTHWOLD JACK, a rare, 15th-century oak figure of a soldier in Wars of the Roses garb who stands at the west end of the magnificent St Edmund's Church and, at the pull of a cord, strikes a bell with his battle-axe to signal the start of special church services. St Edmund's, considered to be THE FINEST MEDIEVAL CHURCH OF ANY SEASIDE TOWN IN ENGLAND, was built in the 15th century on the site of a smaller 13th-century church that burned down. Just over 144 feet (44 m) long with a tower 100 feet (30 m) high, almost matching the lighthouse, the new church is one of the largest in Suffolk, a county renowned for huge churches, and reflects Southwold's status before the fire. Inside, roosting angels look down from the roof. A 15th-century painted rood screen, perhaps the finest in East Anglia, runs the full width of the church. The Cathedral of the Coast, perhaps?

Nearby, at the top of the High Street, is SUTHERLAND HOUSE, where James, Duke of York (later James II), set up his headquarters as High Admiral of the Fleet during the Anglo-Dutch Wars between 1665 and 1672; and it was from here that he went out, with his cousin Prince Rupert and the Earl of Sandwich, to confront the Dutch fleet off Southwold in the inconclusive Battle of Sole Bay in 1672.

While dignified, Southwold is capable of letting its hair down from time to time, and the beach is lined with colourful beach huts of every size and shape that are hugely popular and have to be booked well in advance. Southwold also smiles indulgently upon its unusual pier, which was first built in 1900 as a landing stage for steamships bringing tourists from London. Like all piers it has been damaged by storms and rebuilt over the years, but at present it stands at 620 feet (189 m) long and has pavilions running down the middle for almost the entire length which serve to keep the more vulgar and noisy seaside attractions such as slot machines and candy-floss hidden away. In 2002 a landing stage was put back at the pier-head to allow visits by Britain's only surviving sea-going steam passenger ship, the paddle steamer *Waverley*.

Guarding Southwold on Gun Hill, south of the town centre, are six cannon pointing out to sea. These were given by George II in 1746 to protect the town against pirates from Dunkirk.

Lowestoft

Lowestoft, Suffolk's second largest town, is the first town in Britain to see the sunrise, while LOWESTOFT NESS, just north of the harbour, IS THE EASTERN- MOST POINT OF BRITAIN. In 2005 flint tools over 700,000 years old were found in the cliffs in south Lowestoft, making Lowestoft THE OLDEST INHABITED SITE IN BRITAIN – at least it was until 2010 when tools 800,000 years old were found up the coast at Happisburgh.

Lowestoft is two towns, really, sepa- rated by a narrow body of saltwater called LAKE LOTHING which runs westward into Oulton Broad, part of the Broads, an area of navigable rivers and lakes formed by the flooding of former peat workings. North of Lake Lothing is the older, working part of Lowestoft, which became rich on herring fishing in the 1800s. Here is the harbour and the commercial docks, the town hall and the pretty Georgian High Street. Unique to old Lowestoft are THE

SCORES, a series of ancient, narrow stepped lanes running down from the High Street to the seafront that have been 'scoured' out over the years by people treading paths into the soft cliff- faces. Every year the town holds a Scores Race where competitors race up and the down the remaining 12 Scores, covering a distance of 5 miles and 410 steps.

South of Lake Lothing is the resort part of Lowestoft stretched out along 3 miles of sandy beach. This was largely laid out in the 19th century by SIR SAMUEL PETO, whose family firm Grissell and Peto built Nelson's Column and the Houses of Parliament amongst other projects. He brought the railway to Lowestoft in the 1840s, both to take fish to London and Manchester and to bring tourists to Lowestoft.

In 1843 Peto bought SOMERLEYTON HALL, a large Jacobean house northwest of Lowestoft, which he remodelled in Italianate style. In the 1950s SIR CHRISTOPHER COCKERELL, inventor of the hovercraft, used the lake at Somerleyton Hall to experiment with his early designs.

Lowestoft Lifeboat Station, situated on South Pier at the mouth of the outer harbour, was founded in 1801, over 20 years before the establishment of the Royal National Lifeboat Institution (RNLI), and is one of the oldest lifeboat stations in Britain.

Well, I never knew this about
THE SUFFOLK COAST

George Orwell, author of *Animal Farm* and *1984*, whose real name was Eric Blair, took his pen name from the River

Orwell. He often visited Suffolk to stay with his parents who lived in Southwold.

PIN MILL, a tiny boating haven on the Orwell estuary and home to the sublime BUTT AND OYSTER PUB, was the setting for Arthur Ransome's Swallows and Amazons tale *We Didn't Mean to Go to Sea.*

The medieval church of ST MARY'S IN BAWDSEY IS THE ONLY CHURCH IN ENGLAND KNOWN TO HAVE BEEN BURNED DOWN BY FIREWORKS. It was destroyed, all except for the tower, on Guy Fawkes Night in 1842, when boys letting off fireworks from the top of the church tower set fire to the thatched roof of the nave and chancel.

THE ONLY SURVIVING EXAMPLE OF AN EDWARD VIII WALL LETTER BOX still in use in the world can be found in the wall of the former post office in BAWDSEY.

CHAPTER SIXTEEN
NORFOLK COAST

Great Yarmouth to King's Lynn
90 miles

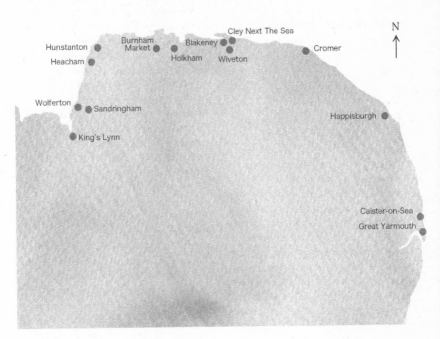

Highlights of the Norfolk coast include the oldest municipal building in England, the birthplace of the fish finger, the world's oldest football stand, the site of England's first holiday camp, the oldest site of human habitation in Britain, Albert Einstein's hiding place, Britain's first nature reserve, the home of the first farmer in England, Lord Nelson's birthplace, unique red-and-white striped cliffs and the Royal Family's favourite home.

Great Yarmouth

Great Yarmouth occupies a narrow spit of land that lies sandwiched between the River Yare and the North Sea. It flourished for over a thousand years as a fishing port, facing inwards to the safe anchorage of the river. When the Victorians bought the railway and the holidaymakers, Yarmouth turned outwards to the sea and the miles of sandy beach along the seashore. Today Great Yarmouth is a vibrant mix of both port – bound to send annually to the sheriffs of Norwich 'one hundred herrings baked in twenty four pasties' – and resort, the largest in East Anglia.

Old Town

Tollhouse

Great Yarmouth suffered quite considerably in both world wars. In the First World War, at 9.20 p.m. on the evening of 19 January 1915, YARMOUTH SUFFERED THE WORLD'S FIRST AIR RAID CASUALTIES as it became the first major town in Britain to undergo aerial bombardment, on this occasion from Zeppelin airship *L3* out of Hamburg, which dropped ten bombs and seven incendiaries, killing two people. The following year the town was bombarded from the sea by the German navy. In the Second World War, being the last significant place the German bombers could drop any remaining bombs on before returning to Germany, Great Yarmouth was heavily bombed.

Despite this, much of the old town survived, including almost a mile of the medieval town wall, which protected the town on three sides and stretched for 1¼ miles between the town and the sea from the mouth of the River Bure in the northwest to the south quay. The wall was begun in 1261 during the reign of Henry III and took 80 years to build. Because there was no building stone on the spit, the wall was made of local flints and pebbles found on the beach, which makes it all the more remarkable that the Great Yarmouth town wall is the second most complete medieval town wall in Britain, 23 feet (7 m) in height and with 11 of the original 16 turrets and towers intact.

Until the 18th century no one was allowed to build outside the wall, and the town within the wall soon became horribly overcrowded, if extremely prosperous. It was divided over time into 145 'Rows', narrow lanes, sometimes only 30 inches (76 cm) wide, that ran east to west, intersected by three long streets running north to south, resembling a medieval Manhattan. The Rows were so narrow – in some of them you could touch the houses either side with your arms outstretched – that a type of two-wheeled barrow called a troll cart had to be invented to transport goods along the alleyways. A number of the Rows survived the bombing and can be seen near the north side of the town.

A genuine survivor of the Old Town is the old stone TOLLHOUSE down by the quay. Yarmouth's coat of arms hangs on the outside wall beneath a figure of Justice, recalling that the tollhouse was also a courtroom and gaol – the dungeons can still be seen beneath. The Tollhouse dates from the 13th century and is THE OLDEST MUNICIPAL BUILDING IN ENGLAND.

SOUTH QUAY, the road that runs alongside the old harbourside on the River Yare, was described by Daniel Defoe as 'the finest key in England, if not in Europe'. It is lined with Elizabethan and Georgian merchants' houses, one of them home to the NELSON MUSEUM, the only museum solely dedicated to Nelson in Britain. Down on the south seafront is the NORFOLK PILLAR, the first of the Nelson's Columns, erected in 1817 as a memorial to the Admiral, who landed back in Great Yarmouth after his victories at the Battle of the Nile in 1798 and the Battle of Copenhagen in 1801. On receiving the Freedom of Great Yarmouth after the Battle of the Nile, Nelson put his left hand on the Bible. 'Your right hand, my lord,' said the clerk. 'That,' replied Nelson, 'is in Tenerife.' Atop the 144 foot (44 m) high Doric column stands a figure of Britannia facing towards Nelson's birthplace at Burnham Thorpe, 50 miles northwest. The pillar is open on occasion for those prepared to climb the 217 steps to the viewing platform at the top.

Great Yarmouth's minster church of ST NICHOLAS was founded in 1101. It was rebuilt and added to over the centuries and greatly restored by the Victorians before being almost completely destroyed by bombing during the Second World War. It was reconstructed and reopened in 1961 and vies with Holy Trinity in Hull to be THE LARGEST PARISH CHURCH IN ENGLAND.

In contrast to its Elizabethan and Georgian Old Town, Great Yarmouth's seaside town is Victorian and Edwardian. And a lot more frivolous. As well as miles of sandy beach Yarmouth's 'Golden Mile' seafront offers the second oldest wooden rollercoaster in Britain (after Margate), built in 1928 and found in the Pleasure Beach at the south end of the waterfront. There are two piers, neither of which actually reaches the sea, the WELLINGTON PIER, which was first opened in 1853, and the BRITANNIA PIER, which was first opened in 1858 and has one of Britain's few surviving end-of-the-pier theatres, the BRITANNIA THEATRE.

Next to the Wellington Pier are the WINTER GARDENS, a vast palace of glass and cast iron which was built in Torquay in 1878 and later shipped to Great Yarmouth without a pane of glass being broken, and reconstructed on the seafront. THE LAST SURVIVING SEASIDE VICTORIAN CAST-IRON AND GLASS WINTER GARDENS IN BRITAIN, this is currently one of the most endangered buildings.

Just back from the seafront is the Hippodrome Circus, THE ONLY FULL-TIME CIRCUS LEFT IN BRITAIN.

Caister-on-Sea

The name Caister, meaning camp, or castle, refers to a Roman fort built here in about AD 200 that became a supply base for subsequent Roman forts built later in the 3rd century to defend the Saxon Shore.

ENGLAND'S FIRST HOLIDAY CAMP was founded at Caister-on-Sea in 1906 by socialist and former grocer JOHN FLETCHER DODD, who so enjoyed Caister when he visited on holiday that he bought a house on the front. He pitched some tents in the garden and invited some poor working families from London's East End to come and join him for a week or so beside the seaside. It proved so popular that Dodd started building wooden accommodation huts and people came from all across the country. Within ten years there were beach huts, a shop, sports facilities, entertainments, a communal dining hall and opportunities for bus trips, picnics and rambles. Dodd ran his camp according to strict socialist rules; Rule No. 12, for instance, prohibited 'intoxicants, gambling, rowdy conduct and improper language'. Everyone had to pitch in with the cooking and cleaning, lights out at 11 p.m. It was not until the 1960s that these rules were relaxed, having helped give rise to the popular impression of regimented holiday camps.

Socialist worthies such as George Bernard Shaw, Herbert Morrison, George Lansbury and Keir Hardie were amongst those who indulged in the delights of Caister, and the camp eventually spread to over 100 acres (40 ha). It was sold by the family after the Second World War and is now a Haven Holiday Park.

Happisburgh

During the 20th century Happisburgh, or Hazeboro as the inhabitants call it, lost over 50 acres (20 ha) of land to the sea as its soft cliffs, a mixture of sand, silt and gravel, eroded. One positive of this erosion is the uncovering of some remarkable archaeological finds. In 2010 tools said to be 800,000 years old were discovered on the beach, making Happisburgh the THE OLDEST SITE OF HUMAN HABITATION IN BRITAIN. In 2013 the oldest human footprints ever discovered outside the Great Rift Valley of Africa, 850,000 years old, were uncovered on the same site.

Happisburgh's strikingly banded red-and-white lighthouse, built in 1790 and the oldest working lighthouse in East Anglia, stands in the middle of fields and is presently about 600 feet (180 m) back from the cliff edge. The tower is 85 feet (26 m) high while the lantern is 134 feet (41) above sea level. The lighthouse is run by a local trust and is THE ONLY INDEPENDENTLY OPERATED LIGHTHOUSE IN BRITAIN. It is open to the public on occasional Sundays in summer.

Cromer

The magnificent Perpendicular tower of Cromer's church of ST PETER AND ST PAUL stands 160 feet (49 m) high, THE TALLEST CHURCH TOWER IN NORFOLK.

CROMER PIER, like Great Yarmouth's Britannia Pier, has one of Britain's last remaining end-of-the-pier theatres.

Coxswain of Cromer's lifeboat from 1909 to 1947 HENRY BLOGG, along with his crew, saved a record 873 people during his years of service.

Cromer is best known today for its crabs, considered the best crabs in Britain because of the shallow water and mud-free chalky seabed off Cromer which allows the crabs to filter in good clean water, in the same way that clean chalky streams are best for trout. But should Cromer be known for much, much more?

For instance, could Cromer be the birthplace of *The Hound of the Baskervilles?* In 1901 Sherlock Homes author Sir Arthur Conan Doyle came to Cromer for a golfing holiday and was invited by Benjamin Cabbell to dinner at his home, the Tudor Gothic Cromer Hall. During dinner Cabbell apparently recited the story of his ancestor Richard Cabbell, Lord of Buckfastleigh on Dartmoor, in Devon. Richard Cabbell's wife had been unfaithful and Cabbell beat her and chased her out on to Dartmoor where he stabbed her to death. The wife's loyal hound then attacked Cabbell and tore his throat out. The dog's ghost is said to have haunted Dartmoor ever since and to reappear to kill each new generation of the Buckfastleigh Cabbells. Just to add to the plot, Benjamin Cabbell's coachman was called Baskerville. And Conan Doyle's description of Baskerville Hall sounds remarkably similar to Cromer Hall ... Cromer Hall is still privately owned.

And could Cromer be the birthplace of the atomic bomb? For a while in 1933 Cromer was the home of the world famous scientist Albert Einstein,

after he was smuggled out of Nazi Germany and taken into hiding in a small hut on Roughton Heath in Cromer. His benefactor was eccentric MP Oliver Locker-Lampson who had planned with Winston Churchill to send an agent into Ostend to rescue Einstein and bring him to England. A bounty of 1,000 guineas was put on Einstein's head by the Nazis, and while he was in his Norfolk hideout Einstein was guarded by Locker-Lampson and two female secretaries armed with rifles. When the celebrated sculptor Jacob Epstein came to make a bust of Einstein the scientist spoke out against Hitler and exhorted the world to take up arms against fascism. Who knows what world-changing scientific theories Einstein worked on while confined to his hut, but he went to America a few weeks later, and in 1939, despite being an ardent pacifist, wrote to Franklin Roosevelt urging the President to build an atomic bomb because Hitler was developing such a bomb in Germany and must be stopped.

Beacon Hill, just south of West Runton near Cromer, is 338 feet (103 m) high and the highest point in Norfolk, just 23 feet (7 m) higher than the spire of Norwich Cathedral. In the 1990s the largest and most complete

mammoth skeleton ever discovered was found in the cliffs at West Runton. Various parts of the skeleton can be seen in museums around Norfolk.

Blakeney Haven

Blakeney Haven was a deep inlet running east to west that was protected by a sand and shingle spit and created a safe harbour for a number of ports such as Cley next the Sea, Wiveton and Blakeney. In the 17th century the inlet silted up, gradually cutting the ports off from the sea.

Cley Marshes lie inland of the spit and in 1926 became BRITAIN'S FIRST NATURE RESERVE when they were leased from the National Trust to be held in perpetuity as a bird breeding sanctuary by BRITAIN'S OLDEST WILD-LIFE TRUST, THE NORFOLK WILDLIFE TRUST, which was founded in the same year by Dr Sydney Long.

Overlooking Cley Marshes on the edge of Cley next the Sea is CLEY WINDMILL, an 18th-century, five-storey, brick tower mill which was in operation until 1910. It was restored and lived in for many years by the family of singer-songwriter JAMES BLUNT (real name Blount) and they eventually converted the mill for use as a guest-house.

Cley next the Sea

Cley next the Sea was a busy fishing port until cut off from the sea by the spit, and the large number of houses with Dutch gables in the town signify that much of its trade was done with the Low Countries. In one of the windows of Cley's St Margaret's Church, the largest of the Blakeney Haven churches, there is a depiction of a white-crowned sparrow, an American bird never before seen in Britain, that was spotted in Cley in 2008. Birdwatchers who flocked to Cley to try and catch sight of the rarity donated more than £3,000 towards the church's restoration, and the window was put there as a thank you to the little bird for its generosity.

Wiveton

Wiveton is a small former port that lies between Blakeney and Cley. In 1779 it came to prominence when the newly appointed Rector of Wiveton, JAMES HACKMAN, shot dead Martha Reay, mistress of the 4th Earl of Sandwich (see page 185) in the foyer of the Theatre Royal in Covent Garden. Martha, the fabulously beautiful daughter of a corset maker, once ran a tea shop in the Naze Tower in Essex but had lived with the Earl of Sandwich for 19 years and borne him many children – she is thought by some to have been the inspiration behind George Bernard Shaw's *Pygmalion*, later to become *My Fair Lady*. James Hackman had become infatuated with her, and when she refused to leave Sandwich he snapped and murdered her. He was hanged two days later at Tyburn.

WIVETON HALL is a glorious 17th-century Dutch gabled Jacobean manor house situated right on the edge of the marshes north of Wiveton village. It is now lived in by DESMOND MACCARTHY, grandson of Sir Desmond MacCarthy, literary and drama critic of *The Sunday Times* and member of the Bloomsbury Group, and is the setting for the BBC2 documentary series *Normal for Norfolk*.

Blakeney

Blakeney is the largest and longest-lasting of the three 'Haven' ports, remaining a working port until the early 20th century. In an alleyway just off the quay is the 14th-century Guildhall of Blakeney's fish merchants, roofless now but with an almost perfect brick-vaulted undercroft. Standing higher up the village, 100 feet (30 m) above the marshes, with its splendid 15th-century Perpendicular tower soaring a further 125 feet (38 m) into the sky, ST NICHOLAS CHURCH is half-way to being the highest point in Norfolk. No one seems to know what the slender, rather curious octagonal tower tacked on to the east end of the church is for, although perhaps it is designed to lend St Nicholas a uniquely distinctive profile from the sea. Inside, St Nicholas is famed for its rare 13th-century vaulted chancel, which is graced by an east window that is one of only two medieval seven-light windows in England (the other being at Ockham in Surrey).

BLAKENEY POINT lies at the western end of the sand and shingle spit that now runs for 9 miles west from Sheringham. A National Nature Reserve, it has been owned by the National Trust since 1912, and the sandbanks off the point are home to THE LARGEST SEAL COLONY IN ENGLAND, with some two thousand grey seal pups born each winter.

Holkham

HOLKHAM NATIONAL NATURE RESERVE comprises of 10,000 acres (4,050 ha) of unspoiled salt marsh, sand dunes, fields and woodland lying between Blakeney and Burnham Overy Staithe on the north Norfolk coast and is THE LARGEST COASTAL NATURE RESERVE IN ENGLAND.

West of the resort and former seaport of Wells-next-the-Sea is HOLKHAM HALL, the magnificent Palladian palace home of the Earls of Leicester. Built for the FIRST EARL OF LEICESTER, THOMAS COKE (1607–1776), by WILLIAM KENT, it was begun in 1734 and finished in 1764. A few years later, in 1777, it became only the second stately home of England to open to the public, after Wilton House in Wiltshire.

Thomas Coke's nephew and heir, another THOMAS COKE (1754–1842) was an innovative landowner and farmer who changed English farming for ever. Known as the 'first farmer in England', he pioneered the rotation of crops and the enriching of the soil with manure, as well as building comfortable homes for his farm workers. His success at turning the inhospitable sands and salt marshes of north Norfolk into fertile crop-growing fields encouraged farmers throughout Britain to follow his methods, as they still do today.

Thomas's heir, WILLIAM COKE, was THE FIRST MAN IN ENGLAND TO

WEAR A BOWLER HAT. In 1849 he placed an order with Lock & Co. of St James's for a hard hat that would protect his head from overhanging branches while he was out shooting on his Norfolk estate. Lock passed his requirements on to felt hat makers Thomas and William Bowler, who devised a new kind of hard hat ready for Coke's approval in December 1849. Coke travelled up to London, walked into Lock & Co., placed the hat on the floor and proceeded to jump up and down on it. He then picked it up and inspected it for damage. There was none, so he placed it on his head, enquired of the price and departed with the hat. To this day, if you go into Lock & Co. and ask for a 'bowler' they will politely correct you and show you what they prefer to call a 'coke'.

Burnham Market

The Hoste Arms in the Burnham Market village square is named after CAPTAIN WILLIAM HOSTE, a protégé of Lord Nelson and heroic frigate captain during the Napoleonic Wars. Born in nearby Ingoldsthorpe, he joined Nelson as captain's servant on HMS *Agamemnon*, Nelson's favourite ship, and went on to fight with Nelson at many battles including the Battle of Cape St Vincent and the Battle of the

Nile. Hoste is said to be the model for Jack Aubrey, the hero of Patrick O'Brian's naval stories.

Lord Nelson himself was born at BURNHAM THORPE, where his father was the Rector. The rectory in which Nelson was born is gone, but the church where he was baptised in 1758 remains, and the pub where he dined the men of the village before he departed to join HMS *Agamemnon* is also still there. In Nelson's day it was called the Plough; now it is the Lord Nelson.

Hunstanton

Hunstanton – or 'Sunny Hunny' as it likes to be known – looks out across the Wash towards distant Boston in Lincolnshire and is one of only two seaside towns on the east coast of England that face west, the other being Heacham, a mile to the south. As with many east coast resorts there are two Hunstantons, old and new.

Old Hunstanton is a quiet, venerable place of stone cottages that lies near the northern end of the PEDDARS WAY, an ancient track that comes up across Norfolk from near Thetford on the Suffolk border. The village sits on top of a section of vivid red-and-white striped cliffs that are unique in Britain, red limestone at the bottom and a band of white chalk above. Up to 60 feet (18 m) high, they are an extraordinary sight and even the boulders on the beach at the bottom of the cliffs are mixed red and white. Stark on the cliff top are the ruins of ST EDMUND'S CHAPEL, built in 1272 to mark where the Saxon nobleman Edmund the Martyr, the original patron saint of England, landed from Germany in AD 850 to take up the crown of East Anglia. He was martyred by the Danes in AD 869. Close by, on a spot where there has been a lighthouse since 1665, is OLD HUNSTANTON LIGHTHOUSE. The present building, put up in 1840, was decommissioned as a lighthouse in 1922 and is now privately owned. The previous lighthouse on the site had THE WORLD'S FIRST PARA-BOLIC REFLECTOR, installed in 1776.

New Hunstanton was begun in the mid 19th century by the local land-owners the LE STRANGE family as a resort for day-trippers brought in on the new railway from King's Lynn. William Butterfield, the eminent Victorian architect who was the first to introduce polychrome brickwork into architecture, was asked to help design the first few buildings of the new town, and an example of his work is the restrained GOLDEN LION HOTEL which sits across the new village green from the seafront. Nearby, just to emphasise the more light-hearted nature of New Hunstanton, is BRITAIN'S LARGEST JOKE SHOP.

Much-loved comic writer P.G. WODEHOUSE visited Hunstanton frequently to stay with his friend

Charles Le Strange at HUNSTANTON HALL, which lies in its own park east of the town. Hunstanton Hall, a Victorian Tudor Gothic pile, was the model for Woollam Chersey, the country lair of Bertie Wooster's terrifying Aunt Agatha, while the 17th-century Octagon summerhouse set in the middle of the lake at Hunstanton became the setting for Wodehouse's sublime short story *Jeeves and the Impending Doom*.

Heacham

Heacham, the other east coast town to face west, is at the centre of Norfolk's lavender trade, the first fields of lavender being planted there in 1936.

Hanging in the cupola on the tower of Heacham's Norman Church of St Mary is THE OLDEST BELL IN EAST ANGLIA, dating from 1100.

HEACHAM HALL was the ancestral home and birthplace, in 1585, of JOHN ROLFE, the English settler who married Native American princess Pocahontas in Jamestown, Virginia, in 1614. The couple came to England in 1615 with their young son Thomas and visited Rolfe's parents at Heacham Hall on more than one occasion. Pocahontas died at Gravesend as they were preparing to return to Virginia in March 1617, and Rolfe went back to America with his son, never to return to his family home at Heacham. The Hall was burned down during the Second World War.

Wolferton

Wolferton lies on what was the King's Lynn to Hunstanton railway, and in 1862 a station was built there to serve the small seaside village. In that same year Queen Victoria bought the neighbouring estate of Sandringham for her eldest son Albert, the Prince of Wales, later EDWARD VII, and members of the Royal Family started to use the station. In view of its royal patronage it was decided to upgrade the station in 1898 and new, Elizabethan-style black-and-white platform buildings, complete with clock tower, were put up along

with traditional white-painted canopies. The waiting room, where the Royal Family members would sit while their transport to Sandringham was prepared, was fitted with oak panelling and comfortable chairs. The result was one of the most beautiful little railway stations in Britain, and although the station was closed along with the railway in 1969, the whole complex has been refurbished and preserved under private ownership as a delightful, unspoiled example of a Victorian railway station.

Sandringham

Sandringham House sits on a site occupied since Elizabethan times. The estate was purchased by Queen Victoria in 1862 as a wedding present for her eldest son the Prince of Wales and he moved in the following year with his new bride Alexandra. It soon became clear that the simple Georgian villa that was there was too small for the Prince's growing family and so it was demolished and a new grand house in the Victorian 'Jacobethan' style was put up between 1870 and 1900 to replace it.

For the Prince of Wales Sandringham became 'the house I like best'. A huntin' and shootin' man, he devised Sandringham Time, whereby the clocks

at Sandringham were all put half an hour fast so that he could make the most of the winter daylight hours for outdoor pursuits.

GEORGE V established the tradition of spending Christmas and New Year at Sandringham, a tradition still followed by the Royal Family today. On Christmas Day in 1932 he made THE FIRST CHRISTMAS BROADCAST live on the radio from Sandringham, with a speech written by Rudyard Kipling. Three years later, in January 1936, George V died at 'dear old Sandringham, the place I love better than anywhere in the world'.

EDWARD VIII only spent one day at Sandringham and swore he would 'fix those bloody clocks' on his accession. He duly abolished Sandringham Time in 1936.

GEORGE VI was born in York Cottage on the Sandringham estate in 1895 and, like his father, came to love Sandringham, writing to his mother, 'I have always been so happy here, I love the place.' He died there in 1952.

His daughter ELIZABETH II continues to enjoy Sandringham and in 1957 made THE FIRST TELEVISED CHRISTMAS BROADCAST live from the library.

The gardens at Sandringham were first opened to the public by Edward VII in 1908, and Elizabeth II opened the house up in 1977 in celebration of her Silver Jubilee. It is now open regularly in the summer months.

On the edge of the grounds is the Tudor parish church of ST MARY MAGDALENE, attended by the Royal Family when they are in residence at Sandringham. Made from carstone, a rich brown sandstone seen in the cliffs at Hunstanton, it is considered to be the finest carstone building in Britain. The interior of the church is a good example of opulent Victoriana, with a sumptuous painted roof, gilded woodwork and wood panelling everywhere, and an extraordinary and unique silver altar and reredos and silver pulpit given by American department store owner Rodman Wannamaker in memory of Edward VII.

King's Lynn
'Beautiful, well-built and well-situated'
Daniel Defoe

Lynn, then Bishop's Lynn, and finally King's Lynn when Henry VIII got his hands on it during the Dissolution of the Monasteries in 1539, was at one time England's third largest port and grew rich as a trading base for the Hanseatic League, a powerful confederation of merchant guilds and trading towns in Germany and the Baltic that was finally revoked by Elizabeth I. The legacy of this prosperity is a handsome town with more listed buildings than York. Poet John Betjemen thought the walk through King's Lynn's quiet Elizabethan and Georgian streets such as Nelson Street, Queen Street and King Street the 'finest town walk in Europe'.

The main part of the town is sandwiched between two markets, the Saturday and Tuesday markets. Saturday Market is dominated by the imposing west towers of ST MARGARET'S CHURCH, the second biggest church in East Anglia. A Norman foundation, it has been rebuilt many times and lost its spire in 1741, but retains a number of interesting features including some fine carved misericords, a Georgian pulpit and THE TWO BEST AND BIGGEST 14TH-CENTURY FLEMISH BRASSES IN ENGLAND. Across the road is the GUILDHALL OF THE HOLY

TRINITY, built in 1423 and recognisable by its striking chequerboard façade of dark flint and pale stone, while next door and built to match is the Victorian TOWN HALL of 1895. Leading away from the church down St Margaret's Lane to the quayside is the HANSEATIC STEELYARD, or Warehouse, a long, two-storey building constructed in 1475 after the Treaty of Utrecht which allowed the Hanseatic League to establish a trading base in Lynn for the first time. It is THE ONLY SURVIVING HANSEATIC BUILDING IN THE WHOLE OF BRITAIN.

In Queen Street is CLIFTON HOUSE, a red-brick Elizabethan merchant's house heralded by twisting barley sugar pillars holding up the portico and with a five-storey Tudor watchtower from where the owner could scan the horizon for his ships. ST GEORGE'S GUILDHALL in King Street dates from 1410. TUESDAY MARKET, which is the Town Square, is overlooked by the Victorian CORN EXCHANGE of 1854, now a concert hall, and the smart 17th-century Duke's Head Hotel, named in honour of the Duke of York (later James II).

The most famous building in King's Lynn and a fitting tribute to the town's mercantile prestige is the CUSTOM HOUSE on Purfleet Quay, built in 1683 by HENRY BELL, twice Mayor of King's Lynn.

Standing in front of the Custom House is a statue of GEORGE VANCOUVER (1757–1798), who was born in King's Lynn, the son of the Collector of Customs. As a boy of 13 he went off round the world with Captain Cook and witnessed cook's death on the beach at Hawaii in 1779, all the while gaining a taste for exploration and adventure. His lasting legacy was the charting of the west coast of America from Alaska to Mexico, and in 1792 he negotiated with the Spanish for Nootka Island, which was renamed Vancouver Island. In 1885 the Canadian city of Vancouver was named in his honour as well.

Well, I never knew this
about
THE NORFOLK COAST

ANNA SEWELL (1820–1878), the author of *Black Beauty*, was born in a tiny 17th-century black-and-white house in the close beside the minster church of St Nicholas in GREAT YARMOUTH.

In the early part of the 20th century Great Yarmouth was THE BIGGEST HERRING FISHING PORT IN THE WORLD, and on one day in 1907 fishermen brought home over 80 million herring. Yarmouth had a vast fishing fleet, made up mainly of steam drifters, and the last surviving one of these steam drifters, the *Lydia Eva*, can be seen moored at Great Yarmouth today.

The grandstand at Great Yarmouth Town Football Club's WELLESLEY RECREATION GROUND was built in 1892 and is THE OLDEST FOOTBALL STAND STILL IN REGULAR USE IN THE WORLD.

Great Yarmouth is the BIRTHPLACE OF THE FISH FINGER, which was first produced at Birds Eye's Yarmouth factory in 1955.

Resting on lion's paws in the churchyard of ST MARY'S IN WEST SOMERTON is the massive sarcophagus of ROBERT HALES, THE NORFOLK GIANT, tallest man in Britain at that time. Born in West Somerton in 1820, Hales grew to be 7 feet 8 inches (2.34 m) tall and weighed more than 32 stone (203 kg). He toured Britain with his sister Mary who was also over 7 feet tall, and in 1849 went with showman P.T. Barnum to the USA, where he married Elizabeth Simpson from County Cork, who was 8 feet tall – later this was revealed to be a publicity stunt.

CHAPTER SEVENTEEN
LINCOLNSHIRE COAST

Sutton Bridge to Barton-upon-Humber
100 miles

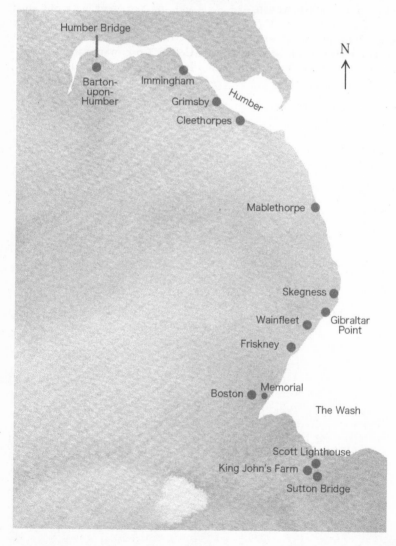

Highlights of the Lincolnshire coast include the lonely lighthouse that inspired the world's conservation movement and one of the greatest novels of all time, the place where King John lost the Crown Jewels, the tallest medieval tower in England, the birthplace of the United States of America, the tallest working windmill in Britain, a rare Georgian hudd, a jolly fisherman, the highest concentration of holiday caravans in Europe, the sand dunes that inspired one of England's greatest poets, the largest fish and chip shop in Britain, Britain's foremost trading gateway, the oldest and biggest surviving ice factory in the world and Britain's longest suspension bridge.

The Wash

England's second biggest bay, covering some 100 square miles, the Wash separates Lincolnshire from East Anglia and stretches from Gibraltar Point south of Skegness in Lincolnshire to Hunstanton in Norfolk. The Romans built embankments around the margins of the Wash to protect the agricultural land from flooding, but these defences decayed after the Romans left and much of the Fens as far as Peterborough and Cambridge were inundated, enabling the Vikings to sail far inland when invading East Anglia and the Midlands during the 9th and 10th centuries. Large-scale drainage of the Wash and land reclamation was carried out in the 16th and 17th centuries by Dutch engineers and has continued to the modern day, and the Wash is now contained by sea walls on all three sides.

Sutton Bridge

Four rivers feed into the Wash, the Witham, Welland, Nene and Great Ouse. Two of these form commercial shipping lanes, the Great Ouse leading to the docks at King's Lynn and the River Nene to Sutton Bridge and on to Wisbech. About a mile inland from where the Nene meets the Wash, two lonely 19th-century lighthouses act as gatekeepers, one on either side of the channel. From 1933 to 1939 the lighthouse on the east bank was the home of conservationist SIR PETER SCOTT (1909–1989), son of Antarctic explorer Robert Falcon Scott. Peter Scott was a great wildlife painter and built himself a studio next to the lighthouse and also created a series of ponds for the various wildfowl that lived or migrated in the wetlands. Inspired by his time at this solitary, atmospheric place, one of the richest wildfowl preserves in the world, Scott went on to found the World Wildlife Fund and the Wildfowl and Wetlands Trust. The American novelist PAUL GALLICO was a friend of Peter Scott, and Scott's romantic lighthouse home inspired his novel *The Snow Goose*.

The lighthouse was commandeered by the Army during the Second World War and has since been restored as a private home.

A little further downstream, on the west bank, is KING JOHN'S FARM, said to be on the site of where King John lost the Crown Jewels in October 1216. He was travelling from King's Lynn (then Bishop's Lynn) to Spalding in Lincolnshire, and while he himself took a safer but longer route via

Wisbech, he ordered his baggage train to take a short cut along a tidal causeway that forded the Wellstream (now the River Nene) at the point where King John's Farm now stands. The slow, heavily-laden horse-drawn wagons got bogged down in the mud and were caught by the incoming tide. The horses and wagons, still tied to each other, were all lost and so were many of the men. King John was heart-broken at the symbolic loss of his Crown and died a week later of dysentery at Newark. Bounty hunters still come from far and wide in search of King John's treasure but nothing has ever been found.

Before the 19th century what is now Sutton Bridge was just a small collection of cottages beside the muddy track across the treacherous Cross Keys Wash through which the River Nene made its way to the Wash. Those who wanted to cross the marsh could hire a guide at the Wash House, now the Bridge Hotel. In 1831 a raised embankment was built to carry the road above the marsh, and a wood and cast-iron bridge, which opened like Tower Bridge in London, was flung over the Nene by John Rennie the Younger and

Thomas Telford. This was replaced in 1850 by a swing bridge built by Robert Stephenson, which in turn was replaced by the present swing bridge, known as Cross Keys Bridge, in 1894. The first dock at Sutton Bridge collapsed a month after opening in 1881, while the present dock, which is able to accommodate small vessels, opened in 1987.

Boston

Boston sits on the River Witham at the head of The Haven, a tidal inlet of the Wash into which the Witham drains. It grew up around a monastery founded in AD 654 by St Botolph, hence the name 'Botolph's Town' which becomes Boston. By the 15th century Boston had become the chief port of England, grown prosperous on the export of wool from the sheep that grazed on the fertile Lincolnshire pastures. Its prosperity is reflected in the magnificent church of St Botolph, one of the largest parish churches in England. The church tower, known as the BOSTON STUMP for its profile from a distance, is Boston's trademark. Completed in 1510, it is 272 feet (83 m) high, THE TALLEST MEDIEVAL TOWER IN ENGLAND. The lantern at the top once served as a beacon for sailors on the Wash and the Stump still acts as a prominent landmark. A climb of 365 steps (one for each day of the year) gives access to a viewing gallery from where it is possible to see Hunstanton across the Wash in Norfolk and the towers of Lincoln Cathedral 30 miles to the north.

Boston could arguably be called THE BIRTHPLACE OF THE UNITED STATES OF AMERICA, for it was here that the movement began which led to the founding of the USA. In 1607, the earliest of the Pilgrim Fathers, a group of 13 English Protestant separatists from Lincolnshire and the Midlands, attempted to set sail from Boston for the Netherlands where they could live free from persecution, but they were betrayed by the Dutch captain of the ship they had chartered, who was paid to inform the authorities. THE PILGRIM FATHERS MEMORIAL at SCOTIA CREEK, about a mile outside Boston on The Haven, marks the spot where they were arrested as they waited to board ship, and they were taken back from there by boat to the BOSTON GUILDHALL and put in prison to await trial for trying to emigrate illegally. The cells where they were held can still be seen in the Guildhall, which is now run as a museum. The pilgrims were released after a month and the following year they tried again from the Humber and this time made it to Holland. In 1620 many of them, including WILLIAM BREWSTER and future governor WILLIAM BRADFORD, sailed from Southampton on the *Mayflower* to found the colony of Plymouth. Ten years later more pilgrims set sail from Boston and founded the city of Boston, Massachusetts. JOHN COTTON, Puritan minister of St Botolph's from 1612 to 1632, encouraged members of his congregation to emigrate to America, and in 1633 he went there himself to become one of Boston's first and most influential ministers. With him was fellow Bostonian RICHARD BELLINGHAM, who would become the first of five Governors of Massachusetts from Boston, Lincs.

In the Market Place by the church there is a statue of HERBERT INGRAM, founder in 1842 of the *Illustrated London News*, THE WORLD'S FIRST ILLUSTRATED MAGAZINE, who was born in Boston in

1811, while a plaque on the Stump and Candle pub indicates that this was the birthplace of JOHN FOXE (1517–1578), author of the *Book of Martyrs*.

Boston to Skegness

FREISTON SHORE is the southernmost of the villages that shelter behind a sea wall that runs 22 miles from here all the way to Skegness along the western shore of the Wash.

FRISKNEY'S claim to be the largest village in England by land area is disputed, but what can't be argued is that All Saints Church is in possession of ONE OF THE ONLY SIX HUDDS IN EXIST-ENCE. A hudd is a small portable wooden hut, a bit like a sentry box, where the priest can shelter from the rain while conducting a funeral by the graveside. This one dates from the 18th century.

WAINFLEET ALL SAINTS was the birthplace of WILLIAM WAYNFLETE (1398–1486), Bishop of Winchester and founder of Magdalen College, Oxford in 1458. He also founded Magdalen College School in Wainfleet in 1484 to prepare students for the college, and although the school has now moved, its lovely old red-brick building survives and is now run as a museum. Wainfleet is also the home of BATEMAN'S BREWERY, founded in 1874 by GEORGE BATEMAN to supply the local farmers and still independent to this day.

Gibraltar Point, a long sand dune ridge, is the northernmost extent of the Wash and the point where the Lincolnshire coast turns north and then northwest towards the Humber.

Skegness

Skegness was a tiny fishing village until the railway from the Midlands arrived in 1875. The resort was laid out by Lord Scarborough as one of the first planned towns and in 20 years it grew from a population of five hundred to some two thousand people. By 1881 it had the fourth longest pier in Britain, 1,844 feet (562 m) in length. This was destroyed by gales in 1978. The most prominent landmark today is the DIAMOND JUBILEE CLOCK TOWER, put up in 1989 to celebrate Queen Victoria's Diamond Jubilee in 1897. Nearby is the statue of the town's mascot, THE JOLLY FISHERMAN, designed for an advertising poster for the Great Northern Railway in 1908 by John Hassall. On the poster a smiling fisherman is seen skipping along the beach above the

slogan 'Skegness is SO bracing' – a nod, perhaps, to the invigorating east wind that can blow in off the North Sea all too frequently.

At the north extent of Skegness's 6 miles of sandy beach is INGOLDMELLS, which in 1936 became the site of THE FIRST BUTLIN'S HOLIDAY CAMP. Ingoldmells has THE HIGHEST CONCENTRATION OF HOLIDAY CARAVANS IN EUROPE, and Fantasy Island's JUBILEE ODYSSEY, built in 2002 and named after Queen Elizabeth II's Golden Jubilee of that year, is THE LARGEST SUSPENDED LOOPING ROLLERCOASTER IN THE WORLD as well as the third tallest rollercoaster in Britain, 167 feet (51 m) high.

Mablethorpe

Lincolnshire-born poet ALFRED, LORD TENNYSON, and his brother Charles came to wander amongst the sand dunes of Mablethorpe on the day their first book of poems, *Poems by Two Brothers*, was published in 1827, and they spent the time reciting their verses into the wind.

The first Mablethorpe, along with its church of St Peter, was lost to the sea in the 1540s, with now just a few tree stumps revealed at low tide to remember it by; but a new Mablethorpe has grown in its place, protected by a sea wall promenade, that attracts thousands of tourists to tread the dunes in the summer months. In D.H. Lawrence's novel *Sons and Lovers* the Morel family come to Mablethorpe for their first holiday.

The Humber

The Humber is an estuary, not a river, and is formed by the confluence of the Ouse and Trent rivers, being joined by the River Hull at Kingston-upon-Hull. It has long been a major boundary, in Saxon times between the kingdoms of Northumbria (north of the Humber) and Mercia and today between Yorkshire and Lincolnshire. The mouth of the Humber lies between Cleethorpes in Lincolnshire to the south and Spurn Head in Yorkshire to the north. Between the two are the Humber forts, Bull Sand Fort and Haile Sand Fort, built to protect the entrance to the Humber during the First World War. Thanks to the ports of Grimsby, Immingham and Kingston-upon-Hull the Humber is BRITAIN'S LARGEST AND BUSIEST CARGO PORT COMPLEX.

Cleethorpes

While physically joined to Grimsby, Cleethorpes is determined to remain separate. A fishing village grown into a resort, it used to have a pier 1,200 feet (366 m) long to reach the sea at low tide. This was cut during the Second World War to prevent a German invasion using it as a landing point, and today just a short section remains on the beach. The pavilion on the pier is now occupied by PAPA'S FISH AND CHIPS, which claims to be THE LARGEST FISH AND CHIP SHOP IN BRITAIN. To the south is the Cleethorpes Coast Light railway, which runs south from the leisure centre to the Pleasure Island theme park. Between the sea and the theme park terminus is a metal plate running along the line of the PRIME MERIDIAN which cuts through Cleethorpes and a signpost giving distances to such places as the North Pole (2,517 miles), London (143 miles), New York (3,481 miles), and the South Pole (9,895 miles).

Grimsby

Grimsby was founded in the 10th century by a Lincolnshire fisherman called Grim who rescued the son of an assassinated Danish king from drowning at sea and brought him up as his son. When the prince grew up and won back his kingdom, Grim was rewarded handsomely and used his riches to found the fishing town that became Grimsby. King John gave the town a charter in 1201, making Grimsby THE OLDEST CHARTERED TOWN IN ENGLAND.

After a period of decline due to silting, the port was revived by the arrival of the railway and was opened up again by dredging, and in 1856 Grimsby got THE WORLD'S FIRST PURPOSE-BUILT FISH DOCK. By the end of the 19th century Grimsby had become THE LARGEST FISHING PORT IN THE WORLD WITH THE WORLD'S LARGEST FISHING FLEET, but after the imposition of the Common Fisheries Policy in the 1970s the fleet declined

dramatically. All that remains of the largest fishing fleet in the world is the *Ross Tiger*, THE WORLD'S LAST SURVIVING SIDE WINDING FISHING TRAWLER, which is berthed in Grimsby's Alexandra Dock and has been converted into a museum ship.

One of the most distinctive landmarks on the English coast, and iconic to Grimsby, is the startling 309 foot (94 m) tall GRIMSBY DOCK TOWER, built in 1852 at the entrance to Grimsby's Royal Dock. This was the hydraulic accumulator tower that provided hydraulic power to operate the dock gates and locks. In order to achieve sufficient pressure the tower had to be built high enough to contain 30,000 gallons of water at a height of 200 feet (61 m). The Victorians loved to disguise their functional buildings and architect JAMES WILLIAM WILD based the appearance of the tower on that of the Torre del Mangia in Siena.

Although most of the rest of Grimsby's Victorian dock buildings have been razed, one has survived, the GRIMSBY ICE FACTORY, built in 1898 to provide crushed ice with which to preserve the fish stored aboard the fishing boats. When it was built it was THE LARGEST ICE FACTORY IN THE WORLD and today it is THE OLDEST AND BIGGEST SURVIVING ICE

FACTORY IN THE WORLD. It is also the only surviving ice factory to retain its machinery, much of which is unique. The factory is in a dilapidated state and considered 'at risk', but development plans are being discussed.

Today Grimsby handles car imports and business associated with THE WORLD'S BIGGEST OFFSHORE WIND FARM located at the DOGGER BANK some 70 miles off the Yorkshire coast.

Immingham

The village of Immingham developed as a port with the arrival of the railway in the 19th century and has since grown to be BRITAIN'S LARGEST PORT BY TONNAGE HANDLED.

In 1608, long before it became an international port, the village of Immingham played an important part in the story of the early Pilgrim Fathers who, the year before, had been arrested and imprisoned in Boston while trying to emigrate to Holland. Their second attempt began at Immingham where their ship was anchored while awaiting fair weather. The womenfolk were offered shelter in the village church of St Andrew's, but once again the pilgrims were betrayed and the ship had to set sail leaving the women behind. The women were arrested but, after an outcry, were released and allowed to join the other pilgrims in Holland. Twelve years later many of them were aboard the *Mayflower* when it sailed for the New World. In 1924 members of the Anglo-American Society erected a granite memorial to the Pilgrim Fathers beside the creek from which they sailed. On top they placed a piece of stone cut from Plymouth Rock in New England, where the Pilgrim Fathers made their first landfall in America in 1620. When the creek was filled in for Immingham's new docks the memorial was moved to a small park, Pilgrims Park, opposite St Andrew's Church.

Barton-upon-Humber

Barton was once the biggest port on the Humber but now lies inland and is better known as the place where the A15 takes flight over the Humber Bridge. Nonetheless it remains a pleasant, self-contained Georgian market town with a church that is amongst the greatest of England's treasures, the Saxon church of St Peter, whose 10th-century tower is one of the wonders of Saxon architecture. The lower two thirds of the tower are decorated with stone arcading, both round arched and triangular, but while the arcading appears to be made from strips of stone it is in fact formed of the projected ends of large blocks of stone embedded in the wall. There is only one other tower like it in England, at Earls Barton in Northamptonshire.

Humber Bridge

For more than nine hundred years the only way to cross the Humber was by ferry from Barton. This was superseded in the 19th century by the ferry from New Holland to Hull, which ran until 1981 when the HUMBER BRIDGE was opened. With a central span of 4,626 feet (1,410 m), the Humber Bridge was THE LONGEST SUSPENSION BRIDGE IN THE WORLD until 1997 when it was overtaken by the Great Belt Bridge in Denmark. There are 44,000 miles of cable holding up the bridge and as a result of the earth's curvature, the twin towers, both 533 feet (162 m) high, are 1.4 inches (36 mm) further apart at the top than at the bottom. The Humber Bridge is still THE LONGEST BRIDGE IN THE WORLD THAT CAN BE CROSSED ON FOOT – and it is also one of the most beautiful bridges in the world.

Well, I never knew this about
THE LINCOLNSHIRE COAST

The 11th-century spire of ST MARY'S CHURCH in LONG SUTTON, 3 miles west of Sutton Bridge south of the Wash, is 162 feet (49 m) high and THE TALLEST LEAD SPIRE IN BRITAIN.

CROSS KEYS BRIDGE at Sutton Bridge was used as a target by 617 Squadron when they were practising low-level flying before their daring Dambusters raid on the Ruhr Valley in 1943. They would fly their Lancaster bombers along the Nene Channel at low level and then skim the bridge, deliberately missing it by just a few feet.

The brick-built MAUD FOSTER MILL, which sits beside the Maud Foster Sluice, a man-made waterway running through Boston, is 80 feet (24 m) tall and THE TALLEST WORKING WINDMILL IN BRITAIN. It was built in 1819 for Lincolnshire-born ISAAC RECKITT, founder of Reckitt & Sons, which would go on to become Reckitt & Colman.

In September every year MABLETHORPE hosts BRITAIN'S ONLY BEACH HUT FESTIVAL, called Bathing Beauties, for which prizes are awarded for the most imaginatively decorated beach huts.

Between 1880 and 2013 GRIMSBY MINSTER was THE ONLY PARISH CHURCH IN BRITAIN TO HAVE ITS OWN CHOIR SCHOOL.

CHAPTER EIGHTEEN
YORKSHIRE COAST

Kingston-upon-Hull to Middlesbrough
110 miles

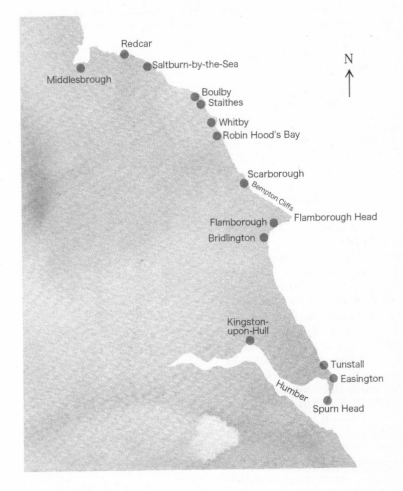

Highlights along the Yorkshire coast include Britain's busiest port complex, England's oldest brick building, the northernmost settlement on the Prime Meridian, the inspiration for toad in the hole, England's oldest lighthouse, the largest mainland breeding ground for birds in England, the first seaside resort in England, the birthplace of English poetry, the highest cliffs on England's east coast, the world's only polyhalite mine, Britain's oldest hydraulic lift, Lillie Langtry's love nest, the world's oldest lifeboat and the world's biggest transporter bridge.

Kingston-upon-Hull

Kingston-upon-Hull, or Hull, sits on the north bank of the Humber, and forms a part of BRITAIN'S BUSIEST CARGO PORT COMPLEX. Once the biggest fishing port in the world it was founded in the 12th century by monks from the Cistercian Meaux Abbey 6 miles to the north near Beverley. The monks built a quay at the point where the River Hull joins the Humber from where they could ship the wool from their estates. In 1293 Edward I acquired the harbour and laid out around it the King's Town upon the Hull. The town really began to flourish from 1331 onwards when the richest merchant of the day, William de la Pole, shifted his patronage from nearby Hedon and was appointed as Hull's first mayor.

In 1642 Hull saw THE FIRST ACTION OF THE ENGLISH CIVIL WAR when, on the orders of Parliament, the Governor of Hull, SIR JOHN HOTHAM, closed the gates of the town against Charles I, sparking the Siege of Hull. THE PLOTTING PARLOUR, a wood-panelled room in the White Harte Inn, in the old town centre, where Sir John

and his associates met to agree the fateful decision, is still there.

Hull has long been a pioneer in the development of docks. In 1778 THE WORLD'S FIRST ENCLOSED DOCK, THE QUEEN'S DOCK, was constructed at Hull, with THE WORLD'S FIRST BUCKET-CHAIN DREDGER being used to clear away the silt. When constructed in 1881, Hull's ALEXANDRA DOCK was the first dock in the world to be built with the help of a hydraulic excavator.

William Wilberforce

The Queen's Dock has now been filled in to create the Queen's Gardens, which are gazed down upon by a statue of Hull's most famous son, WILLIAM WILBERFORCE (1759–1833), which stands on top of a pedestal 100 feet (30 m) high. Wilberforce was born in a beautiful early Georgian house in the High Street, the son of a merchant and Mayor of Hull made wealthy by the Baltic trade. He was elected to Parliament at the age of 21 and his life and career culminated in one of the greatest political achievements of human history, the Abolition of Slavery. His birthplace, WILBERFORCE HOUSE, is now a museum showcasing his life and work. The High Street, swept with sea breezes, drunkenly follows the course of the River Hull and is narrow, cobbled and lined with Georgian houses and warehouses, a glorious evocation of what the old port of Hull must once have been like.

Although Hull was the most heavily bombed place in Britain after London in the Second World War, with some 95 per cent of the town centre damaged or destroyed, the heart of the old town, gathered around the parish church of HOLY TRINITY, somehow survived. Holy Trinity vies with Great Yarmouth Minster to be ENGLAND'S LARGEST PARISH CHURCH and is THE OLDEST BRICK BUILDING IN BRITAIN STILL SERVING ITS ORIGINAL PURPOSE. Dating from 1285, it was THE FIRST MAJOR BUILDING TO BE BUILT OF BRICK SINCE ROMAN TIMES.

Spurn Head

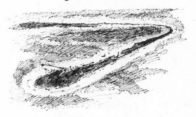

Spurn Head is a thin tongue of land, at places just 30 feet (9 m) wide, made up of shingle and sand, that juts out for 3½ miles into the mouth of the Humber. Every 250 years or so the spit gets washed away and then re-establishes itself a few yards further west for the next 250 years. Spurn Head today is a wild and windswept place but not quite devoid of human life. The lighthouse on the point has been inactive since 1986 but is now used as a visitor centre for the nature reserve run by the Yorkshire Wildlife Trust. Cars are no longer allowed to drive along the spit; access is by bike, on foot or by special shuttle. As well as the lighthouse at Spurn Point there is a jetty from which pilots race out to assist ships wishing to navigate the hazardous channels of the Humber, and a lifeboat station which is home to BRITAIN'S ONLY FULL-TIME PAID LIFEBOAT CREW.

Bridlington

The Perpendicular west window of Bridlington Priory is THE LARGEST WEST WINDOW IN THE NORTH OF ENGLAND. In medieval times Bridlington's priory church, founded for the Augustinians in 1113, was the grandest church in Yorkshire after York Minster, until the last prior joined the Pilgrimage of Grace in defiance of Henry VIII and lost his head. His priory suffered too, losing much of its size, only the nave surviving to serve as the parish church of St Mary. Today the church, still impressive, slumbers in the quiet of Old Bridlington's 17th-century High Street, in the company of the priory's 14th-century gatehouse, now a museum. Both of them keep a haughty distance from the candy-floss and kiss-me-quick of New Bridlington's once genteel seaside.

Flamborough

The most interesting tomb in Flamborough's Norman church of St Oswald is that of 'Little' SIR MARMADUKE CONSTABLE (d. 1518), commended by Henry VIII for bravery at the Battle of Flodden in 1513, who died in agony after swallowing a toad while drinking a glass of water – an easy mistake. The toad proceeded to gnaw its way out of Sir Marmaduke by eating his heart. This cautionary tale is graphically illustrated on the tomb by a sculpture showing the ribcage laid open to reveal a bulbous heart. Could this be the inspiration for the delicious English dish of toad-in-the-hole?

Flamborough Head

Before his unfortunate end, Sir Marmaduke would come up to Flamborough Head every Christmas to fire an arrow with a gold coin attached to it out to sea and call for the King of the Danes to come and collect it – his reasoning being that the Constables had been prominent in Flamborough for so long that they no longer knew who to pay their rent to. Flamborough is thought to have been founded by the Danes and lies at the centre of an area known as Little Denmark.

A little way back from the cliff edge is one of the oldest lighthouses in England, an octagonal chalk tower erected in 1673.

Scarborough

The view from Scarborough's castle, standing 300 feet (90 m) above the sea, is spectacular: golden beaches curving away to jagged cliff headlands, smart white terraces, the jumbled red roofs of the old town tumbling down towards the harbour filled with fishing boats and pleasure craft. Scarborough is the largest of Yorkshire's coastal towns and is a town of many faces. For five hundred years from 1253, Scarborough held ONE OF THE LARGEST TRADE FAIRS IN EUROPE, attended by merchants from all across the Continent and commemorated in song by Simon and Garfunkel.

Scarborough takes great pride in being THE FIRST ENGLISH SEASIDE RESORT. In 1626 Elizabeth Farrow discovered a spring at the base of a cliff on the south beach which she believed had health-giving properties. Her claim was confirmed in 1660 when a DR WITTIE wrote a book about the medical benefits of the spa waters of Scarborough, attracting people with ailments from all over Yorkshire and beyond.

THE FIRST BATHING MACHINES IN ENGLAND were introduced at Scarborough in 1735 and in 1845 visitors were welcomed into ONE OF ENGLAND'S FIRST PURPOSE-BUILT HOTELS, the Crown, overlooking South Bay.

In 1829 THE WORLD'S FIRST DEDICATED MUSEUM OF GEOLOGY was opened in Scarborough to showcase the work of the 'Father of Geology', WILLIAM SMITH, who produced THE FIRST GEOLOGICAL MAP OF BRITAIN (a copy of which is on display in the museum), and came to Scarborough to examine the geologically rich and fossil-laden Yorkshire coastline. The museum is housed in a unique circular building called THE ROTUNDA, one of the world's first purpose-built museums.

On 25 May 1849 author ANNE BRONTË came to Scarborough with her sister Charlotte, in the hope that the fresh sea air might help her to recover from her consumption. Alas, she was already too weak and died three days later. True to Charlotte's desire to 'lay the flower where it had fallen', Anne is buried in the churchyard of St Mary's, high above the bay in the shadow of the castle. A blue plaque outside the Grand Hotel marks the site of Wood's Lodgings, where Anne died.

The Grand Hotel, when it opened in 1867, was THE LARGEST HOTEL IN EUROPE and one of the largest brick buildings in the world. It has a distinctive V-shape design and was built around the theme of the calendar, with 365 bedrooms, 52 chimneys, 12 floors and 4 towers. In 1914 the top two

floors had to be demolished after being damaged by a bombardment from offshore by two cruisers of the German navy. Scarborough thus became THE FIRST TOWN IN ENGLAND TO BE FIRED ON BY THE GERMAN NAVY.

In 1955 STEPHEN JOSEPH established BRITAIN'S FIRST THEATRE-IN-THE-ROUND on the first floor of Scarborough's public library. In 1996 the Stephen Joseph Theatre moved into its own premises under the direction of playwright ALAN AYCKBOURN, THE WORLD'S MOST PERFORMED LIVING PLAYWRIGHT, who has premiered over 70 of his plays there. Scarborough was the birthplace of both LORD LEIGHTON (1830–96), THE FIRST ARTIST TO BE MADE A PEER, and CHARLES LAUGHTON (1899–1962), THE FIRST ENGLISH ACTOR TO BE AWARDED AN OSCAR.

Robin Hood's Bay

Once a more important fishing port than Whitby, just up the coast, Robin Hood's Bay cascades red-roofed down a fissure between two steep cliffs, creating one of Yorkshire's most attractive coastal villages. The connection with Robin Hood is dubious but comes from a medieval ballad recounting how Robin Hood came here to help the fishermen see off some French pirates. The village was a vibrant smuggling centre and there is said to be a network of underground passageways running between the houses, through which smuggled goods could pass from one end of the village to another without ever being seen. Robin Hood's Bay sits at the eastern end of the 190 mile Coast to Coast Walk from St Bees in Cumbria.

Whitby

Wonderful Whitby is THE BIRTH-PLACE OF ENGLISH POETRY, THE BIRTHPLACE OF THE ENGLISH CHURCH and the place from where the English explorer Captain Cook sailed into immortality. Cottages laced with narrow alleyways are pooled high on the steep banks of the River Esk and tumble down the valley towards the harbour, where fishing boats bob and seagulls squabble.

A steep staircase of 199 steps climbs the east cliff to the sturdy parish church of ST MARY, with its massive low tower and slightly disconcerting mix of Norman, Gothic and Georgian architecture. Inside is a riot of box pews, galleries and pillars, all fashioned and carved by different shipbuilders for different families and crammed in haphazardly at different times over the centuries – a rare example of a church interior left completely untouched by Victorian restoration. The whole interior is presided over by a whopping triple-decker pulpit built in 1748, THE ONLY TRIPLE-DECKER PULPIT TO BE FOUND STANDING IN THE MIDDLE OF A CHURCH anywhere in the world.

Above the church lie the spectacular 13th-century ruins of WHITBY ABBEY, founded in AD 657 by St Hilda, in thanks for King Oswy of Northumbria's victory over the heathen King Penda of Mercia. In AD 664 King Oswy convened

THE FIRST EVER CHURCH SYNOD at Whitby, bringing together Christians from the south, who followed the Roman traditions of St Augustine, and Celtic Christians from Scotland and the north, who believed in a more monastic form of Christianity as introduced by monks from Ireland. Their purpose was to decide which of these traditions should prevail. King Oswy, ever practical, came down in favour of the Roman Church, whose leader Wilfrid claimed that his authority came straight from St Peter, holder of the Keys to Heaven. 'Then I will obey St Peter,' Oswy declared, 'lest when I come to the Gates of Heaven there be none to open to me.' Thus was established the supremacy of the Roman Church in England, which would last for almost a thousand years, until the English Reformation. Also fixed was the date of Easter, the most important celebration of the Christian calendar.

Another remarkable inhabitant of Whitby from those momentous days was the poet CAEDMON, an uneducated cowherd who tended the abbey's cattle on the cliff-top pastures. He had a dream in which an angel commanded him to compose a song about the Glory of Creation, and he set to work and came up with THE 'SONG OF CREATION', THE FIRST POEM EVER WRITTEN IN ENGLISH. Caedmon thus became THE FIRST ENGLISH POET AND THE FATHER OF ENGLISH LITERATURE. His vision of Creation influenced Milton's epic *Paradise Lost* and still resonates today in the lively debate between Creationists and Evolutionists. A tall stone cross commemorating Caedmon, unveiled in 1898 by Poet Laureate Alfred Austin, stands in St Mary's churchyard. Carved on the base of the column are the first words of English poetry,

Now must we praise the
Guardian of Heaven's realm.
The Creator's might and
His Mind's thought.

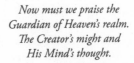

The great explorer CAPTAIN JAMES COOK, who was born in Marton in Middlesbrough, served a three-year apprenticeship in Whitby sailing in Whitby 'cats', sturdy vessels used for coastal work. All four ships in which he later sailed on his epic explorations were built in Whitby. The *Endeavour*, in which he made his first voyage of discovery in 1768–71, during which he discovered Botany Bay and became THE FIRST MAN TO MAP AND CIRCUMNAVIGATE NEW ZEALAND, was a converted Whitby cat. The house in Grape Lane on the east side of the river where Cook lived (in the attic) during his apprenticeship survives today as the CAPTAIN COOK MEMORIAL MUSEUM, and there is a bronze statue of him looking out to sea on top of the western cliff.

Near the Cook statue is a whalebone arch which commemorates the fact that between 1780 and 1840 Whitby was a major whaling centre. Whitby's most famous whaling captain was WILLIAM SCORESBY (1760–1829) who, in search of whales, sailed to 81 degrees 30 north, further north than anyone had previously sailed, a record he kept for 21 years. He was also THE INVENTOR OF THE 'CROW'S NEST', a half-covered lookout fixed near the top of the mast that protected seamen from severe weather conditions when on watch in the cold northern seas.

In the mid 19th century GEORGE HUDSON, the Railway King, brought the railway to Whitby and began to develop Westcliff as the 'Bath of the North'. He only managed to half finish the Royal Crescent before his money ran out but, even so, the half crescent high up above the town is one of the sights of Whitby.

Author BRAM STOKER came up with the idea for *Dracula* while he was staying in Whitby. In his story Count Dracula comes ashore in Whitby in the form of a black dog and climbs the 199 steps to St Mary's Church, after his ship, the *Demeter*, is wrecked off the Whitby coast. This scene was no doubt inspired by a real-life incident that had occurred a few years earlier when a ship called *Demetrius* was wrecked off Whitby and its cargo of coffins, laden with bodies, was found floating in the sea. These Dracula connections were influential in the choice of Whitby as the location for the twice yearly Whitby Goth Weekend, held in the town since 1994.

Whitby is also home to one of England's most ancient traditions, the PLANTING OF THE PENNY HEDGE, which takes place every year on the eve of Ascension Day. It dates from 1159 when a boar, being hunted by three men in the woods of the Esk valley, took refuge in the small chapel of a hermit monk. The monk refused to let the men kill the boar and they were so enraged that they set about the monk and beat him to death. As he lay there dying the monk forgave the men on the condition that every year at sunrise on Ascension Eve they planted a hedge made of staves worth no more than a penny in Whitby Harbour. If it was washed away before three tides the men or their descendants would forfeit their land and property to the Abbot of

Whitby. This penance has been carried out every year since 1159 and the hedge has not yet been swept away ...

Staithes

In the 19th century Staithes, pronounced 'Steeres', was one of England's busiest fishing ports. Today, fishing has been replaced by tourism, which is hardly surprising as the old part of Staithes is like a film set of an archetypal fishing village, squeezed into a narrow cleft between enormous red cliffs and intoxicating in its loveliness. There is one extremely steep cobbled street that winds down to the harbour which is watched over by the Cob and Lobster pub – at least three of the pub's predecessors have been washed away. Narrow passages and alleyways snake in and out of cottages and shops and the breeze is always off the sea.

Captain Cook lived for 18 months in Staithes, working as a grocer's boy when he was 16. Seduced by the lure of the sea at Staithes, he soon began to fret in the confines of William Sanderson's grocery shop and one morning he gathered up his possessions and walked out of the door to make his way across the moor to Whitby and his awesome destiny. The shop was swept away in 1812, but some of its materials were saved and used in a new building that now houses the CAPTAIN COOK AND STAITHES HERITAGE CENTRE.

Artists have long been drawn to Staithes, and when the railway arrived at the end of the 19th century it brought

with it a flock of painters, inspired by the French Impressionists, who became known as the Staithes Group. In 1898 artists LAURA JOHNSON and HAROLD KNIGHT set up home in the village and joined the STAITHES GROUP. They married in 1903 and lived there for ten years. Laura Knight, as she became, was THE FIRST ARTIST TO BE MADE A DAME OF THE BRITISH EMPIRE, in 1929, and THE FIRST WOMAN TO BE ELECTED A FULL MEMBER OF THE ROYAL ACADEMY, in 1936.

Boulby

BOULBY CLIFFS, 1 mile west of Staithes, rise to 666 feet (203 m) and are THE HIGHEST CLIFFS ON THE EAST COAST OF ENGLAND. A few hundred yards inland from the cliffs is BOULBY MINE, THE WORLD'S FIRST AND ONLY POLYHALITE MINE. Polyhalite, which has been mined here since 2016, is a mineral used in fertilisers. The mine is over 4,500 feet (1,400 m) deep, THE DEEPEST MINE IN BRITAIN AND THE SECOND DEEPEST MINE IN ALL OF EUROPE. It takes seven minutes to reach the bottom of the mine where there are some 600 miles of tunnels, many of which run out under the North Sea. Because there is virtually no background radiation that far below the surface, there is also an underground laboratory in the mine run by the Scientific and Technologies Facilities Council for conducting experiments on the nature of dark matter.

A little further west at HUMMERSEA SCAR are the remnants of BRITAIN'S FIRST CHEMICAL INDUSTRY, THE MINING AND PURIFICATION OF ALUM, a blue stone used for dying wool and tanning leather. Alum mining took place all along the Yorkshire coast, and here in Hummersea cliffs it is possible to see the scars of the mine workings and the remains of a small harbour.

Saltburn-by-the-Sea

The pier at the charming Victorian resort of Saltburn-by-the-Sea is the only remaining pleasure pier on the east coast of England north of the Humber. When it opened in 1869 it was 1,500 feet (457 m) long but after being shortened by a series of accidents and fires, it is now 681 feet (208 m) long. In 1884 a funicular railway was built to take people between the pier and the cliff top and this is now THE OLDEST SURVIVING HYDRAULIC LIFT IN BRITAIN.

At the top of the cliff is a private house called TEDDY'S NOOK, built in 1862 as a holiday home by the railway magnate HENRY PEASE, director of the world's first public railway, the Stockton and Darlington Railway, who was responsible for the development of the modern town of Saltburn. Pease named it, modestly enough, The Cottage. In the late 1870s the actress LILLIE LANGTRY was wont to stay there so that the Prince of Wales, later EDWARD VII, could visit her for rest and relaxation while a guest at the ZETLAND HOTEL just up the road. Hence the house became known as Teddy's Nook.

The imposing Victorian Italianate-style Zetland Hotel was opened by the local landowner the Earl of Zetland in 1863; it was ONLY THE SECOND PURPOSE-BUILT RAILWAY HOTEL after the one in Derby. The hotel had its own station stop, and the platform and canopy of the station can still be seen behind the building, which is now apartments.

Middlesbrough

Middlesbrough today is a vast sprawling industrial landscape of belching chimneys and smoke that fills the wide vale below the high Cleveland Hills. It was not so long ago a peaceful place of churches and water meadows. The oldest remnant of a settlement in the area is a Norman font from the church of St Hilda, part of a Benedictine priory founded in what is now the centre of Middlesbrough in the 12th century. The font is now in the city's Dorman Museum.

Mydilsburgh was originally the 'middle place' between the great abbeys of Whitby and Durham. In 1801 it was a hamlet of four farms and 25 people. Within 150 years it had grown into THE BIGGEST PRODUCER OF IRON AND STEEL IN BRITAIN and THE LARGEST PETRO-CHEMICAL CENTRE IN EUROPE.

This remarkable expansion began in 1830 when a group of Quaker businessmen, led by JOSEPH PEASE of the pioneering Pease railway family, bought some land at Middlesbrough where they could build a port on the River Tees for shipping out coal from their Durham coalfields. They also extended the Stockton and Darlington Railway to bring the coal to the port. In 1841 JOHN VAUGHAN (1799–1868) and HENRY BOLCKOW (1806–1878), the founders of modern Middlesbrough, established the first iron foundry. Ten years later they built Middlesbrough's first blast furnace to exploit the iron ore recently found in the Cleveland Hills. And in 1863 Vaughan and Bolckow, who had become Middlesbrough's first mayor in 1853, began to extract rock salt from a rich seam they had discovered beneath their ironworks, thus building the foundations of Middlesbrough's mighty chemicals industry.

By 1865 Middlesbrough was producing one third of Britain's iron and had become THE WORLD'S BIGGEST PRODUCER OF IRON, manufacturing the iron rails for railway tracks across the globe. Steel production began in 1879 and Middlesbrough quickly became THE WORLD LEADER IN STEEL PRODUCTION. As the commentator Sir H.G. Reid put it, *The iron of Eston ... has crept out of the Cleveland Hills, where it has slept since Roman days, and now, like a strong and invisible serpent, copulas itself around the world.'*

Middlesbrough gained a particular reputation for building bridges, with DORMAN LONG, founded in 1875, being perhaps the greatest of the bridge builders. They made bridges to span the Bosporus, the Nile, the Yangtze, the Thames at Lambeth and the Zambezi at Victoria Falls. Two iconic bridges that proudly bear the stamp 'Made in Middlesbrough' are the Tyne Bridge in Newcastle, built in 1928, and the Sydney Harbour Bridge, built in 1932.

Middlesbrough's Tees Newport Bridge, also built by Dorman Long, was opened in 1934 and was not only BRITAIN'S FIRST VERTICAL LIFT BRIDGE but THE HEAVIEST BRIDGE IN THE WORLD. The central lifting span is 270 feet (82 m) long and rises to leave a clear headway of 126 feet (38 m) above high water. At its peak in the 1940s the bridge was raised three hundred times a year, but owing to declining traffic on the river it was raised for the last time in 1990 and then sealed in the down position to serve as a conventional road bridge.

The most famous symbol of Middlesbrough today is THE WORLD'S LARGEST AND LONGEST TRANSPORTER BRIDGE, built by Sir William Arrol & Co. in 1911. It is one of only two transporter bridges in Britain, the other being in Newport, South Wales, and is the lowest bridge spanning the River Tees, linking Middlesbrough with Port Clarence on the north bank. The gondola, which is suspended from the bridge's main crossbeam, is designed to carry up to two hundred people or nine cars across the river in 90 seconds and provides one of Yorkshire's most enjoyable and exhilarating jaunts.

In 2015 the huge Redcar steelworks, HOME OF EUROPE'S BIGGEST BLAST FURNACE, was closed, leaving the production of steel on Teeside with an uncertain future.

Being an almost entirely Victorian creation, Middlesbrough is not renowned for its ancient architectural gems, particularly as it was the first industrial centre to be bombed in the Second World War. It has only one Grade 1 listed building, ACKLAM HALL, built in 1678 by draper Sir Wiliam Hustler. It remained in the Hustler family until 1928 when it was

sold to Middlesbrough Corporation and used as a school. It is now a conference centre, wedding venue and restaurant.

Well, I never knew this about

THE YORKSHIRE COAST

In 1989 HULL became THE FIRST CITY IN BRITAIN TO HAVE A FULLY DIGITAL TELEPHONE NETWORK. It is the only city in Britain not to be served by BT and to have its own independently operated telephone system. This is run by Kingston Communications, which took over the system from Hull City Council in 2007. Hull is also THE ONLY CITY IN BRITAIN TO HAVE WHITE-PAINTED TELEPHONE BOXES.

The village of EASINGTON, a few miles north of Spurn Head, has the best preserved timber-framed thatched tithe barn in the North of England. It dates from the 16th century. One mile north

of the village is THE EASINGTON GAS TERMINAL, WHERE NORTH SEA GAS CAME ASHORE FOR THE FIRST TIME, in 1967.

The village of TUNSTALL, 2 miles north of Withernsea, is the northernmost settlement on the Prime, or Greenwich, Meridian. An Ordnance Survey trig point used to mark the actual place, about 1 mile north of Tunstall, where the Prime Meridian leaves Britain, but it fell into the sea due to coastal erosion and there is no longer a marker to indicate that this is THE PRIME MERIDIAN'S MOST NORTHERLY LANDFALL – there is no land along the Meridian between here and the North Pole.

ST JOHN OF BRIDLINGTON, prior from 1362 until his death in 1379, was canonised by Pope Boniface IX in 1401, THE LAST ENGLISHMAN TO BE CANONISED BEFORE THE REFORMATION.

WILLIAM KENT (1685–1748), THE FIRST ARCHITECT TO DESIGN FURNITURE as well as houses and gardens, was born in Bridlington.

The BEMPTON CLIFFS, north of Flamborough Head, rise to a height of 400 feet (122 m) and make up THE LARGEST BREEDING GROUND FOR BIRDS ON THE ENGLISH MAINLAND. They are also the home of Britain's only mainland colony of gannets.

The first passenger to die in a plane crash in England lost his life on FILEY SANDS in 1911, when the plane he was in came down there, killing both passenger and pilot.

REDCAR is home to THE WORLD'S OLDEST LIFEBOAT, THE *Zetland*, which is displayed in a dedicated museum on the Esplanade. Built in 1800 and named after the local landowner the 1st Earl of Zetland, she served Redcar for 78 years and saved over five hundred lives. THE CLEVELAND GOLF CLUB at Redcar was THE FIRST GOLF CLUB IN YORKSHIRE and is the only true links course in Yorkshire. Redcar racecourse is one of the few racecourses in England to have a 'straight mile'.

CHAPTER NINETEEN

DURHAM COAST

Hartlepool to South Shields
40 miles

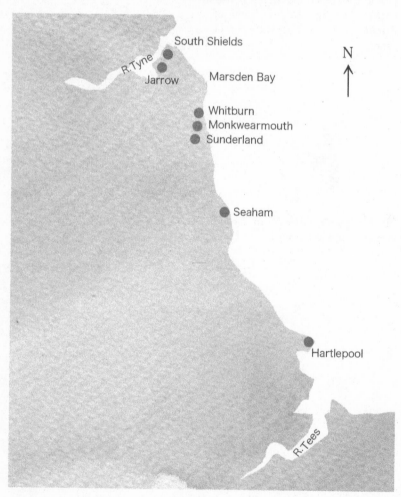

Highlights of the Durham coast include Europe's oldest warship, the oldest Saxon vaulting in the world, Britain's largest car factory, Britain's only cave bar, the second oldest lifeboat in the world, the birthplace of English literature, England's oldest dedication stone, the oldest stained-glass window in the world and the longest wooden escalators in the world.

Hartlepool

There is Hartlepool (the pool where harts drank), a small walled town of Victorian and Georgian seafront houses gathered on a headland around a mighty church, and then there is West Hartlepool. In 1945 West Hartlepool was no more than a single farm. By 1878, and for some years afterwards, it was THE LARGEST SHIPYARD IN THE WORLD, by tonnage launched. This was all the work of RALPH WARD JACKSON, local solicitor and railway owner who brought the railway to the coast here and began the docks in 1847, and local store owner SIR WILLIAM GRAY, who founded WILLIAM GRAY & COMPANY to build the ships. Today the old docks are a marina and JACKSON DOCK is home to the NATIONAL MUSEUM OF THE ROYAL NAVY HARTLEPOOL, whose collection includes HMS *Trincomalee*, launched in 1817 and THE OLDEST WARSHIP STILL AFLOAT IN EUROPE.

Old Hartlepool grew up around a Saxon monastery founded in AD 640 by St Aidan, Bishop of Lindisfarne, and put under the charge of Northumbria's first nun, an Irish abbess called HIEU. The monastery was what was known as a double monastery, that is a monastery containing both monks and nuns whose communities lived separately but were run jointly. Hieu was THE FIRST FEMALE ABBESS EVER TO BE IN CHARGE OF A DOUBLE MONASTERY. The next abbess was HILDA who would later go on to found Whitby Abbey.

Hilda is commemorated by the imposing 12th-century Norman church of St Hilda's which stands in a commanding position on Hartlepool's headland on the site of the Saxon monastery. The church was rebuilt in the 13th century by the de Brus family to become what Sir Alec Clifton-Taylor described as 'a glory of Early English architecture in its earliest and purest phase'. Behind the altar is the Bruce Chapel and Tomb, most likely that of ROBERT DE BRUS IV, great-grandson of the Robert de Brus who came over with William the Conqueror. Hartlepool was for some two hundred years a possession of the de Brus family, who built themselves a vast fortified manor house in the village of HART, northwest of Hartlepool, but this was taken off them by Edward I after Robert de Brus rebelled and became King of Scotland in 1306.

During the Norman and medieval era Hartlepool served Durham, mainly as a fishing port, and by the early 19th century had become what Isambard Kingdom Brunel described as 'a curiously isolated old fishing town'. Then West Hartlepool happened, and the two were eventually merged.

Seaham

'But I saw the sea once more in all the glories of surf and foam'
Lord Byron, in a letter written at Seaham

The glorious old Saxon church of St Mary the Virgin, its long, low buttressed walls standing stark on the cliff top north of the small town of Seaham, is all that is left of the original village of Seaham. It is ONE OF THE TEN OLDEST CHURCHES IN ENGLAND, with a Saxon nave, Saxon and Norman splayed windows, a 700-year-old font, an Elizabethan carved wooden pulpit and gorgeous creaking Georgian box pews with brass name plates recording previous owners such as Mr Bewick Seaton 1811.

One couple who sat in these pews, and whose signatures grace the marriage register of St Mary's, are the poet LORD BYRON and his bride ANNE ISABELLA MILBANKE. On 2 January 1815 they were married in the drawing room of SEAHAM HALL, next door to the church, then owned by Anne's father. 'I shall never forget the 2nd of January 1815,' wrote Byron. 'Lady Byron was the only unconcerned person present. Lady Noel, her mother, cried. I trembled like a leaf, made the wrong responses, and after the ceremony called her Miss Milbanke.' The marriage lasted not much more than a year, but long enough for the couple to produce ADA, who grew up to become the Countess of Lovelace and a good friend of the mathematician Charles Babbage, inventor of the Analytical Engine, a calculating machine operated with punch cards and regarded as the first computer. She and Babbage had many discussions about things that could be done with this amazing machine and programmes that could be created for it, and Ada is recognised as THE FIRST EVER COMPUTER PROGRAMMER. One of the first modern computer programmes, ADA, was named in her honour.

A few years later the Milbankes sold the Seaham estate to the 3RD MARQUESS OF LONDONDERRY, who built a harbour to handle coal from the local coal-mines. The town that grew up by the harbour was at first known as Seaham Harbour, but as the original village disappeared so the town took the name Seaham. The harbour is unusual in that, rather than having two sea walls, it is made up of a series of small docks interlinked by locks.

Seaham Hall is now a luxury hotel and Seaham has become a prime location to live for wealthy footballers and industrialists from Middlesbrough and Sunderland.

Sunderland

Sunderland got its name because it was the built on land 'sundered' from the monastery at MONKWEARMOUTH by the River Wear. The monastery was founded on the north bank of the mouth of the River Wear in AD 674 by a Northumbrian noble turned monk called BENEDICT BISCOP, who had returned from a pilgrimage to Rome determined to promote Christianity in Northumbria. Since there were no stonemasons or glass makers in Anglo-Saxon England at this point, Biscop imported them from France, and the church that he built for his monastery, St Peter's, had THE FIRST GLASS WINDOWS KNOWN IN ENGLAND. Not much is left of the monastery except for the 10th-century church tower of St Peter's. The lower, vaulted portion of the tower was the actual church porch built by Biscop in the 7th century and is POSSIBLY THE OLDEST SURVIVING SAXON STONEWORK IN BRITAIN – there is certainly no other Saxon vaulting above ground anywhere else in Britain. Standing in the porch it is spine-tingling to think that the VENERABLE BEDE walked through this very porch, for he was born in Monkwearmouth in 672 and began his monastic life at St Peter's.

Next door to St Peter's, on the water-front, is the glass-roofed NATIONAL GLASS CENTRE, sited appropriately close to the spot where glass making was introduced into Britain. Thanks to the abundance of high-grade sand and coal, Sunderland became Britain's chief glass making centre in the 18th century and for over 90 years between 1915 and 2007 ALL PYREX GLASS-WARE WAS MADE IN SUNDERLAND. The National Glass Centre tells the story.

The 'sundered land' south of the river grew up as a fishing village for the monastery and by the 14th century had taken up shipbuilding. By the mid 19th century Sunderland was THE BIGGEST SHIPBUILDING CENTRE IN THE WORLD. By the end of the 20th century ship-building had declined dramatically and the old shipyards were transformed into a mix of commercial and residential sites. Sunderland is now one of Britain's largest IT and automotive centres, with BRITAIN'S LARGEST CAR FACTORY, Nissan Motor Manufacturing UK.

WEARMOUTH BRIDGE is the lowest bridge across the River Wear and links Sunderland with Monkwearmouth. The present steel arch bridge was built in 1929 by William Arrol & Co, builders of the Forth Railway Bridge, and is the third bridge on the site. The first bridge, built in 1796, was only the second iron bridge ever built, after that at Ironbridge, but at 240 feet (73 m) was twice as long and at the time was THE LARGEST SINGLE SPAN BRIDGE IN THE WORLD. The first Wearmouth Bridge was a catalyst for the growth of Sunderland and a proud symbol of the town, appearing frequently as a subject on Sunderland's famous 19th-century lustre-ware pottery.

Marsden Bay

The Souter Lighthouse, south of Marsden Bay, was THE FIRST LIGHTHOUSE IN THE WORLD DESIGNED SPECIFICALLY TO USE ALTERNATING ELECTRIC CURRENT. Although it stands on Lizard Point it takes its name from Souter Point, a mile to the south, to avoid confusion with the Lizard Lighthouse off Cornwall. It was decommissioned in 1999 and is now owned by the National Trust and open to the public.

MARSDEN ROCK is a sea stack that lies about 100 yards off the beach. In 1911 some of the stack collapsed, leaving an arch not dissimilar to Durdle Door in Dorset, which became a much-loved local landmark. In 1996 the arch collapsed, splitting the stack in two, and eventually the smaller stack disintegrated.

Marsden Rock can be seen from the MARSDEN GROTTO, BRITAIN'S ONLY CAVE BAR, a pub dug into the cliffs and reached from the cliff top via a lift housed in a brick shaft. It was started in 1782 by a lead miner called JACK BATES who blasted a small cave into the cliff where he and his wife could live rent free. The eccentric accommodation attracted curious visitors and Bates started to offer them the chance to buy refreshments.

South Shields

The site on which South Shields now stands has been occupied since the Stone Age. The Romans built a fort here called Arbeia in AD 160 and expanded it in 208 to supply the soldiers along Hadrian's Wall. King Oswald of Northumbria turned the abandoned fort into a palace in the 7th century and his son Oswin was born there.

In AD 647 Oswin gave some land nearby to St Hilda to build a monastery, the site of which is today occupied by St Hilda's Church, which dates mainly from the early 19th century. Suspended from the ceiling of the nave is a model of a boat designed in 1802 by WILLIAM WOULDHAVE, said to be the world's first practical lifeboat, a claim disputed by supporters of Kent's Lionel Lukin who patented a lifeboat in 1785. The story of Wouldhave's lifeboat begins in 1789 when a Newcastle ship *The Adventure* was wrecked on the Herd Sands at the mouth of the River Tyne and thousands stood on the shore watching as the ship was torn to pieces and men died because the seas were too rough for any boat to attempt a rescue. A competition was set up amongst the people of South Shields to design a rescue boat that could operate and be self righting in the stormy seas, and Wouldhave came up with a boat lined with cork that couldn't sink. Another successful competitor who shared the prize with Wouldhave was HENRY GREATHEAD, who improved on Wouldhave's design and whose boat *The Original* would go on to serve for 40 years, saving many hundreds of lives. All three, Lukin, Wouldhave and Greathead, were responsible for the invention of the lifeboat although Greathead's *Original* is generally accepted as THE FIRST PURPOSE-BUILT LIFEBOAT. Greathead's second boat, built in 1802, was the *Zetland*, which is now housed in Redcar.

Both William Wouldhave and Henry Greathead are commemorated on the Jubilee Clock Tower down by the south pier which was built to celebrate Queen Victoria's Golden Jubilee in 1887. Displayed next to the clock is THE SECOND OLDEST SURVIVING LIFEBOAT

IN THE WORLD, the *Tyne*, built in 1833 by South Shields engineer J. Oliver, which served for 60 years and saved over a thousand lives.

South Shields's South Pier was completed in 1895 and, along with its counterpart Tynemouth's North Pier, was designed to protect ships entering the Tyne. The South Pier is almost a mile long and has a lighthouse at its tip. The full length is accessible to the public, although walking to the end is perhaps a little too exhilarating in stormy weather.

A little north of the South Pier is the Herd Groyne, a short pier built in 1861to prevent the sands of Littlehaven beach being washed into the mouth of the Tyne and silting it up. Perched on the end is one of South Shield's best-loved landmarks, the bright red HERD GROYNE LIGHTHOUSE, standing 42 feet (13 m) high on 12 iron legs and looking for all the world like the Lunar Landing Module.

Jarrow

The origin of Jarrow was a monastery founded in AD 682 by BENEDICT BISCOP, the twin to St Peter's Monastery at Monkwearmouth which he had founded eight years earlier. St Paul's Monastery at Jarrow was, for 50 years, the home of the VENERABLE BEDE, the first person to write extensively in the English language. Bede's *Ecclesiastical History of the English People* is THE FIRST WRITTEN RECORD OF THE ENGLISH PEOPLE AND OF ENGLISH HISTORY and tells us about the beginnings of Christianity in these islands up to the Synod of Whitby in AD 664. Bede was also THE FIRST PERSON TO DATE EVENTS FROM ANNO DOMINI (AD), THE YEAR OF OUR LORD. He

was buried at Jarrow, but 30 years later his relics were stolen by a monk who took them to Durham, where they now lie in the cathedral's Galilee Chapel.

The CHURCH OF ST PAUL, attached to the monastery, was dedicated in AD 685 and the original dedication stone is still in place above the chancel arch, which has survived, along with much of the chancel itself, from Bede's day. The stone is THE OLDEST SURVIVING DEDICATION STONE IN ENGLAND. One of the windows in the south wall of the church, a roundel produced in the monastery's workshop in the 7th century, is THE OLDEST STAINED-GLASS WINDOW IN THE WORLD. A battered wooden seat,

Bede's Chair

some 1,100 years old and called BEDE'S CHAIR, stands beside the altar.

Two of the world's most precious books were produced at St Paul's Monastery in the late 7th and early 8th century, the CODEX AMIATINUS, now THE WORLD'S OLDEST BIBLE, and the ST CUTHBERT'S GOSPEL, now THE OLDEST INTACT BOOK IN EUROPE. The Codex Amiatinus was taken to Rome by Abbot Ceolfrith as a gift for the Pope and ended up in the Biblioteca Medicea Laurenziana in Florence. In 2018 it came back home to England for the first time in over 1,300 years for display in the British Library's Anglo-Saxon Kingdoms exhibition, alongside the St Cuthbert's Gospel.

Jarrow remained a small community until the arrival in 1852 of CHARLES PALMER, who founded THE PALMER SHIPBUILDING AND IRON COMPANY, THE WORLD'S FIRST MANUFACTURER OF ARMOUR PLATE, and, in 1875, became the first Mayor of Jarrow. In the year that it opened the Palmer shipyard produced THE WORLD'S FIRST IRON SCREW-POWERED COLLIER, the *John*

Bowes, which almost single-handedly revived the Tyneside coal trade by enabling it to compete with the coal-mines of the Midlands, where they were using the steam railways to get their coal to market more rapidly. The shipyard became ONE OF THE BIGGEST AND MOST PROLIFIC SHIPBUILDING YARDS IN THE WORLD, building hundreds of colliers as well as passenger ships and cargo steamers, while the Crimean War led to lucrative orders for warships, and by the time the yard closed in 1933 it had built over a thousand ships.

The shipyard's closure in 1933, in the same year that the *John Bowes* was lost at sea off the Spanish coast after a working life of 81 years, put three quarters of Jarrow's population out of work and led directly to the JARROW MARCH of 1936, when two hundred men marched from Jarrow to London to protest to the government about the unemployment caused by the closure. Although the march did not have any immediate effect, it is regarded as a defining moment in the progress towards industrial reform in the 20th century.

Well, I never knew this
about

THE DURHAM COAST

During the Napoleonic Wars a French warship was wrecked off HARTLEPOOL and the only survivor to reach land was the ship's monkey. The citizens of Hartlepool didn't get out much and had never seen a 'Frenchie' before and, assuming that this poor ape must be one, they took him into the town square and hanged him. As a result, the town's football team, Hartlepool United, is nicknamed THE MONKEY HANGERS. In 2002 the club mascot, H'Angus the Monkey, was elected as the Mayor of Hartlepool.

BRITAIN'S FIRST KEEP FIT CLASSES took place in SUNDERLAND in 1929, when physiotherapist NORAH REED set up The Keep Fit Adventure for the ladies of Sunderland, based on her philosophy that 'Keeping Fit' was for everyone.

A disaster at SUNDERLAND'S VICTORIA HALL in 1883, when 183 children died after being crushed against an inward-opening door while rushing downstairs to collect treats, led to THE INVENTION OF PUSH BAR OUTWARD-OPENING DOORS. It was the worst disaster of its kind in British history. Victoria Hall was destroyed by a bomb in the Second World War.

THE SUNDERLAND EMPIRE THEATRE is THE BIGGEST THEATRE BETWEEN EDINBURGH AND LONDON. Comic actor SID JAMES died of a heart attack on stage there in 1976.

It is thought that LEWIS CARROLL wrote 'The Walrus and the Carpenter' while staying in WHITBURN. His sister Mary was married to the Rector of Southwick in Sunderland, and in the rectory there was said to be a stuffed walrus that may have given Carroll the idea. He visited Whitburn regularly to stay with his cousins the Misses Wilcox and would walk on the beach which, at low tide, is a wide expanse of sand, possibly the inspiration for the lines

> *The Walrus and the Carpenter*
> *Were walking close at hand*
> *They wept like anything to see*
> *Such quantities of sand*

The *Shields Gazette*, established in SOUTH SHIELDS in 1849, is THE OLDEST PROVINCIAL NEWSPAPER IN BRITAIN.

THE TYNE CYCLIST AND PEDESTRIAN TUNNEL linking Jarrow with Howdon opened in 1951 as Tyneside's contribution to the Festival of Britain. Consisting of two parallel tunnels, one for pedestrians and a larger one for cyclists, it was THE FIRST PURPOSE-BUILT CYCLE TUNNEL IN BRITAIN. The escalators at the entrance climb 85 feet (26 m), are 197 feet (60 m) long and at the time of their construction were THE HIGHEST SINGLE-RISE ESCALATORS IN BRITAIN. In 2019 two of the escalators were replaced by lifts, but the remaining two were preserved as THE LONGEST WOODEN ESCALATORS IN THE WORLD.

CHAPTER TWENTY

NORTHUMBERLAND COAST

Tynemouth to Berwick-on-Tweed
70 miles

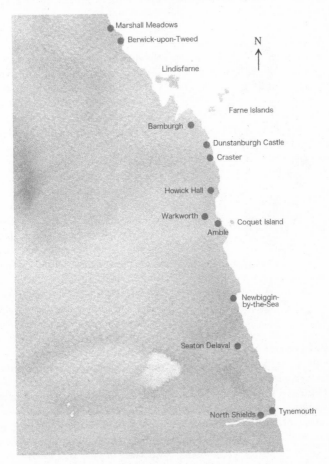

Highlights of the Northumberland coast include the steps that inspired a comedy film classic, the burial place of the saint who sank William II's fleet, the birthplace of a courageous warrior who gave his name to a famous football club, the longest Norman nave in Northumberland, the only surviving fortified bridge gatehouse in England, the home of Earl Grey tea, the birthplace of the kipper, the largest castle in Northumberland, the home of a Victorian hero, the ancient capital of Northumbria, the site of the first Viking raid on England, and Britain's most northerly town.

North Shields

North Shields began life in the 13th century as the fishing port of Tynemouth Priory and then developed to handle to export of coal and salt from local salt-pans. The original town grew up along a narrow strip of land next to the river, hemmed in by a steep bank, but as it became busier a new town was built on the plateau above and the old and new

towns were linked by a series of long, steep staircases cut into the hillside. Comedian STAN LAUREL, the thin half of the comedy duo Laurel and Hardy, lived in North Shields as a boy in DOCKWRAY SQUARE at the top of the hill, and his memories of climbing up and down the stairs between his home and the quayside inspired the famous piano moving scene from their 1932 film *The Music Box*. Dockwray Square has been redeveloped with a park in the middle called Laurel Park which has a statue of Stan Laurel at its centre.

Tynemouth

Standing on a headland at the landward end of the half-mile long North Pier and surrounded on three sides by the sea, are the impressive ruins of TYNEMOUTH CASTLE AND PRIORY. The priory was founded in the 7th century by Edwin of Northumbria and became for a while a place of pilgrimage as the burial place of two martyred Saxon kings, ST OSWIN OF DEIRA (a small kingdom which later joined with Bernicia to become Northumbria) in AD 651 and OSWIU OF NORTHUMBRIA in AD 790. During the 9th century the priory was attacked by the Danes nine times and left derelict. In 1050 Earl Tostig, brother of King Harold I, made himself a wooden fortress beside the ruins before being killed at the Battle of Stamford Bridge in 1066. The Scottish king MALCOLM III, who defeated Macbeth for the Scottish crown, was initially buried in the priory grounds at Tynemouth after being killed at the Battle of Alnwick in 1093, before being taken for reburial in Dunfermline Abbey.

In the 13th century a strong stone castle was built on the headland and it was here, in 1312, that Edward II and his favourite Piers Gaveston hid from

the disapproving barons Henry Percy and Robert Clifford before fleeing by sea to Gaveston's castle at Scarborough. Edward's illegitimate son ADAM FITZROY, mother unknown, was buried at Tynemouth in 1322.

The priory was then dismantled at the Dissolution of the Monasteries and all that remains intact of the priory church of St Mary is the tiny but exquisite PERCY CHAPEL with its stone vaulted ceiling and mini rose window, which was built on to the east end of the church in the 15th century as a chantry for the mighty Percy family.

Gazing out to sea across the mouth of the River Tyne is a vast statue of ADMIRAL COLLINGWOOD, born in Newcastle in 1748. Sculpted by JOHN GRAHAM LOUGH the statue stands 23 feet (7 m) tall. Collingwood was Nelson's second-in-command at the Battle of Trafalgar in 1805 and his ship the *Royal Sovereign* fired the first shots. When Nelson was mortally wounded, Collingwood took control and saw the English fleet through to victory without the loss of a single ship. Four guns from the *Royal Sovereign* stand at the base of the monument.

Tynemouth has long been a popular holiday resort for the people of Newcastle, and Long Sands beach, which stretches for a mile north from Tynemouth to Whitley Bay, is frequently voted one of the top ten beaches in England.

Amble

Once a busy coal port, Amble is now a smart resort town with a small boat-yard and marina. Visible to the east is COQUET ISLAND, owned by the Duke of Northumberland and now a bird reserve run by the RSPB. In 1091 ships taking corn to provision William II's troops in Scotland were wrecked on the island after plundering the priory at Tynemouth and being cursed by the monks. A penitent William paid homage to St Oswin of Tynemouth for the rest of his life. The island's light-house, built in 1841, was once tended by Grace Darling's brother, and it is thought that she contracted the pneu-monia that led to her death after rowing out to visit him here in a small boat (*see* Longstone, page 245).

Visible to the west from Amble is WARKWORTH CASTLE, which sits on a hill overlooking the pleasant town of WARKWORTH, protected on three sides by the River Coquet. A stronghold of the Percy family, the castle was begun by Henry II, while the impressive keep was added by Henry Percy, 1st Earl of Northumberland. His eldest son Harry 'Hotspur' Percy was born in the castle

and here the two of them plotted the downfall of Richard II and rise to power of Henry Bolingbroke as Henry IV. Hotspur later rebelled against Henry and was slain at the Battle of Shrewsbury, it is said by the hand of the Prince of Wales, later Henry V. Hotspur, consid-ered THE BRAVEST KNIGHT OF HIS DAY, and so named because he dug his spurs into his horse to make it charge faster into battle, appears as an impor-tant character in Shakespeare's *Henry IV Part I*. Tottenham Hotspur Football Club, or 'Spurs', are named after Hotspur, whose family owned the land on which the club first played.

The castle gazes down the fine Georgian High Street to ST LAWRENCE'S CHURCH, set upon a shady lawn that runs down to the River Coquet. St Lawrence's is a large Norman church with a deeply satisfying 14th-century spire, one of only two medieval stone spires in Northumberland. The nave, showing deeply splayed Norman windows, is 90 feet (27 m) long, THE LONGEST NORMAN NAVE IN NORTHUMBERLAND. The Norman chancel has a superb stone rib-vaulted roof in the style of Durham Cathedral. On the morning of 9 October 1715 General Forster of Bamburgh Castle arrived with an army of Northumbrian Jacobites and attended a service in St Lawrence's taken by the Old Pretender's chaplain. Afterwards the General led the congregation into the market square and proclaimed the Pretender King James III, making Warkworth THE FIRST TOWN IN ENGLAND TO DECLARE FOR JAMES STUART.

The town still retains its rare medieval 'stints', long strips of land that can be cultivated in one stint, or allotted time.

Guarding Warkworth's 14th-century stone bridge is a gatehouse tower, THE

ONLY SURVIVING FORTIFIED BRIDGE
GATEHOUSE IN ENGLAND.

Howick

From the seaside at Howick a mile-long footpath winds its way through beautiful woods to HOWICK HALL, home of the 2ND EARL GREY who, as Prime Minister, forced through the Great Reform Act of 1832, ONE OF THE MOST SIGNIFICANT ADVANCES IN THE CAUSE OF UNIVERSAL SUFFRAGE. It considerably extended the electorate and abolished the rotten boroughs, whereby one wealthy patron could elect an MP to send to Parliament. It was this same Earl Grey for whom Earl Grey tea was blended, especially to suit the water at Howick. He was apparently given the recipe, a blend of Indian and Ceylon teas subtly flavoured with a type of orange called bergamot, by a Chinese mandarin whose life he had saved.

The first Grey to live at Howick was Sir Edward Grey from Morpeth, who moved into the large pele tower that was there in 1597. This was knocked down in 1780 and replaced with a classical house designed by Newcastle architect William Newton. This in turn was enlarged for the 2nd Earl by George Wyatt in 1809 and then rebuilt by Sir Herbert Baker in 1928 after a fire. The house is still lived in by descendants of the Grey family and is private, but the magnificent gardens are open to the public.

Dunstanburgh Castle

Dunstanburgh
castle

The bleak, brooding clifftop ruins of Dunstanburgh Castle, standing proud and broken on its bare rock promontory, its dark, stark shards of ruin piercing the sky, are one of the wonders of the Northumberland coast. The curtain walls enclose 10 acres (4 ha) and Dunstanburgh is thus THE LARGEST CASTLE IN NORTHUMBERLAND BY AREA. It was built in the early 14th century by THOMAS, EARL OF LANCASTER, second richest man in England after the king and most powerful baron of the North. His refusal to join Edward II undoubtedly contributed to Edward's defeat at the Battle of Bannockburn, but when Lancaster rebelled directly against the King in 1322 he was killed in battle and Dunstanburgh came into the hands of another Lancaster, JOHN OF GAUNT, later Duke of Lancaster. He abandoned the castle when his son became Henry IV and it was then besieged, captured and recaptured several times during the Wars of the Roses.

A splintered tower in the southeast corner of the castle, above the sea, is named QUEEN MARGARET'S TOWER after the story that Henry VI's wife Margaret of Anjou, trapped in the castle under siege, was lowered from the tower by a rope to the beach below so she could escape on to a boat waiting in QUEEN MARGARET'S COVE. After these adventures Dunstanburgh was left to moulder, and by 1550 had become, in the words of Sir Robert Bowes, 'in wonderful great decay'.

The most impressive feature left to us is the GREAT GATEHOUSE in the southwest corner, converted by John of Gaunt into a defensive keep against the Scots, and ONE OF THE MOST FORMI-DABLE STRUCTURES EVER BUILT IN ANY CASTLE IN ENGLAND.

The remote grandeur of Dunstanburgh is only enhanced by the fact that the castle is 1½ miles from the nearest road and can only be reached on foot from Craster or Dunstan Steads.

Farne Islands

The Farne Islands consist of a scattering of treeless rocky outcrops that lie between 1 and 5 miles off the Northumberland coast between Seahouses and Bamburgh. Some of the islands disappear at high tide and some are joined by causeways at low tide. The islands are a haven, in particular, for eider ducks and grey seals and are run as a nature reserve by the National Trust. They can be visited by boat from Seahouses, although visitors can only be landed on two of the islands, Staple Island and Inner Farne, which is the largest island at 16 acres (6.5 ha) and the nearest to the mainland.

Inner Farne

The first person known to have visited the Farne Islands, between AD 635 and 651, was ST AIDAN, the first Bishop of Lindisfarne, who liked to retreat there to pray and meditate. He was followed in 676 by ST CUTHBERT, who retired as Prior of Lindisfarne and built himself a cell dug out of the turf on Inner Farne, where he lived the life of a hermit for eight years. He was eventually persuaded to become Bishop of Lindisfarne but after two years, feeling his days were coming to a close, he returned to Inner Farne to die in 687. While living on Inner Farne, St Cuthbert instituted laws to protect the eider ducks and other nesting birds on the islands, THE FIRST LAWS FOR THE PROTECTION OF THE NATURAL WORLD ever introduced anywhere in the world.

Remains of St Cuthbert's cell on Inner Farne are still visible beside tiny ST CUTHBERT'S CHAPEL, built on the site in his memory in the 14th century. Nearby is PRIOR CASTELL'S TOWER, built in 1550 by the Prior of Durham. Before the lighthouse was built on the far corner of the island at the end of the 18th century, the prior's pele tower served as a lighthouse, with a fire kept lit on the roof to act as a beacon.

Longstone

The furthest of the Farne Islands from the mainland is Longstone. The lighthouse on Longstone was built in 1826 and is the setting for one of the most astonishing tales of heroism in our island story. In the early days of Queen Victoria's reign, the keeper of the Longstone lighthouse was WILLIAM DARLING, who lived there with his family. One early morning in September 1838 one of William's three daughters, GRACE, who was 23 at the time, was woken by a violent storm. As dawn broke she looked out of her bedroom window and spotted the wreck of a paddle steamer, the *Forfarshire*, bound for Hull from Dundee, being pounded on the rocks of BIG HARCAR, a neighbouring island about half a mile to the west. As the light improved she was able to make out figures clinging to the wreckage, and so Grace roused her father and together they clambered into their tiny coble and rowed through the mountainous seas to the scene of the wreck. They had to take a long detour to keep to the lee of the islands, which made it a distance of over a mile, but they got there and while Grace fought to keep the boat afloat William helped five survivors off the *Forfarshire* and into the rowing boat, including a woman who was holding on desperately to her two dead children. After delivering them safely to the lighthouse,

Grace's father went back for the remaining four survivors.

It was three days before the weather abated and the rescued men and women could be taken to the mainland. The rescue captured the imagination of Victorian England. Grace, who was pretty and slight and endearingly modest, became one of the first celebrities, with her picture on the front page of all the newspapers and reporters clamouring for her story. To escape all the attention she continued to live in the lighthouse on Longstone but tragically, in 1842, at the age of 26, after visiting her brother William on Coquet Island she caught pneumonia and died. She was buried in the churchyard in Bamburgh, the village where she was born, in front of a huge crowd of mourners, and even Queen Victoria sent her personal condolences, while Poet Laureate William Wordsworth penned a tribute to her. Grace's deeds were captured in paintings and songs, lifeboats were named after her, and to this day she is honoured as an example of heroism and courage.

The LONGSTONE LIGHTHOUSE where she lived still stands and her bedroom window, from where she spotted the *Forfarshire*, can be identified as the upper window in the white-painted part of the lighthouse. To see this window from a bucking boat on a stormy day brings home the magnitude of Grace Darling's extraordinary bravery.

Bamburgh

Majestic Bamburgh Castle crowns a spur of rock that rises 150 feet (46 m) from the wide sandy beach, creating an unsurpassed sight that has long attracted painters and poets and film producers. Bamburgh was the first capital of Northumbria and has been fortified since at least AD 547 when Bamburgh Castle became the seat of the Kings of Bernicia and later Northumbria. The castle is identified as Joyous Guard, the formidable fortress captured single-handedly by Sir Lancelot in Thomas Malory's *Morte d'Arthur*, and Lancelot is said to be buried there.

In 1464, during the Wars of the Roses, Henry VI held court in Bamburgh Castle after his defeat at the Battle of Hexham, and the castle was besieged by Edward IV's right-hand man Warwick the Kingmaker, who used cannon to bring down the defences, making Bamburgh THE FIRST CASTLE IN ENGLAND TO BE OVER-POWERED BY ARTILLERY.

The oldest part of the spectacular castle we see today is the keep, which is 12th-century Norman, built probably during the reign of Henry II. The rest of the castle was restored in the 19th century by Tyneside industrialist WILLIAM ARMSTRONG who was, appropriately

enough, the inventor of modern artillery. The Armstrong family still own the castle today and it is open to the public.

At the other end of Bamburgh is ST AIDAN'S CHURCH, one of England's most important religious sites whose story comes down to us from the earliest days of English Christianity. The church was founded by St Aidan as a place of worship for King Oswald of Northumbria, who had appointed Aidan as first Bishop of Lindisfarne and whose seat was at Bamburgh. The present building seems to have been rather flung together over the years. The square west tower is mostly 13th century, with Victorian battlements, the long low nave is 12th century, while tacked on to the east end, seemingly as an afterthought, is the chancel, laid out in 1230 on the footprint of Aidan's original wooden church.

At 60 feet (18 m) in length the chancel is THE SECOND LONGEST CHANCEL OF ANY PARISH CHURCH IN ENGLAND. Set against the north wall is the simple shrine of St Aidan marking the exact spot where he died in 651, leaning against the wall of his own church. The forked wooden beam against which he rested, the only part of his original church that survives,

can now be seen in the ceiling of the tower.

In the north aisle is an effigy of Grace Darling, which originally lay beneath the canopy of her memorial in the churchyard but was replaced with a copy and brought inside the church in 1885 when it had begun to weather badly. The distinctive memorial to Grace outside in the churchyard was designed by the prominent architect Anthony Salvin and was placed so as to be visible from passing ships. The canopy had to be rebuilt after a fierce storm in 1893 which sank 48 ships off the east coast. Grace actually lies nearer to the church, in a family plot alongside the rest of her family.

Lindisfarne

Life on Lindisfarne, or Holy Island, is controlled by the tides, for the island is joined to the mainland north of Bamburgh by a mile-long causeway that disappears under the water for 11 hours every day. It is a beautiful, haunting place that is one of the cradles of English Christianity. In AD 634 ST AIDAN, a monk from Iona in Scotland, crossed the sands and founded a monastery on Lindisfarne at the request of King Oswald of Northumbria. He was followed by ST CUTHBERT, sent to help the Celtic monks learn about the ways of Roman Christianity as settled on at the Synod of Whitby in 664. He gained a reputation for healing and miracles and brought great fame to Lindisfarne as a place of sanctuary and peace. Cuthbert was eventually buried on Lindisfarne in 687 and his grave became a place of pilgrimage. His life was recorded in a book written at the end of the 7th century at St Paul's monastery in Jarrow and placed in Cuthbert's coffin. Known as St Cuthbert's Gospel, it was discovered when the coffin was

moved to Durham and reopened and can now be found in the British Library, THE OLDEST INTACT BOOK IN EUROPE.

Not long after Cuthbert's death, in about AD 715, the monks of Lindisfarne themselves produced one of the wonders of the Saxon age, a gloriously illustrated manuscript now known to the world as THE LINDISFARNE GOSPELS, which can also be seen in the British Library.

In 793 Lindisfarne was the victim of the first Viking raid on England's coast, during which Aidan's monastery was looted and burned but, fortunately, Cuthbert's grave was overlooked. In 875 Lindisfarne was again threatened by Viking invaders and this time the monks fled the island, taking with them Cuthbert's coffin and the Lindisfarne Gospels, and eventually, after seven years of wandering through the north of England, they ended up at Durham, where Cuthbert was safely laid to rest.

In 1093 Lindisfarne once more became a Holy Island when a new monastery was built there by the monks of Durham. The red sandstone ruins of the Norman priory church still stand today, surrounded by the huddled houses of the fishing village that grew up around the monastery. Beyond the harbour, set high upon a conical mound at the island's highest point, is LINDISFARNE CASTLE, a ruined 16th-century fort transformed into a romantic castle home by Sir Edwin Lutyens in 1903 and now owned by the National Trust.

Berwick-upon-Tweed

Berwick-upon-Tweed, England's most northerly town, had changed hands between the Scots and the English 14 times before being settled in England in 1482. It is THE ONLY ENGLISH TOWN THAT LIES NORTH OF THE RIVER TWEED, which forms the border between England and Scotland for 17 miles west of Berwick.

Berwick's Elizabethan town walls are unique in Britain and amongst the best preserved town walls in the whole country. They were built in 1558 as a defence against the Auld Alliance of France and Scotland and were designed by Italian engineers as THE FIRST ENGLISH TOWN WALLS TO BOTH WITHSTAND AND MAKE FULL USE OF ARTILLERY – they are also amongst the earliest such walls in all of Europe. The ramparts are thick and massive and originally included five huge projecting bastions which allowed the artillery to provide cover to every part of the wall. Three of the bastions survive, as well as one of the original gates, the tunnelled COW PORT, and you can walk the entire circuit of walls around the town.

Huddling within the walls near the Cow Port on the north side of town is HOLY TRINITY CHURCH, built in 1652 and ONE OF ONLY TWO TOWN CHURCHES BUILT DURING THE COMMONWEALTH. The church has no stained glass, no steeple and no bells, all banned by the Puritans, and had to rely on the ring of eight bells in the 150 foot (46 m) high steeple of the 18th-century neo-classical Guildhall by the central market-place. The steeple also includes a curfew bell, still rung every evening at eight o'clock, maintaining a tradition begun in the days of William the Conqueror. Held every year in July is the BERWICK CURFEW RUN in which competitors attempt to complete the 1-mile circuit of the Elizabethan town walls before the bell stops ringing.

Across the Parade Ground from Holy Trinity Church are BERWICK BARRACKS, built in 1721, possibly to a design by Sir John Vanbrugh and THE EARLIEST PURPOSE-BUILT BARRACKS IN BRITAIN. Before they were built, the garrison's soldiers would be put up at inns or in people's homes, and in the close confines of the enclosed town this began to lead to trouble and so it was decided the troops needed their own accommodation, an idea that was taken up with alacrity in towns and cities across Britain.

There is little left of Berwick's 13th-century castle, which was demolished by the Victorians to make way for the railway station. Buried somewhere beneath the platforms is the Great Hall where, in 1292, Edward I weighed up the competing claims to the Scottish throne of John Balliol and Robert the Bruce. He came down in favour of Balliol, thus precipitating the Scottish Wars of Independence.

Three Bridges

Trains are brought into the station across the ROYAL BORDER BRIDGE which carries the railway at a height of 126 feet (38 m) above the River Tweed. The bridge is a third of a mile long, has 28 arches and was designed by Robert Stephenson and opened in 1850 by Queen Victoria herself. It is one of three spectacular bridges that cross the Tweed at Berwick. BERWICK'S OLDEST AND

LOVELIEST BRIDGE, completed in 1634, carried the Great North Road from London to Edinburgh into Berwick over its 15 crooked arches. It was built on the orders of James VI of Scotland, who apparently found the previous bridge precariously unstable when he rode across it on his way to London to accept the crown of England as James I in 1603. Although the OLD BRIDGE, as it is known, still carries one-way traffic, the main A1 bypasses the town to the west and two-way local traffic uses the ROYAL TWEED BRIDGE, which when it was completed boasted THE LONGEST CONCRETE SPAN IN THE WORLD.

Well, I never knew this
about

THE NORTHUMBERLAND COAST

SEATON DELAVAL HALL, half a mile inland, was built in 1728 for ADMIRAL GEORGE DELAVAL by SIR JOHN VANBURGH, architect of Blenheim Palace and Castle Howard, and is considered to be Vanburgh's finest work, the definitive example of English Baroque. The Hall, which consists of a central block for the state rooms and matching wings for the stables and servants' quarters, has had an unpromising history. Neither Delaval nor Vanbrugh lived to see it finished and it has rarely been lived in. The central block was gutted by fire in 1822 and although it has been stabilised since the National Trust took over the property in 2009 the block is still just a shell.

The lifeboat station at NEWBIGGIN-BY-THE-SEA opened in 1851 and is THE OLDEST OPERATIONAL LIFEBOAT STATION IN BRITAIN. Newbiggin was also at the British end of THE FIRST TELEGRAPH CABLE FROM SCANDINAVIA, which was laid in 1868 from Jutland, in Denmark.

THE PLESSEY WAGGONWAY, which ran for 5½ miles from the coalfields at Plessey to the harbour at BLYTH, was opened some time in the late 17th century and was POSSIBLY THE EARLIEST 'RAILWAY' IN BRITAIN, IF NOT THE WORLD. It was built of beechwood rails laid on oak sleepers and was used to transport coal on horse-drawn wagons. It closed in 1812 but parts of the line can still be seen in various places in the form of 6 foot (1.8 m) high earthworks.

CRASTER is claimed as THE BIRTH-PLACE OF THE KIPPER, and over-looking the harbour are the smoke houses where the herring are flavoured to produce the famous Craster Kipper acknowledged by many to be THE BEST KIPPER IN THE WORLD.

BAMBURGH'S LIGHTHOUSE was built in 1910 and is ENGLAND'S MOST NORTHERLY LAND-BASED LIGHTHOUSE.

BERWICK-UPON-TWEED is the only English town whose football team plays in the Scottish Football League.

MARSHALL MEADOWS BAY, 2½ miles north of Berwick-upon-Tweed, is THE NORTHERNMOST POINT OF THE COAST OF ENGLAND, while the hamlet of MARSHALL MEADOWS is THE NORTHERNMOST SETTLEMENT IN ENGLAND and the MARSHALL MEADOWS COUNTRY HOUSE HOTEL, just 300 yards from the border with Scotland, is both ENGLAND'S MOST NORTHERLY HOTEL AND MOST NORTHERLY INHABITED BUILDING.

Gazetteer

1-CUMBRIA

ST BEES PRIORY –
OPEN DAILY, DAWN TO DUSK

Roman Bath House EH Open daily
    Walls Dr, CA18 1SR
    Tel: 0370 333 1181
    www.english-heritage.org.uk/visit/
    places/ravenglass-roman-bath-house

RAVENGLASS AND ESKDALE
RAILWAY

    Ravenglass CA18 1SW
    ravenglass-railway.co.uk

FURNESS ABBEY EH OPEN DAILY

Manor Road, Barrow in Furness,
    Cumbria, LA13 0PJ
    www.english-heritage.org.uk/visit/
    places/furness-abbey

CONISHEAD PRIORY

Conishead Priory, Ulverston,
    Cumbria, LA12 9QQ
    Tel: 01229 584029
    www.manjushri.org

LAUREL AND HARDY MUSEUM

The Roxy, Brogden Street, Ulverston
    LA12 7AH
    www.laurel-and-hardy.co.uk

HOAD MONUMENT OPEN DAILY

Hoad Hill, Ulverston LA12 7LD
    Tel: 01229 585778

2-LANCASHIRE

CARNFORTH STATION HERITAGE
CENTRE OPEN DAILY

Carnforth LA5 9TR
    www.carnforthstation.co.uk

LANCASTER CASTLE OPEN DAILY

2 Castle Park, Lancaster LA1 1YQ
    www.lancastercastle.com
    Tel: 01524 735165

NORTH PIER, BLACKPOOL

North Pier Promenade, Blackpool
    FY1 1NE
    Blackpoolpiers.co.uk

BLACKPOOL TOWER

Promenade, Blackpool FY1 4BJ
    www.theblackpooltower.com
    Tel: 01253 622242

CENTRAL PIER, BLACKPOOL

Promenade, Blackpool FY1 5BB
    www.visitblackpool.com/detail/
    central-pier-5896

SOUTH PIER, BLACKPOOL

Promenade, Blackpool FY4 1BB
    www.attractionsblackpool.co.uk/
    South_Pier.htm

PLEASURE BEACH, BLACKPOOL

525 Ocean Blvd, Blackpool FY4 1EZ
    www.blackpoolpleasurebeach.com

ASHTON MEMORIAL

Williamson Park, Quernmore Road,
  Lancaster, LA1 1UX
  Open October to March: 10am – 4pm
  (April to September: 10am – 5pm)
  www.lancaster.gov.uk/sites/
  williamson-park/ashton-memorial
  Tel: 01524 33318

3 – MERSEYSIDE

SOUTHPORT PIER

Promenade, Southport
  www.visitsouthport.com/things-to-
  do/southport-pier-p92273
  Tel: 01704 539701

RED SQUIRREL RESERVE NT

www.nationaltrust.org.uk/formby/
  trails/formby-red-squirrel-walk

ROYAL ALBERT DOCK

3–4 The Colonnades, Liverpool L3 4AA
  albertdock.com/

CAVERN CLUB

10 Mathew Street, Liverpool L2 6RE
  www.cavernclub.com
  Tel: 0151 236 1965

FORT PERCH

Marine Promenade, Wirral CH45 2JU
  http://www.fortperchrock.org/
  Fort_Perch_Rock/Home.html
  Tel: 07976 282120

4 – BRISTOL AND SOMERSET

SS GREAT BRITAIN OPEN DAILY

Great Western Dockyard, Gas Ferry
  Rd, Bristol BS1 6TY
  www.ssgreatbritain.org

CLEVEDON COURT NT

Tickenham Rd, Clevedon BS21 6QU
  www.nationaltrust.org.uk/clevedon-
  court
  Tel: 01275 872257

CLEVEDON PIER OPEN DAILY

The Toll House, The Beach, Clevedon
  BS21 7QU
  Clevedonpier.co.uk

WOODSPRING PRIORY MUSEUM,
KEWSTOKE LANDMARK TRUST

www.landmarktrust.org.uk/news-and-
  events/visiting-landmarks/visiting-
  woodspring-priory/

GRAND PIER, WESTON-SUPER-
MARE OPEN DAILY

Marine Parade, Weston-super-Mare
  BS23 1AL
  www.grandpier.co.uk/
  Tel: 01934 620238

BURNHAM-ON-SEA PIER

www.burnham-on-sea.com/history/
  burnham-pier

DUNSTER CASTLE NT

Dunster, Minehead TA24 6SL
  www.nationaltrust.org.uk/dunster-
  castle
  Tel: 01643 821314

ALLERFORD MUSEUM OPEN DAILY

The Old School, Minehead TA24
  8HN
  www.allerfordmuseum.org.uk
  Tel: 01643 862529

NEW ROOM, BRISTOL

The Horsefair, Bristol, BS1 3JE
  www.newroombristol.org.uk

5 – DEVON NORTH

LYNTON AND LYNMOUTH CLIFF
RAILWAY

Lee Rd, Lynton EX35 6HW
www.cliffrailwaylynton.co.uk
Tel: 01598 753486

LUNDY ISLAND NT

www.landmarktrust.org.uk/lundyisland

CHAMBERCOMBE MANOR

Chambercombe Ln, Ilfracombe EX34
9RJ
www.chambercombemanor.org.uk
Tel: 01271 862624

6 – CORNWALL NORTH

HAWKER'S HUT NT OPEN 24
HOURS

Morwenstow, Bude EX23 9JG
www.nationaltrust.org.uk/morwen-
stow/trails/hawkers-hut-walk

BUDE CASTLE OPEN DAILY

The Wharf, Bude EX23 8LG
thecastlebude.org.uk
Tel: 01288 357300

TINTAGEL CASTLE EH

Castle Road, Tintagel, Cornwall,
PL34 0HE
www.english-heritage.org.uk/visit/
places/tintagel-castle

OLD POST OFFICE, TINTAGEL NT

Fore St, Tintagel PL34 0DB
www.nationaltrust.org.uk/tintagel-
old-post-office
Tel: 01840 770024

PRIDEAUX PLACE, PADSTOW

Prideaux Place, Padstow PL28 8RP

www.prideauxplace.co.uk
Tel: 01841 532411

BARBARA HEPWORTH MUSEUM,
ST IVES OPEN DAILY

Barnoon Hill, Saint Ives TR26 1AD
www.tate.org.uk/visit/tate-st-ives/
barbara-hepworth-museum-and-
sculpture-garden
Tel: 01736 796226

GEEVOR MINE OPEN DAILY
(EXCEPT SATURDAYS)

Pendeen, Penzance TR19 7EW
www.geevor.com/
Tel: 01736 788662

BOTALLACK MINE NT

www.nationaltrust.org.uk/botallack

LEVANT MINE

Levant Rd, Pendeen, Trewellard,
Penzance TR19 7SX
www.nationaltrust.org.uk/levant-
mine-and-beam-engine

MUSEUM OF WITCHCRAFT AND
MAGIC, BOSCASTLE OPEN DAILY

The Harbour, Boscastle PL35 0HD
museumofwitchcraftandmagic.
co.uk/
Tel: 01840 250111

7 – CORNWALL SOUTH

MINACK THEATRE OPEN DAILY

Porthcurno, Penzance TR19 6JU
https://www.minack.com/
Tel:01736 810181

EGYPTIAN HOUSE, PENZANCE
LANDMARK TRUST

Chapel St, Penzance TR18 4AJ

St Michael's Mount NT
www.stmichaelsmount.co.uk

CORNISH SEAL SANCTUARY OPEN
DAILY

Gweek TR12 6UG
www.sealsanctuary.co.uk/cornl
Tel: 01326 221361

PENDENNIS CASTLE EH

Castle Dr, Falmouth TR11 4LP
www.english-heritage.org.uk/visit/
places/pendennis-castle

MOUNT EDGCUMBE HOUSE OPEN
DAILY

Cremyll, Torpoint PL10 1HZ
www.mountedgcumbe.gov.uk
Tel: 01752 822236

ANTONY HOUSE NT

Ferry Ln, Torpoint PL11 2QA
www.nationaltrust.org.uk/antony
Tel: 01752 812191

ST MAWES CASTLE EH OPEN
DAILY

Castle Dr, St Mawes, Truro TR2 5D
www.english-heritage.org.uk/visit/
places/st-mawes-castle

THE MONKEY SANCTUARY OPEN
SUMMER WEEKENDS

Murrayton House St Martins, Looe
PL13 1NZ
www.monkeysanctuary.org

8 – DEVON SOUTH

DEVONPORT GUILDHALL AND
COLUMN OPEN DAILY (EXCEPT
SUNDAYS)

Ker St, Plymouth PL1 4EL

www.devonportguildhall.org
Tel: 01752 395028

SMEATON'S TOWER OPEN DAILY

Hoe Rd, Plymouth PL1 2NZ
plymhearts.org/smeatons-tower

ROYAL CITADEL

Lambhay Hill, Plymouth PL1 2PD
www.english-heritage.org.uk/visit/
places/royal-citadel-plymouth

PLYMOUTH GIN DISTILLERY OPEN
DAILY

60 Southside St, Plymouth PL1 2LQ
www.plymouthdistillery.com
Tel: 01752 665292

GREENWAY, NR DARTMOUTH NT

www.nationaltrust.org.uk/greenway

DARTMOUTH CASTLE EH

Castle Road, Dartmouth, Devon,
TQ6 0JN
www.english-heritage.org.uk/visit/
places/dartmouth-castle
Tel: 01803 834445.

NEWCOMEN MEMORIAL ENGINE

Royal Avenue Gardens, Dartmouth
www.devonmuseums.net/Thomas-
Newcomen-Engine

GOLDEN HIND, BRIXHAM OPEN
DAILY (EXCEPT FRIDAYS)

The Quay, Brixham TQ5 8AW
www.goldenhind.co.uk
Tel: 01803 856223

TORRE ABBEY OPEN DAILY
(EXCEPT MONDAYS)

The King's Drive, Torquay TQ2 5JE
www.torre-abbey.org.uk

KENT'S CAVERN

91 Ilsham Rd, Torquay TQ1 2JF
www.kents-cavern.co.uk
Tel: 01803 215136

A LA RONDE NT

Summer Ln, Exmouth EX8 5BD
www.nationaltrust.org.uk/a-la-
ronde
Tel: 01395 265514

SEATON TRAMWAY OPEN DAILY

Harbour Rd, Seaton EX12 2WD
www.tram.co.uk

NATIONAL MARINE AQUARIUM OPEN DAILY

Plymouth PL4 0LF
www.national-aquarium.co.uk

9 – DORSET

ABBOTSBURY SWANNERY OPEN DAILY

New Barn Rd, Abbotsbury DT3 4JG
abbotsbury-tourism.co.uk/swannery
Tel: 01305 871858

POOLE MUSEUM OPEN DAILY

4 High St, Poole BH15 1BW
www.poolemuseum.org.uk

BOURNEMOUTH PIER OPEN DAILY

Pier Approach, Bournemouth BH2 5AA
www.thebournemouthpier.com
Tel: 01202 983983

BOSCOMBE PIER OPEN DAILY

2494 Undercliff Dr, Bournemouth
BH5 1BN
www.visitbournemouth.com/attrac-
tions/boscombe-pier
Tel: 01202 451773

CHRISTCHURCH PRIORY

www.christchurchpriory.org

LULWORTH CASTLE AND ESTATE OPEN DAILY (EXCEPT SATURDAYS)

East Lulworth, Wareham BH20 5QS
www.lulworth.com

BROWNSEA ISLAND NT

www.nationaltrust.org.uk/
brownsea-island

10 – HAMPSHIRE

HURST CASTLE OPEN DAILY

Milford on Sea, Lymington SO41
0TP
www.hurstcastle.co.uk

CALSHOT CASTLE EH OPEN DAILY

Jack Maynard Rd, Calshot,
Southampton SO45 1BR
www.english-heritage.org.uk/visit/
places/calshot-castle
Tel: 0370 333 1181

TUDOR HOUSE, SOUTHAMPTON OPEN DAILY (EXCEPT FRIDAYS)

Bugle St, Southampton SO14 2AD
www.Tudorhouseandgarden.com

NETLEY ABBEY EH OPEN DAILY

Abbey Hill, Netley, Hampshire,
SO31 5FB
www.english-heritage.org.uk/visit/
places/netley-abbey

ROYAL NAVY SUBMARINE MUSEUM

Haslar, Jetty Road, Gosport PO12 2AS
https://www.nmrn.org.uk/subma-
rine-museum

PORTCHESTER CASTLE EH OPEN
DAILY

Church Ln, Portchester, Fareham
    PO16 9QW
    www.english-heritage.org.uk/visit/
    places/portchester-castle

PORTSMOUTH HISTORIC
DOCKYARD

www.historicdockyard.co.uk

SPINNAKER TOWER OPEN DAILY

Portsmouth PO1 3TT
    www.spinnakertower.co.uk

SOUTHSEA CASTLE OPEN DAILY
(EXCEPT MONDAYS)

Clarence Esplanade, Portsmouth PO5
    3PA
    www.southseacastle.co.uk

CHARLES DICKENS' BIRTHPLACE
MUSEUM OPEN FRIDAY TO
SUNDAY

393 Old Commercial Rd, Portsmouth
    PO1 4QL
    charlesdickensbirthplace.co.uk
    Tel:023 9282 7261

11 – ISLE OF WIGHT

THE NEEDLES

www.theneedles.co.uk

SHANKLIN CHINE OPEN DAILY IN
SUMMER (APRIL-SEPTEMBER)

3 Chine Ave, Shanklin PO37 6BW
    www.shanklinchine.co.uk
    Tel: 01983 866432

OSBORNE HOUSE EH

www.english-heritage.org.uk/visit/
    places/osborne

BLACKGANG CHINE AMUSEMENT
PARK OPEN APRIL TO SEPTEMBER

www.blackgangchine.com

QUARR ABBEY

Quarr Rd, Ryde PO33 4ER
    www.quarrabbey.org
    Tel: 01983 882420

12 – SUSSEX

ARUNDEL CASTLE

Arundel BN18 9AB
    www.arundelcastle.org
    Tel: 01903 882173

MARLIPINS MUSEUM OPEN
TUESDAY TO FRIDAY

36 High St, Shoreham-by-Sea BN43 5DA
    www.sussexpast.co.uk/properties-
    to-discover/marlipins-museum
    Tel: 01273 462994

BRIGHTON PAVILION OPEN DAILY

4/5 Pavilion Buildings, Brighton BN1
    1EE
    www.brightonmuseums.org.uk/
    royalpavilion

BRITISH AIRWAYS i360
OPEN DAILY

Lower Kings Road, Brighton BN1 2LN
    www.britishairwaysi360.com

VOLKS RAILWAY

Madeira Dr, Brighton BN2 1EN
    www.volkselectricrailway.co.uk

PEVENSEY CASTLE EH OPEN DAILY

Castle Rd, Westham, Pevensey BN24
    5LE
    www.english-heritage.org.uk/visit/
    places/pevensey-castle

HASTINGS CASTLE

Castle Hill Rd, Hastings TN34 3JL
www.visit1066country.com/things-
to-do/attractions/hastings-castle-
and-1066-story-p44433
Tel: 01424 422964

13 – KENT

DOVER CASTLE OPEN DAILY

Castle Hill Rd, Dover CT16 1HU
www.english-heritage.org.uk/visit/
places/dover-castle

ROMAN PAINTED HOUSE OPEN TUESDAY TO SATURDAY

25 New St, Dover CT17 9AJ
www.whitecliffscountry.org.uk/
Things-to-do/Attractions/History-
and-Heritage/Roman-Painted-
House.aspx
Tel: 01304 203279

GRAND SHAFT

Drop Redoubt Rd, Dover CT17 9DY
www.doverwesternheights.org/
grand-shaft

WALMER CASTLE EH OPEN DAILY

58 Ledbury Rd, Notting Hill, London
W11 2AJ
www.english-heritage.org.uk/visit/
places/walmer-castle-and-gardens
Tel 020 7229 4620

DEAL CASTLE EH OPEN DAILY

Marine Rd, Walmer, Deal CT14 7BA
www.english-heritage.org.uk/visit/
places/deal-castle

RICHBOROUGH CASTLE EH OPEN DAILY

Richborough Rd, Sandwich CT13 9JW

www.english-heritage.org.uk/visit/
places/richborough-roman-fort-
and-amphitheatre
Tel: 01304 612013

THE GRANGE, RAMSGATE LANDMARK TRUST

Open Wednesday afternoons for
pre-booked tours
www.visitkent.co.uk/attractions/
the-grange-2670
Tel: 01628   825925   (Mon-Fri
9am-5.30pm)

DICKENS HOUSE MUSEUM OPEN WEEKEND AFTERNOONS

2 Victoria Parade, Broadstairs CT10
1QS
www.thanet.gov.uk/info-pages/
dickens-house-museum
Tel: 01843 861232

THE SHELL GROTTO OPEN FRIDAY TO SUNDAY

Grotto Hill, Margate CT9 2BU
shellgrotto.co.uk
Tel: 01843 220008

ROMNEY, HYTHE & DYMCHURCH RAILWAY OPEN DAILY

New Romney Station, 2 Littlestone
Rd, Littlestone, New Romney
TN28 8PL
www.rhdr.org.uk

14 – ESSEX

COLCHESTER CASTLE OPEN DAILY

Colchester CO1 1TJ
colchester.cimuseums.org.uk/visit/
colchester-castle

HARWICH REDOUBT OPEN SUNDAYS

Main Road, Harwich CO12 3LT

www.harwich-society.co.uk
Tel: 01255 553610

15 – SUFFOLK

LANDGUARD FORT EH OPEN DAILY

View Point Rd, Felixstowe IP11 3TW
www.english-heritage.org.uk/visit/
places/landguard-fort

ORFORD CASTLE EH OPEN DAILY

Castle Hill, Orford, Woodbridge IP12
2ND
www.english-heritage.org.uk/visit/
places/orford-castle

THE RED HOUSE, ALDEBURGH CLOSED MONDAY

Golf Ln, Aldeburgh IP15 5PZ
www.brittenpears.org/visit
Tel: 01728 451700

SOMERLEYTON HALL AND GARDENS

Open April to September Tues,
Thurs, Sundays and Bank
Holidays
www.somerleyton.co.uk/somer-
leyton-hall/visitor-info

16 – NORFOLK

NELSON MUSEUM CLOSED SATURDAYS

26 S Quay, Great Yarmouth NR30
2RG
www.nelson-museum.co.uk
Tel: 01493 850698

HOLKHAM HALL OPEN DAILY

Holkham Rd, Wells-next-the-Sea
NR23 1AB
www.holkham.co.uk

SANDRINGHAM HOUSE

Sandringham PE35 6EN
www.sandringhamestate.co.uk
Tel: 01485 545400

17 – LINCOLNSHIRE

BOSTON GUILDHALL OPEN WEDNESDAY TO SATURDAY

South St, Boston PE21 6HT
www.mybostonuk.com/boston-
guildhall
Tel: 01205 365954

MAUD FOSTER WINDMILL OPEN WEDNESDAYS AND SATURDAYS

16 Willoughby Rd, Boston PE21
9EG
www.maudfoster.co.uk
Tel: 01205 352188

18 – YORKSHIRE

WILBERFORCE HOUSE OPEN DAILY

23–25 High St, Hull HU1 1NQ
www.hcandl.co.uk/museums-and-
galleries/wilberforce-house
Tel: 01482 300300

ROTUNDA MUSEUM, SCARBOROUGH OPEN DAILY (EXCEPT MONDAYS)

Vernon Rd, Scarborough YO11 2PS
www.scarboroughmuseumstrust.
com/rotunda-museum

CAPTAIN COOK MEMORIAL MUSEUM

Grape Ln, Whitby YO22 4BA
www.cookmuseumwhitby.co.uk
Tel: 01947 601900

19 – DURHAM

National Glass Centre Open Daily

Liberty Way, Sunderland SR6 0GL
www.nationalglasscentre.com
Tel: 0191 515 5555

St Paul's, Jarrow EH Open Daily

Church Bank, Jarrow NE32 3DY
www.english-heritage.org.uk/visit/
places/st-pauls-monastery-jarrow
Tel: 0370 333 1181

20 – NORTHUMBERLAND

Tynemouth Priory EH

Pier Road, Tynemouth, Tyne and
Wear, NE30 4BZ
www.english-heritage.org.uk/visit/
places/tynemouth-priory-and-castle

Warkworth Castle EH Open Daily

Castle Terrace, Warkworth, Morpeth
NE65 0UJ
www.english-heritage.org.uk/visit/
places/warkworth-castle-and-
hermitage
Tel: 0370 333 1181

Dunstanburgh Castle EH Open Weekends

Dunstanburgh Rd, Alnwick NE66
3TT
www.english-heritage.org.uk/visit/
places/dunstanburgh-castle

Farne Islands, Inner Farne NT Open April to November

www.nationaltrust.org.uk/farne-
islands

Bamburgh Castle Open Daily

Bamburgh NE69 7DF
www.bamburghcastle.com/
Tel: 01668 214515

Lindisfarne Castle NT

https://www.nationaltrust.org.uk/
lindisfarne-castle

Seaton Delaval Hall NT Open Thursday to Sunday

The Avenue, Seaton Sluice, Whitley
Bay NE26 4QR
www.nationaltrust.org.uk/seaton-
delaval-hall

Index of People

Index of Places